Beautiful Solidarity, Symbolic Impacts

SERIES EDITORS

David L. Brunsma
David G. Embrick

SERIES ADVISORY BOARD

Margaret Abraham
Elijah Anderson
Eduardo Bonila-Silva
Philomena Essed
James Fenelon
Evelyn Nakano Glenn
Tanya Golash-Boza
David Theo Goldberg
Patricia Hill Collins
José Itzigsohn
Amanda Lewis
Michael Omi
Victor Rios
Mary Romero

Beautiful Solidarity, Symbolic Impacts

2020 Racial Justice Uprisings

Eileen O'Brien

The University of Georgia Press
ATHENS

Sociology of Race and
Ethnicity web page

© 2025 by the University of Georgia Press
Athens, Georgia 30602
www.ugapress.org
All rights reserved
Designed by Kaelin Chappell Broaddus
Set in 10.5/13.5 Garamond Premier Pro Regular
by Mary McKeon

Most University of Georgia Press titles are
available from popular e-book vendors.

Printed digitally

EU Authorized Representative
Easy Access System Europe--Mustamäe
tee 50, 10621 Tallinn, Estonia,
gpsr.requests@easproject.com

Library of Congress Cataloging-in-Publication Data
Names: O'Brien, Eileen, 1972– author
Title: Beautiful solidarity, symbolic impacts : 2020
racial justice uprisings / Eileen O'Brien.
Description: Athens : The University of Georgia
Press, 2025. | Series: Sociology of race and ethnicity |
Includes bibliographical references and index.
Identifiers: LCCN 2024060644 | ISBN 9780820373720
hardback | ISBN 9780820373737 paperback | ISBN
9780820373744 epub | ISBN 9780820373751 pdf
Subjects: LCSH: Racial justice—United States | Anti-racism—
United States | United States—Race relations | Protest
movements—United States—History—21st century | African
Americans—Violence against—History—21st century
Classification: LCC HT1561 .O27 2025 | DDC
305.800973/09052—dc23/eng/20250409
LC record available at https://lccn.loc.gov/2024060644

For Darnella Frazier (Minneapolis) and Kris Smith (Louisville), I honor your courage.

For Kaya and Kaden, may your children's youth not be interrupted by having to march in the streets over yet another senseless life taken. May you always have the courage to stand up when needed.

CONTENTS

ACKNOWLEDGMENTS IX

CHAPTER 1. The Perfect Storm: Why Now? 1

CHAPTER 2. Similar but Different: Something Old, Something New 27

CHAPTER 3. Protect and Serve: But for Whom? 57

CHAPTER 4. Discordant Harmonies: Age, Gender, and Race 92

CHAPTER 5. Beyond Marching: "A Beautiful Uprising," an Antiracist Racial Project 127

CHAPTER 6. After 2020: What's Next? 151

APPENDIX Respondent Demographics Table 189

REFERENCES 191

INDEX 205

ACKNOWLEDGMENTS

This project has been a labor of love that I could never have finished without the support of many others. First and foremost, my children, Kaya Faith and Kaden Robert, who were passionate about protesting after being isolated at home and not always appreciating what they saw on social media, were my catalysts. Although I took them to many marches over the years, this time was different. They were leading the way. Terrified of COVID-19 and planning to only stay in the "drive-by" contingent, when I saw their souls being fortified the minute they exited the car, I knew I had to stand with them. Day after day, our faithful companions were the Gist family—Terrence, Shana, Isaiah, and Linda; we hugged, we cried, we screamed, we looked out for each other. I am so grateful to you all for etching this onto my heart. My "sis" and colleague Dr. Ebony Perez, as we continued our conversations about why so many people cared now who didn't care before, you excited my curiosity as your cautious optimism confronted my skeptical pessimism, and I wanted to know how the rest of the world was working this out! These catalysts and a sabbatical from Saint Leo University (thank you, Chair Janis Prince, and Dean Heather Parker, for your support) all helped birth this baby!

Of course, the others making this possible were thirty brave protesters who volunteered their time to speak with me about their experiences. Only eight of them had I ever met previously. So I have so many thoughtful referrers to thank—including Ebony Perez, Chris Dovi, Lori Janke, Ainsley Lambert-Swain, Charlotte and Alexis Braziel, Anna Potter, Kaya O'Brien-James, Reverends Laura Horton-Ludwig and Ashley Moran, Nathaniel Sawyer, LaToya Henderson, Devin Wynne, and Michelle Owen. All of you referred me at least one person who gave me an interview, and some, it was many more than one interview referral. I so appreciate your assistance with making connections!

Dale Wimberley of Virginia Tech, I appreciate being able to speak on your SSS panel about sociology and activism. Joe Feagin, I appreciate your being my mentor for so long—some people have a PhD program mentor, but I have a lifelong mentor and friend in you and I am eternally grateful. I am also grateful to the members of your Texas A&M University graduate seminar in December 2021 who listened to my earliest and first presentation of this work. I am also thankful to Ruth Triplett for the invitation to present this research to the Old Dominion University community. And also my colleague and brilliant dear friend Deirdre Royster for your suggestions along the way. But reading all my words, I mean ALL my words, that is a serious commitment! For that I especially thank Drs. Ebony Perez, Ainsley Lambert-Swain, and Megan Underhill for giving me such thoughtful feedback that improved my work. This project was also especially strengthened from the feedback of two anonymous reviewers for the University of Georgia Press—especially the one who had a long list of bullet points that pushed me so hard on all I missed at first, you truly made me better by identifying all the work I still had to do. To "the Davids," David Embrick and David Brunsma, I was so honored for you to consider my work for this amazing powerhouse series and so fortified by your generous and heartwarming encouragements all along the way when it was far from polished. I appreciate your willingness to see its potential. I am grateful to everyone at the University of Georgia Press especially Mick Gusinde-Duffy. And E Mackey, thank you for being such a brilliant, passionate photographer who puts your whole heart into it and for picking up the phone the day I dared to call you. Your work makes this project pop, and I hope we both are giving proper tribute to all who keep fighting for the better world we deserve. The photos from Nate and Rachael Sawyer as well as Latanya Wallace-Conyers, I appreciate you all also. I wanted to visually represent both small towns and big cities, and your generosity allowed me to do so.

And although many inquired how my sabbatical project was going, no one did so more frequently and more passionately than D'Shawn Wright. Everyone needs a hype man like you! You brought that same gusto you use coaching clients to the finish line of their workouts to me with this project. Every day, it was "What number interview is it?" "What did you learn?"—all the perfect questions you ask and all the ways you celebrate the little wins is what kept me going, all the way. Thank you for everything.

Beautiful Solidarity, Symbolic Impacts

CHAPTER 1

The Perfect Storm

Why Now?

And I remember thinking to myself, man, the one good thing about us being shut down and trapped in the house is that at least Black people can't get killed. I literally had this thought, like, at least we can't get killed now. And maybe a week or two later, the video came out.

—Photographer E Mackey on the video of Georgia runner Ahmaud Arbery being shot and killed by Travis McMichael on February 23, 2020, Choose Your Weapon: How It Began on Vimeo.

2020—The perfect vision year. A year for reflection. A time to contemplate what came before and what is ahead. Days into its sixth month, one thing is certain: 2020 has laid bare the results of an uncured and oft ignored disease that pervades our society—racism. Whether we are talking about the disproportionate rates of COVID-19 contraction and related deaths, the weaponizing of white privilege/whiteness, or the senseless deaths resulting from police brutality, racism is the ultimate underlying cause, and these are merely symptoms of the larger disease.

—Tekisha Dwan Everette, PhD, Yale University School of Public Health, June 16, 2020 Ahmaud Arbery. Breonna Taylor. George Floyd. Say Their Names, Yale School of Public Health

The year 2020 was the culmination point of several global crises that all seemed to explode at once. A public health crisis (COVID-19) that at first appeared to be only affecting China and Italy would soon disable the world, while also laying bare the preexisting inequalities in health care and resources between groups. A power-hungry tyrannical U.S. president, espousing the most blatant racism the nation had seen at its helm in decades, had already wreaked nearly four years of havoc but now facing the prospect of reelection would support a coup attempt/terrorist attack on his behalf. And the modern-day lynching of African Americans (from killings to terrorism, threats, and harassment), whether at the hands of police or everyday citizens, was becoming a steady drumbeat that more people than ever could hear, thanks to cell phone cameras and social media momentum building since the 2013 advent of the Black Lives Matter movement.

Which day or event in 2020 was the one that changed everything? The precise power of this racial justice uprising resides in the fact that there is not one unifying answer to this question. The journalistic shorthand of calling the racial justice uprising of 2020 the "George Floyd protests" camouflages the reality that much was brewing before May 25, 2020, when Mr. Floyd was murdered by police officer Derek Chauvin, and much occurred afterward as well. Certainly, one unprecedented peak of protest occurred between May 26 and June 6, 2020, where it estimated between 15 to 26 million people participated in Black Lives Matter (BLM)–related protests in the United States, across as many as 550 different locations (Buchanan, Bui, and Patel 2020). Because this peak occurred just after Floyd's murder, it is understandable that some may infer that this was the catalyst for the largest social movement in U.S. history (Buchanan, Bui, and Patel 2020). June 2020 was also an important moment for white Americans recognizing racism was a problem—an unprecedented 91 percent of Americans felt racism was a serious problem at that time, and 67 percent supported the BLM protests. However, by September 2020, these proportions were already falling back down (Smith 2020; Thomas and Horowitz 2020). Because this rise and fall in demonstrations and support for racial justice is timed closely with the death of George Floyd, one could assume it is this one atrocity alone that drove so many people to suddenly care about racial justice. But such an assumption ignores many other concurring conditions that created this "perfect storm" of factors.

For those who had dedicated their entire lives, even decades, to racial justice work, this new surge of activity and interest presented exciting possibilities. Having encountered so much resistance to even small antiracist reforms and simple basic accountability for racist actions, the prospect of suddenly enough popular support for antiracist policy to accomplish real social change was a pregnant moment indeed. None of the demands made by 2020 protesters were anything new;

all had been proposed countless times before. What was different were the sheer *numbers* of people protesting and also the *scope* and *spread* of the protest activity. Protests were held in all fifty U.S. states, including many places where protests are rare. "The United States rarely has protests in this combination of size, intensity and frequency; it usually has big protests or sustained protests, but not both" (Putnam, Chenoweth, and Pressman 2020). It was a moment of great potential in antiracist history. To what extent did 2020 live up to its antiracist potential? And to the extent that it fell short, why?

Interest Convergence, Racial Realism, and an Antiracist Racial Project

Any number of critical race scholars, particularly Derrick Bell, could have told us before it even started not to get too excited about this "temporary peak" in seemingly widespread conviction to reduce and eradicate racism. In his book *Faces at the Bottom of the Well: The Permanence of Racism*, Bell (1992, 12) wrote,

> Black people will never gain full equality in this country. Even those herculean efforts we hail as successful will produce no more than temporary "peaks of progress," short-lived victories that slide into irrelevance as racial patterns adapt in ways that maintain white dominance.

There is no denying that the racial justice uprising of 2020 was a "herculean effort" of unprecedented proportions. As the uprising raged on, Brookings Institution policy fellow and sociologist Rashawn Ray (2020) suggested it was a "policy window" within which to capitalize on the recent surge of support for antiracist change, and the window metaphor was clear —a situational opening to quickly make the most of before the return to the status quo. This framing is quite different than the idea of a permanent awakening from which there is no turning back. To approach the 2020 racial uprisings from the perspective of racial realism theory, we must understand that the baseline, the default, the norm is white supremacy and systemic racism. If history is any guide, no matter how monumental or unprecedented the change, there is a tendency for it to eventually "slide into irrelevance." Or as journalist Amy Harmon and her colleague Audra D. S. Burch observed in June 2020, "It is as though the ability of white people to collectively ignore the everyday experience of black people has been short-circuited, at least for now" (Harmon and Burch 2020).

Although he did not live to see the 2020 racial justice uprising, Bell certainly predicted what its ebb and flow would look like with the first fact of four on which he grounded his racial realism theory:

> There has been no linear progress in civil rights. American racial history has demonstrated both steady subordination of blacks in one way or another and, if examined closely, a pattern of cyclical progress and cyclical regression. (Bell 1993, 98)

So if the tendency is to slide back to the norm, what is it that motivates or inspires the momentary progress? According to Bell, it was not at all in whites' interest to end racism; therefore, these temporary peaks when progress happened were the result of a moment of what he terms "interest convergence." In his "Comment" piece about the *Brown v. Board of Education* (1954) ruling in the *Harvard Law Review*, Bell (1980, 523) outlined the principle of interest convergence as follows: "The interest of blacks in achieving racial equality will be accommodated only when it converges with the interests of whites." Much in the same way that slavery ended in 1865, not so much out of concern for the human rights of African Americans as for the goal of preserving the union, Bell argued that it was becoming embarrassing for the United States on the global stage of the mid-twentieth century to be supporting racial segregation on its own shores while intervening abroad to stop fascism and communism. It sought to act to end racial segregation, at least on paper, to retain its global standing in the world. So, as the popular saying goes, "the planets aligned" in favor of African Americans' civil rights but only due to this temporary interest convergence where whites stood to gain from the passage of civil rights laws. Bell also contends that an eventual divergence in interests happens afterward, undermining whatever racial progress had formerly been achieved.

Forty years later, legal scholar Alexis Hoag took to the *Harvard Law Review* to apply these insights from Bell to the 2020 racial justice uprisings. Writing in August 2020, Hoag took note of the outpouring of support for racial justice, which had already started to decline from its June peak, finding the "progress" to be largely performative and symbolic. In this passage, Hoag (2020) pinpointed the reasons for the temporary interest convergence:

> With many Americans either out of work or working from home, we are all glued to pocket-sized screens. . . . Yes, millions marched against anti-Black racism in cities and small towns across the nation, but these demonstrations were largely captured and shared via social media. Appearing at a Black Lives Matter demonstration showed solidarity, but appearing and then posting a photograph of it had measurable social currency. Consumer-driven corporations were all quick to showcase their anti-racist positions. Never mind that some of these corporations had engaged, or continue to engage, in anti-Black practices. Although retail spending decreased during the pandemic, companies could not possibly lose

more money speaking out against racism, but they could by remaining silent, or worse, condoning racism. I argue that a major motivating factor for many white peoples' actions and corporations' pronouncements against racism was not to advance Black equality. Rather, it was the realization that the nation cannot maintain its economic, political, and social superiority over the rest of the world while remaining silent about anti-Black racism in America. Racism is a bad look. Silence in the wake of racist events is even worse. And just as in the 1950s, the world is watching America. Only now, the world is consuming America's hypocrisy in real time on social media.

Put simply, it was evident the world *was* watching and, as Hoag writes, that "racism is a bad look." The COVID-19 pandemic created a global sense of vulnerability; people the world over were confronted with a threat they did not altogether understand or know how to control or contain. Hence, one of the things that made the Floyd protests so compelling was that they appeared to address a pervasive social problem—racism—at a moment in which other threats to human existence seemed uncontrollable.

Racial realism and interest convergence theories help answer the question of why the Floyd protests, which were unprecedented in terms of size and scope, occur in 2020. Like Hoag, I too wondered, "Where were these [Black Lives Matter and White Silence Is Violence] signs when New York City police officers fatally shot Amadou Diallo, unarmed and standing in the doorway of his home, 41 times?" (Hoag 2020). The peak was George Floyd's brutal murder, but unfortunately, there had been so many others, even in much more recent memory than Diallo's killing in 1999. It was exciting, yet curious, that this was the moment so many more people decided to finally care about anti-Black violence in the United States. But upon considering the various economic and political factors, domestically and globally, that converged on this moment, it starts to make more sense; the United States had political and economic incentives to at least look as if it was finally handling its long-standing racism problem.

Thus, the racial justice uprising of 2020 became an antiracist racial project. Omi and Winant's (1994) racial formation theory posits race as a category that is constantly in flux, constructed and reshaped primarily by the state; one of the vehicles by which this is accomplished is through racial projects. A racial project is "simultaneously an interpretation, representation, or explanation of racial dynamics, and an effort to reorganize and redistribute resources along particular racial lines" (Omi and Winant 1994, 56). Racial projects do the ideological work of connecting racial *meanings* to representations and *structure*s. Competing racial projects often exist simultaneously. For example, Carney's (2016) analysis of "hashtag activism" on Twitter demonstrates how #BlackLivesMatter and #AllLivesMatter each present very different analyses of the racial social structure —the former implicating a structure that disregards Black lives, while the latter places a neoliberal faith in a fair social system that seemingly already does the job of valuing all lives equally, presumably needing no further readjustments. As color-blind approaches like "all lives matter" tend to do, it somehow blames Blacks for being "the racist ones" introducing "race" into what might have otherwise been a race-neutral society (Bonilla-Silva 2017, 2020). A racial project does the ideological work of attaching representations to racial groups such that those in the society are more likely to support the particular structural arrangements that go along with those representations. In other words, racial projects signal potentially new meanings of persons racialized as a particular group, and these meanings inevitably have a particular implication for the way power and resources are organized (or reorganized).

Many racial projects are clearly racist, but they do not have to be—some racial projects can be antiracist (Myers and Sbicca 2016; Woodward 2016). For example, in an analysis of 2018 news coverage of Black Lives Matter protests from two different sources, *Slate* and *TheBlaze*, Durham (2022) found that *TheBlaze* undertook a racial project that reproduced white supremacy by problematizing protesters, but *Slate* advanced antiracism with its racial project of "prejudiced police." The latter project advanced the ideology that citizens had every right to protest given the current arrangements. Such protest could potentially lead to a reorganization of policing aimed at reducing prejudice, in this case. Even though it may not critique every aspect of racism, a racial project can be antiracist if it challenges the state's role in reproducing racism in some way, as opposed to merely "celebrating ethnoracial diversity" (Myers and Sbicca 2016, 4). Note that an antiracist project does not have to cover everything, and antiracism and racism can coexist within the same organization or social movement.

These approaches, taken together, can help us make sense of some of the answers to the research questions guiding this project. First, why did so many people suddenly care about racism in 2020 who didn't before? Second, was the racial justice uprising of 2020 truly "unprecedented," and how much of it was just another temporary peak in a cycle of something we have seen before? Third, in what ways was antiracism advanced by this season of racial justice, and what work did it leave undone? Or, put another way, why didn't this phenomenal groundswell of an antiracist racial project accomplish more, given its magnitude? If we understand the racial justice uprising of 2020 as an unprecedented, yet temporary, peak of interest convergence, while also recognizing that this moment was indeed an antiracist racial project that accomplished some but not all of its objectives, we can better make sense of the answers we find to these questions. Racial realism is a useful guide for this journey because Bell (1993) reminds us that realism is different from pessimism—we can acknowledge that the uprising fell way short of its potential, while still appreciating the areas where antiracist progress happened, and participants had fulfilling, even transformative, experiences confronting racism shoulder to shoulder with others in their struggle for justice. As Victor Ray (2022) writes (paraphrasing Bell), that struggle in itself was redemptive. It was a temporary moment of beautiful solidarity, a redemptive struggle—a moment that not surprisingly also left much undone.

Racial Justice Uprising: Key 2020 Event Timeline

Another concept important to define for this project is the event(s) itself that I am analyzing—the racial justice uprising of 2020. This term is selected very specifically—intentionally not using some other terms that are often used to describe the similar event(s), such as "riots," "marches," and "summer." Initially, recruitment was directed toward people who "marched" in the "summer of 2020." But soon enough, subjects volunteered for the study who had participated in 2020 racial justice events either before or after the summer was over. This leads to the larger point that I am not analyzing the "George Floyd protests" in this book. Most participants, even and especially in Minneapolis, for example, described some events in George Floyd Square more as candlelight vigils or community gatherings rather than protests or marches per se—although certainly at times there were also marches, protests, and demonstrations. So the term "uprising" captures all kinds of *social movement activity that required physical presence in a collective, public community space with others for the purpose of recognizing racial injustice, condemning it, and/or collective visioning of a more racially just society.* Chapter 5 details everything besides marches, protests, and demonstrations that participants engaged in within the collective public space of these uprisings, including but not limited to protest art, vigils, yoga, spoken word performance, and mutual aid.

February to Early June 2020: Uprising Catalysts

To fully appreciate why neither "George Floyd" nor "summer" are adequate for describing the racial uprising of 2020, the remainder of this section offers a brief timeline of that particular year in racial justice, which will inevitably be woefully incomplete due to the ubiquity of racism in the United States in 2020 and beyond. Also, it is important to note that any item on this quick 2020 timeline has a long backstory predating 2020. However, I focus on a few key events that are considered catalysts of the 2020 uprisings, beginning with the opening quote of this chapter, several months before Floyd's death.

On February 23, 2020, a young African American man (age twenty-five) named Ahmaud Arbery was going for a run in Brunswick, Georgia, when Travis McMichael, along with his father (former law enforcement) Gregory McMichael, both white men, started following him, then shot and killed him (Lee 2020). Ultimately, much later, it is three men who are arrested and found guilty of Arbery's murder—a third white man, William "Roddie" Bryan, a neighbor, was an accomplice and thus given a shorter sentence than the other two (Griffith 2022). All three were also convicted of federal hate crimes, nearly two years later (Conlon 2022). But many would argue that these convictions may not have ever occurred without the power of the 2020 racial justice uprising. Indeed, most Americans did not even know about this horrific white supremacist attack until seventy-two days later, on May 5, 2020, when video footage was released. It is suspected the Georgia town held back the information because of the law enforcement background of the elder McMichael. Two days after the public release of the video, the men were finally arrested, on May 7, 2020 (Lee 2020). By then, the national shock had gone viral, and it was the day before what would have been Arbery's twenty-sixth birthday, so under the hashtag #IRunWithMaud, runners everywhere ran 2.23 miles (symbolizing the February 23 date Arbery was killed) and posted to social media on May 8, 2020 (Ebrahimji 2021).

Meanwhile, in Louisville, Kentucky, in the early hours of March 13, 2020, a young African American woman, nearly the same age as Arbery (twenty-six years old), Breonna Taylor, laid in her bed asleep when police officers approached her home with a warrant, looking for her ex-boyfriend who was not there. Concerned there were intruders, Taylor's boyfriend (Kenneth Walker III) approached the door with his legally owned weapon, when the officers forced entry, shot Walker in the leg but then went on to shoot and kill Taylor who was still in bed—quite obviously not a threat (Levenson 2020). This is yet another case that local authorities tried to keep quiet—for example, CNN did not first report on the incident until two months later on May 13, 2020, around the same time as the Arbery story was breaking nationally. At this time, no disciplinary action was noted toward the officers, but Taylor's family was pursuing a wrongful death suit against the police department—while the Louisville police union was maintaining on its Facebook page that Walker was the real threat (Jones, Hasan, and Asmelash 2020). Again, we can see the power of the 2020 racial justice uprising in this case—by May 21, the Federal Bureau of Investigation (FBI) began investigating the Louisville Police Department, a new interim police chief placed the officers involved on administrative leave, and one was facing charges of misconduct (but not murder), and by September, Taylor's family won the wrongful death lawsuit. Also, the charges against Walker were dropped, and a "Breonna's Law" was passed banning no-knock warrants (Levenson 2020). Yet we can see that by the middle of May 2020, after two months of pandemic lockdown, the world was already watching the murder of two young, unarmed African Americans in two different U.S. states, for which law enforcement seemed altogether uninterested in pursuing justice or accountability, unless people demanded it.

Regarding the coronavirus (COVID-19) pandemic, Wamsley (2021) identifies March 11, 2020, as "the day that changed everything" in the United States. Even though China and Italy were already grappling with the deadly virus and the first case had been in January in the United States (in Washington State), by March there had already been one thousand cases across forty states, and thirty-one deaths. Some schools were even already closed. But March 11 is when the World Health Organization finally declared it a pandemic. Then-president Trump announced a thirty-day ban on European travel, the stock market plunged, actor Tom Hanks and wife Rita Wilson announced they were sick with the virus, and an NBA game was stopped just before tip-off (Wamsley 2021). All these alarm bells signaled to Americans that something was truly wrong because it sure would take something major to stop all those high-profit margins of capitalism from moving along. Between March 6 and May 19, historic school closures occurred, affecting over 55 million students across 124,000 school districts, and nearly all 50 states eventually declared closing for the rest of that school year (Education Week 2020). Many states issued stay-at-home orders between the months of March and May 2020, ordering temporary closure of many businesses deemed not "essential" (USA Today 2022). So many Americans were trapped, restricted from usual daily activities, out of work, and scared.

While the early March 2020 headlines gave the impression that the virus was limited to wealthy world travelers, by early May it became clear that the social-spatial arrangements of the United States had resulted in disproportionately higher COVID-19 death rate for African Americans and some other people of color—those most likely to be working essential jobs and unable to isolate in ways that privilege allows. By May 11, across thirty-nine states that were reporting data, it was evident that African Americans were dying from COVID-19 at rates more than double their percentage in the population—27 percent of deaths when only 13 percent of the population (Kaur 2020). Add that to the increasing volume of news stories of Asian American discrimination, hate crimes, and even killings in the spring of 2020—due to scapegoating the pandemic as the "China virus" by the president and followers—and there was no denying that COVID-19 was now yet another glaring example of 2020 racism (Bonilla-Silva 2020; Chavez 2020; McTaggart and O'Brien 2021; Pirtle 2020).

Even if racism was not their concern during this time, many Americans were stuck at home with more idle time than before due to school and work closures, and with information changing all the time as scientists and public health experts struggled to make sense of the novel coronavirus, staying on top of the latest news became a life-or-death matter. By the summer of 2020, many more Americans were watching television than previously, and news programs were a top hit, as was social media (Fitzgerald 2020). So by the time May 2020 arrived, over two months into their government-imposed lockdowns, viewers saw in rapid succession a video of Ahmaud Arbery being shot defenseless, news of an African American EMT worker getting shot while sleeping in bed (Breonna Taylor), and then on May 25, 2020, the breaking point occurred. Two different incidents of a Black man assumed to be suspicious, with white social control tactics involving law enforcement, both caught on video—but each very different and one resulting in a coldhearted murder—as the world was watching. The first was white woman Amy Cooper's 911 call on a fellow Central Park dog walker, a Black man also with the last name Cooper, no relation—Christian Cooper recorded the entire interaction himself in New York City, while Amy claimed he was "threatening my life" and "tried to assault" her, he then shared it with the world (Levenson and Sgueglia 2020). A few hours later on the same day, the second incident occurred—the killing of George Floyd (Chavez 2020). So while Floyd's death and its circumstances are horribly egregious on their own, what made it all the more of a tipping point was the buildup in the months leading up to it.

Around the hour of 8:00 p.m. on May 25, 2020, Minneapolis police were called to a Cups corner store, concerned that a shopper, who is an unarmed African American man named George Floyd, had possibly passed a counterfeit $20 bill (Deliso 2021). Four officers—Derek Chauvin, Thomas Lane, J. Kueng, and Tou Thao—were at the scene, and although there was at first a struggle, Floyd was handcuffed and face down on the ground when Chauvin proceeded to kneel on his neck for close to nine minutes. He was taken to the hospital and pronounced dead, and the next day, the first statement police issued was that he died after a "medical incident." But then minutes later, a "bystander video" (taken by now Pulitzer-honoree Darnella Frazier, then just seventeen years old) was posted online, and public outrage began. By the end of the day, protests began, the four officers were fired, but no arrests were yet made, so protests grew. It was not until May 29 that Chauvin was arrested and charged—with third-degree murder and manslaughter (Associated Press 2021). However, by this time, the governor had already called in the National Guard, and protests had erupted nationwide. So on this same day, then-president Trump tweeted, "When the looting starts, the shooting starts," which Twitter flagged for inciting violence (Associated Press 2021; Deliso 2021).

The Armed Conflict Location and Event Data Project (ACLED), along with the Bridging Divides Initiative, both housed at Princeton University, have created the *U.S. Crisis Monitor*, which assembles data from all over the world on political demonstrations. The ACLED website is a treasure trove of maps and charts and an excellent source for comprehensive tracking of types of protests, locations, and numbers of people involved, as well as whether violence was present and by whom it was initiated (i.e., demonstrators as opposed to state actors such as law enforcement). ACLED data show that between May 24 and August 22, over ten thousand protests occurred across the country, and about 95 percent of these were not violent. About 80 percent of those demonstrations were either about the COVID-19 pandemic or BLM-related. During that same period, over 7,700 BLM demonstrations occurred across 2,400 U.S. locations, but the peak day was May 31, when on that day alone over 3,000 protest events took place (Kishi and Jones 2020; Kishi, Stall, and Jones 2020). That same day was when prosecution of the officers in Floyd's murder was transferred from the county prosecutor to state attorney general Keith Ellison. Soon thereafter, on June 2, charges of civil rights violations were filed against the police department (Deliso 2021).

While Floyd's brutal racist murder at the hands of law enforcement was clearly a catalyst for this apex of antiracist movement activity, analysis of the demonstrations supports the conclusion that this unprecedented "showing up" for antiracism was about much more than that one unfortunate death. The world was watching, and the world responded.

> While the U.S. faces a unique combination of overlapping crises, many of these trends are mirrored around the world—and the racism and police brutality exemplified by the killing of George Floyd prompted a global response. In the week's [sic] since Floyd's killing, at least 8,700 demonstrations in solidarity with the BLM movement were reported across 74 countries, including the U.S. Demonstrators focused their outrage on American symbols—including embassies, consulates, and Trump properties—but they also rallied around local cases of police brutality and racial inequality. The BLM movement has offered a "brand" of anti-racism and anti-police violence activism for a range of contexts around the world. In many countries, demonstrators have been "applying their own martyrs" to the solidarity protests, and are using BLM as an inspiration for structuring domestic movements against police violence, discrimination, and political repression. (Kishi and Jones 2020)

Traveling around the world, one could find many more names besides George Floyd on the protest signs. Although May 31 was by far the highest peak of protest activity according to ACLED data, smaller peaks continued to occur in June, July, and into the fall of that year.

By June 2020, words like "never before" and "seismic shift" summed up how the needle had shifted Americans' views on racism. Attributed to the racial justice uprising, a Monmouth University poll found 76 percent of Americans thought racism was a "big problem"—up over 25 percentage points since 2015 (Russonello 2020). Suddenly, businesses wanted to give employees Juneteenth as a holiday, Quaker Oats withdrew their Aunt Jemima logo, NASCAR stopped waving the confederate flag, confederate monuments came down, and even the Washington football team finally gave up its Redskins logo (after decades of protest by Native Americans and allies) (Chavez 2020; Hoag 2020; McTaggart and O'Brien 2021). The pushback the first wave of the Black Lives Matter movement faced seemed it was beginning to subside—even though murders of unarmed African Americans like Trayvon Martin, Eric Garner, Michael Brown, and so many more (as discussed more in the next section) were not all that different from what happened to Arbery, Taylor, and Floyd in 2020, something definitely had shifted in broad support for some measure of racial justice during this period.

Post–George Floyd 2020, Continued Uprising

Although ACLED data show us that late May and early June 2020 was the apex of racial justice uprising activity in terms of protest, so many other unfortunate racist events brought people out to the streets after that time, throughout the remainder of 2020 and beyond. Several of those interviewed for this book were active in the uprising well after the summer was over. Even though certainly not an exhaustive list, a few more questionable police killings of African Americans occurred after June 2020 in several of the cities where participants resided. For example, less than a week after Floyd's murder, during active protesting in Louisville, Kentucky, African American restaurant owner David McAtee was killed by police and National Guard, amid these law enforcement officers attempting to use Pepper-Balls to disperse the crowd (Levenson 2020; Sanchez, Schuman, and Sturla 2020). Also in June 2020 was Rayshard Brooks, a twenty-seven-year-old unarmed African American man killed in a Wendy's parking lot in the Atlanta area. Some may argue that the fact that the officer who shot him (Garrett Wolfe) getting fired and charged with murder (Chavez 2020) was the result of the public pressure mounting from the 2020 uprisings.

Then in August 2020, in Kenosha, Wisconsin, a twenty-nine-year-old African

American man named Jacob Blake was shot by a police officer, Rusten Sheskey, in the back seven times and left paralyzed. This tragedy led to professional athletes, including NBA team Milwaukee Bucks, refusing to play games and intensified protests in the area. As discussed more in chapter 3, some of the 2020 racial justice uprising events attracted white supremacists, who were often not as much counterprotesters as vigilantes, and one such fairly renowned one in Kenosha in August was a white man named Kyle Rittenhouse, who shot and killed two people and wounded a third (Joseph Rosenbaum, Anthony Huber, and Gaige Grosskreutz, respectively—all also white men but there in support of the protests, one a friend of Jacob Blake). Rittenhouse was later found not guilty in these murders (Chavez 2020; Morales 2021; Romo and Pruitt-Young 2021). As with all cases above, the defensive argument was that the victim was resisting arrest, so no officer was convicted in the shooting of Jacob Blake, which left him permanently paralyzed from the waist down (Morales 2021).

Even as the summer of 2020 drew to a close, the racial justice uprising continued, especially in September when a grand jury announced there would be no murder or manslaughter charges filed in the death of Breonna Taylor. The only charges were about "endangerment" of the neighbors with stray shots—no charges relating to the death of Taylor (Chavez 2020; Levenson 2020). Protests extended all the way into December, even as the cold weather made it quite a bit less comfortable to do so, due in part to two different Columbus, Ohio, incidents. The first occurred on December 4, 2020, when twenty-three-year-old Casey Goodson Jr., an African American man was on his grandmother's back porch with Subway sandwiches for his family, was shot seven times in the back and killed by a sheriff's marshal named Jason Meade. He was eventually charged with murder and reckless homicide, and at the time of this writing, the trial is still ongoing. This incident ignited a high volume of protests in the area, even though it did not involve Columbus Police Department (CPD) directly. But less than three weeks later, white CPD officer Adam Coy killed a forty-seven-year-old African American man as he exited his garage, cell phone in hand (Maxouris 2020; Welsh-Huggins 2021). The reality of African Americans not even being safe from police killings while on their own property—the so-called "safe haven" of home—is a particularly jarring injustice indeed. Also note that in many U.S. cities, the "latest incident" is just that; so although even one unjust killing is too many, most locations where protests swell, the residents carry with them a history of multiple incidents of "vicarious victimization," the cumulative impact compelling them to act (Cobbina 2019).

ACLED data identify other smaller peaks after the summer of 2020 and even into 2021, particularly April 2021 when the guilty verdict of Derek Chauvin in the murder of George Floyd was announced, but none even came close to the level of the late-May, early June 2020 participation (Kishi et al. 2021). Likewise, when we examine how big of a concern racism was to Americans, by the fall of 2020, that peak of interest had dropped off as well. For example, Pew found a majority (60 percent) of whites at least somewhat supported the Black Lives Matter movement in June 2020, but by September, that dropped to less than half (45 percent) of white Americans, and support among Hispanics dropped by 11 percentage points as well (Thomas and Horowitz 2020). Reasons for the decline from this peak are many, and some are explored more in the concluding chapter of this book. A vaccine for COVID-19 became widely available in December 2020, prompting much reopening of businesses, schools, and workplaces by 2021. This return to some semblance of prepandemic lifestyles certainly rendered many folks less available for everyday protest activities. However, a more likely explanation is that an illusion of various symbolic concessions to antiracism lulled many into thinking racism was no longer a serious problem by the end of 2020.

Some evidence shows that a number of Americans switched their political party affiliation or voting behavior to Democratic candidates as a result of the 2020 racial uprising, resulting in local- and national-level election shifts (Mutz 2022). After the November 2020 elections and by the end of that year, some celebrated certain political victories as strides toward greater racial equality. For example, with the election of Joe Biden as U.S. president, he selected Kamala Harris as his vice president—the first African American, first South Asian, and first woman to hold that role in U.S. history, and Biden also announced the most diverse cabinet members yet (Chavez 2020). As discussed in greater detail in chapter 5, hundreds of Confederate monuments were targeted in the summer of 2020—either for vandalism, renaming, removing by government officials, or toppling by protesters (Burch 2022). Changing of various names and other logos, and the persons who held certain political positions contributed to "optics" of paying more lip service to dismantling racism. So it could be that once these surface-level changes occurred, this contributed to the drop in the percentage of Americans who perceived racism as a continued problem. In the concluding chapter of this book, I focus more on the actual policy changes that antiracist activists called for during the 2020 racial justice uprisings, none of which included the symbolic, surface-level changes that happened by late 2020. Racial realism theory predicted that the peak of 2020 would likely descend back into exactly this—not as much concern about racism as before. In fact, even a predictable backlash against these optical illusions of progress soon followed, with bills across almost all fifty states proposing bans on any talk of antiracism and diversity whatsoever (Ray 2022). Nevertheless, it is useful to examine what conditions created that brief peak of progress and what that looked like on the ground for those who participated in the uprising, especially if we want to see more peaks of progress in the future.

A Perfect Storm: Building Up to 2020

Even though any one single atrocity of the many listed above was enough to drive an uprising of outrage at racial injustice, most analysts agree it was not these 2020 events alone—which unfortunately were not new—that drove the unprecedented historic crowds of demonstrators. The global pandemic of COVID-19, coupled with the political situation of a U.S. president who had stoked and even openly courted white supremacists throughout his term and beyond, provided the backdrop within which these racist killings and deaths occurred. Furthermore, a new social movement, Black Lives Matter, invented only seven years earlier, had been working hard building an amazing network around the nation and world, standing at the ready to help mobilize the collective fury of 2020. In other words, if it were not for the momentum that had been building up before 2020 of other related social movement activity, the uprising of 2020 could not have happened to the extent that it did. Not only decades of civil rights organizing can be connected to this historic moment, but particularly the years 2013–2019. Note the Trump presidency is certainly a crucial component of this timeline, but again, hardly the only factor. Although I could never hope to cover everything leading up to 2020 in these brief pages, as my primary focus is 2020, I would be remiss not to highlight just a few key events and catalysts relevant to the current analysis, especially Black Lives Matter and white supremacist/nationalist organizing. Because the goal of this book is to explore what, in uprising participants' eyes, made 2020 unprecedented, part of the answer lies within this groundwork laid shortly before it happened.

First-Wave BLM, Obama Era

First and foremost, the 2020 racial justice uprising (which some call the BLM movement) most assuredly would not have been possible, to the extent that it catapulted that year, without Black Lives Matter being founded in 2013. The founding and development period of this movement (2013–2015) is now being referred to by some as the "first wave" (Tillery 2021). The movement began in 2013, when the nation reacted to a not-guilty verdict in the shooting death of a seventeen-year-old African American boy named Trayvon Martin. The shooter, George Zimmerman, a white Hispanic man, claimed he was working in a volunteer neighborhood security capacity in Sanford, Florida, when he deemed Martin was "suspicious" and shot him, despite the fact Martin was unarmed, with even dispatchers directing Zimmerman to leave Martin alone. The nation was watching this case, beginning in 2012 when the shooting occurred, because it was reported that part of what Zimmerman found "suspicious" was that Martin was wearing a hoodie. Even then-president Obama spoke out on the tragedy on March 23, 2012: "If I had a son, he'd look like Trayvon" (Peoples-Wagner and Jerkins 2022). Although Martin's murder occurred on February 26, 2012, Zimmerman was not arrested until April 11, 2012, upon which he quickly raised over $200,000 in donations to pay for his defense. The nation was watching and debating this trial, and when the six-member jury (all women—five white and one Puerto Rican) in Florida declared Zimmerman not guilty in July 2013, outcries of heartbreak and anger ensued. Social media played a crucial role in connecting individuals who wanted to do something about this. In California, two Black women organizers—Alicia Garza and Patrisse Cullors—connected after Cullors posted a "love letter to Black people" with the hashtag #BlackLivesMatter, and a third Black woman organizer out of New York City, Ayo (then Opal) Tometti, joined forces with them (Peoples-Wagner and Jerkins 2022; Vera and Krishnakumar 2022). Black Lives Matter was born.

There were social movement organizations bearing the name Black Lives Matter—the first chapter formed, with the assistance of the three founders listed above, in Los Angeles in 2013—but BLM must be understood also as a broader movement, with which many different racial justice social organizations have affinity (Cobbina 2019). The BLM movement gained momentum when two other police killings of African American men happened in the summer of 2014—Eric Garner in Staten Island, New York, and Michael Brown in Ferguson, Missouri. An unfortunate but all-too-common pattern in these killings is that the initial reason for the police arriving on scene was for minor, nonviolent offenses. Garner, forty-three, was approached by New York Police Department (NYPD) officer Daniel Pantaleo on suspicion of selling stolen cigarettes, yet Pantaleo restrained him in a chokehold that killed him, while he was heard to say, "I can't breathe." Brown, eighteen, was killed by Ferguson police officer Darren Wilson after pursuing him for alleged stolen cigars. Brown's body was left in the street for four hours. Protests ensued in the wake of both of the killings in the summer of 2014 as well as in November and December 2014, when in both cases, it was announced that the officers involved—Pantaleo as well as Wilson—were cleared of any charges (BBC 2021; Peoples-Wagner and Jerkins 2022; Vera and Krishnakumar 2022). The BLM movement and hashtag on social media were instrumental in organizing and raising awareness during this time. Concerned citizens traveled from many places to participate in Ferguson protest events in late 2014, and other related hashtags like #ICantBreathe and #HandsUpDontShoot were worn by athletes, entertainers, and everyday individuals to draw attention to injustices wherever they are (Peoples-Wagner and Jerkins 2022; Vera and Krishnakumar 2022).

The power of this movement resided in its use of social media because the mainstream media often relies on press releases and official statements from police departments and government officials. When there are bystander videos, visual images, or other evidence that is at first concealed from official public statements, social media can be a valuable tool with which to circulate these alternative narratives that reveal more information about the circumstances of these tragedies. In this way, #BLM continued to buttress cases like Tamir Rice and Sandra Bland that might never have been heard of outside their own hometowns without the support of this movement. In November 2014, Tamir Rice, African American and only twelve years old, was killed by Officer Timothy Loehmann in Cleveland, Ohio, while holding a toy gun. No charges were ever filed even though Loehmann had a past history of misconduct. In July 2015, Sandra Bland, a twenty-eight-year-old African American woman, died in her jail cell in Waller County, Texas, three days after an altercation with State Trooper Brian Encina during a routine traffic stop. The family and general public questioned the "suicide" determination as uncharacteristic, suspecting a retaliation killing. BLM helped popularize the hashtag #SayHerName involving this case (BBC 2021; Peoples-Wagner and Jerkins 2022).

However, a case getting more mass media attention during this time, drawing more public protest activity—besides Garner and Brown—was Freddie Gray's death in police custody at the hands of Baltimore police, which occurred in April 2015. Again, the relatively minor charge against the twenty-five-year-old African American man was possessing an illegal switchblade knife, but because he was handcuffed and placed into the back of a police van without a seat belt (in a "rough ride"), he suffered spinal cord injuries, dying a few days later. As in Ferguson just months earlier, protests ensued—first orderly and relatively peaceful, but eventually things became unruly, and the National Guard was called. Ultimately, none of the Baltimore officers involved were convicted of any charges related to Gray's death (Cobbina 2019; Peoples-Wagner and Jerkins 2022).

BLM activists continued to support organizing to raise awareness of these unchecked brutalities, getting a social media assist when Facebook added a "live" function in 2016. Being able to share videos with the public, user to user, via social media allowed the kind of unfiltered content that became harder and harder for police to cover up or deny. Sadly, it was not long after that two other police killings of African American men would get video exposure—Alton Sterling, thirty-seven, in Baton Rouge, Louisiana, and Philando Castile, thirty-two, in Saint Paul,

Minnesota—within twenty-four hours of each other in July 2016. Not only did the world witness Sterling pinned to the ground and shot in the chest at close range (caught on a cell phone camera), but through live stream, Castile's girlfriend, Diamond Reynolds, shared the immediate aftermath of her boyfriend being shot and killed right in front of her four-year-old daughter. The chilling footage of the little girl and her mother in terror, as Castile bled to death from his gunshot wounds and police looked on, brought the empathy-eliciting visual that is often concealed or obscured from view in press conferences and official media reports. Castile was pulled over for a broken taillight, and Sterling was selling used CDs and DVDs in a parking lot. Also, no charges were brought against officers involved in either shooting. From activists to entertainers and politicians, social media statements abounded about the rapid pace of these police murders with no repercussions (BBC 2016; Blades 2016; Peoples-Wagner and Jerkins 2022).

Continued BLM Organizing, More Overt White Supremacy with Trump Presidency

Sadly, that was only a sampling of all the police killings that occurred during the first wave of BLM. Yet racism and white supremacy were on display in other glaring ways leading up to the 2020 uprising, particularly as President Obama's second term drew to a close and the "whitelash" began. In June 2015 in South Carolina—the same state where yet another police killing of a Black man, Walter Scott, had occurred just two months prior—declared-white supremacist Dylan Roof, twenty-one, walked into a Black church during a Bible study meeting, mass murdering nine African Americans. The aftermath of this incident led to the intensification of ongoing debates about all the Confederate monuments and symbols that remain in the U.S. South, especially even on the South Carolina state flag. Then, shortly after Donald J. Trump was elected as the new U.S. president (2016)—a man who had a long history of publicly espousing racist ideologies—a Unite the Right rally took place in Charlottesville, Virginia (August 2017), during which white man and avowed neo-Nazi James Alex Fields Jr. purposely drove into a crowd of peaceful protesters, killing white antiracist Heather Heyer. Then-president Trump publicly commented that there were "very fine people" on "both sides" of this rally, which angered many who felt he did not take a strong enough stance condemning white supremacist violence. However, this was only one of many such related remarks during the Trump presidency (2017–2020). Calling African American athletes like Colin Kaepernick and Lebron James "sons of bitches" for publicly protesting police brutality, calling nations like Haiti and El Salvador "shithole countries" and asking why more immigrants could not come from Norway instead, and tweeting that four female minority members of U.S. Congress (Representatives Tlaib, Omar, Pressley, and Ocasio-Cortez) should "go back" to where they came from were just a few prominent examples (Doane 2020; McTaggart and O'Brien 2021; Peoples-Wagner and Jerkins 2022). By the time of his campaign for reelection in 2020, Trump was practically openly courting white supremacists during nationally televised debates, refusing to denounce known neo-Nazi groups like Proud Boys when asked to do so (McTaggart and O'Brien 2021).

The Trump presidency cannot be ignored as a push factor for the 2020 racial justice uprisings, pulling those who had not been active before that time into action. Despite Black Lives Matter being active since 2013, it definitely picked up momentum due in part to the blatant disregard of the Trump presidency to make even symbolic gestures toward sympathy of the victims of racist violence. The fact that then–presidential candidate Joe Biden even attended the Texas memorial service for George Floyd on June 8, 2020 (Deliso 2021), was a marked departure from any behavior exhibited by Trump during his presidency. As the *New York Times* published when it ran the headline "Black Lives Matter May Be the Largest Movement in U.S. History" on July 3, 2020,

> The adversarial stance that the Trump administration has taken on issues like guns, climate change and immigration has led to more protests than under any other presidency since the Cold War. According to a poll from The Washington Post and the Kaiser Family Foundation, one in five Americans said that they had participated in a protest since the start of the Trump administration, and 19 percent said they were new to protesting. (Buchanan, Bui, and Patel 2020)

A contentious, polarizing presidency became the catalyst for a whole crop of "never before" protesters, even before 2020. In fact, in the present study, quite a few interviewees are not categorized as "first-time protesters" only because of their prior activation in social justice demonstrations during Trump administration and first-wave BLM protests. If it weren't for the couple of years prior to 2020, they would have been first-time protesters in 2020 also.

We cannot limit ourselves to saying Arbery's, Taylor's, and Floyd's deaths set the world afire with protesting. We have to understand them as a product of a very specific social and historical context that consisted of years of anti-Black violence and hardly any accountability for the killings as well as years of tone-deaf remarks and inflammatory encouragement of white supremacy from the highest political office in the nation. A hypothetical tireless soldier in the fight to end racism and stop police brutality since the 1990s, who was accustomed to having dozens, maybe even hundreds, of fellow protesters around them, might be taken aback by suddenly having thousands of allies in 2020. Indeed, some of the protest newcomers might have even been saying, "All lives matter" in 2013, 2014, and 2015 (Carney 2016). But by the time many of the other above atrocities took place, some not even involving African Americans directly (such as the Charlottesville 2017 murder), some of the 2020 uprising participants were saying, "Enough is enough."

In fact, even as 2020 approached, Black Lives Matter activists carefully watched cases that had already occurred, wondering if there would ever be legal accountability or repercussions for the perpetrator. Although I could never hope to cover all those cases here either, a couple stand out because this study includes a look at the communities where they occurred: Botham Jean in Dallas, Texas, and Elijah McClain in Aurora, Colorado. In September 2018, an off-duty Dallas police officer (Amber Guyger) entered the home of Botham Jean, a Black twenty-six-year-old accountant, allegedly mistaking the home for her own apartment one floor below and thinking he was an intruder in her own place, shot and killed him. Guyger, a white woman, was tried for murder and sentenced in 2019 to ten years but was still appealing the case, claiming insufficient evidence, in 2021 (Simon and Killough 2019; Sanchez and Killough 2021).

In August 2019, while walking from a convenience store with iced tea, someone thought Elijah McClain, a small-framed introverted African American young man age twenty-three, looked "sketchy." So when Aurora, Colorado, police approached him, they used a series of questionable techniques to restrain him, including applying a carotid hold (now outlawed) and injecting an excessive amount of a sedative, which ultimately led to his death. Video footage showed three officers saying things like "Stop tensing up" and "Stop messing around" while McClain stated, "I'm sorry" and "I can't breathe correctly." The Aurora Police Department was quite slow to act in this case. Although it led to many subsequent legal reforms, making virtually everything illegal that the officers did to McClain that day, there were no criminal charges in the case ultimately. However, near the end of 2021, it was finally determined that the McClain family would get one of the largest civil suit payouts in history (Franklin 2021; Tompkins 2022). As some aspects of both of these cases were still pending when the 2020 uprisings began and many other cases not mentioned here were ongoing as well, one cannot overstate how much Arbery, Taylor, and Floyd were but only the latest in a long chain of similar atrocities.

As we shall see in the next chapter, "Say their names" became a rallying cry during the uprising to emphasize these were way more than just the "George Floyd protests." Not only was the steady drumbeat of racist killings and police misconduct becoming deafening, but the blatant disregard on the part of the nation's highest leader, was the one-two punch that awakened more people than before. Add that to the global pandemic raging, exacerbating already existing racial and class inequities, and the world was watching the perfect storm unfold in real time. The BLM activism and organizing network stood ready to mobilize its newfound supporters into action.

Uprising Evidence

There are so many studies yet to be done about the 2020 racial justice uprisings. The data collection process and multimethod study design employed here is meant to be exploratory, with both interview and observational data purposely collected toward a particular set of research questions. Since national-level data already exist on basic demographics of 2020 uprising participation, including the size, scope, duration, and overall law enforcement presence (thanks to aforementioned ACLED data set and other recent scholarly work), my aim here is to investigate some more in-depth why questions, with ethnographic data containing rich descriptions of some uprising activities, less apt to be captured in larger quantitative and survey-based projects. Because one of my primary questions is why did so many more people participate in 2020 than before, I sought an interview sample roughly evenly divided between "veteran protesters" and "first timers." In the end, of the thirty participants in these interviews, thirteen of them were first-time protesters.

Interestingly, in her book about the 2014–2015 racial justice protests in Ferguson and Baltimore, Jennifer Cobbina (2019) collects a sample of residents of the two cities, about half who participated in the protests and half who did not, but within this half who participated, she designates three different levels of protest involvement—tourist, intermittent, and revolutionary. Because one of my primary areas of interest is why did so many people come out for the first time in 2020, I was more interested in dividing my sample between first timers and veterans. However, I have a few first timers who dived right in, becoming top-level participants in terms of the frequency of activities they pursued, despite being brand new to this work; all four were in their twenties and thirties. But the majority of the first-time participants (n = 8) participated at the "tourist" level (less than three times) Cobbina described in her work, leaving one first-time participant who attended at the intermediate level (seven different events in the Louisville area). Nearly half (n = 13) of my sample fits the revolutionary category Cobbina identifies in terms of their level of involvement. But nearly that many (n = 11) in my sample would fit the scant "tourist" level of involvement, attending just once or twice total. The smallest group in my sample (n = 6) fits Cobbina's third category of intermittent participation, mainly because the sample was purposively selected to draw as clear a contrast as possible between two groups: (a) those who were veterans and had (ideally many) events before 2020 to compare it to and (b) those who came out for the first time in 2020 (usually attending a small number). Although one might predict that this first-time/veteran distinction is only one of age, there were quite a few younger adults who were also considered veterans because they had participated in first-wave Black Lives Matter demonstrations during the seven years leading up to 2020. However, all of the first-time participants were either in their twenties or thirties, and all ten of the study participants who were over the age of forty were not new to protest activities. So even though age was a pretty strong correlate of whether someone was a first timer or veteran, it was not 100 percent so, especially with some of the younger veterans.

Besides the first-time/veteran distinction, one of the other highest priority concerns in sample selection was to have a variety of U.S. protest locations represented. This is because the major driver of the "unprecedented" claim concerns both the size and the scope of the protest locations. Besides all the major U.S. cities, the 2020 racial justice uprising also included smaller towns in areas where there never had before been demonstrations (Putnam, Chenoweth, and Pressman 2020). Certainly, a very different (and much needed) book would be a sample that examined only protesters in Minneapolis and/or Louisville, the two U.S. cities that were home to the two killings considered to be the biggest catalysts of the uprising. In contrast, the sample for this study attempts to spread across different regions of the country, especially the greater regions (Southeast and Midwest) most affected by the killings on the 2020 timeline. While the interview sample does include five respondents who were active in Minneapolis and three who were active in Louisville, the majority stretches across several other large cities—Atlanta, Georgia; Washington, D.C.; Dallas, Texas; Tampa, Florida; Columbus, Ohio; Detroit, Michigan; Richmond, Virginia; Rochester, New York; and Sacramento, California. A minority of the sample (seven) protested in smaller towns, mostly in North Carolina, Virginia, and Maryland. All the small towns and suburbs are majority-white areas, with the exception of Aurora, which is discussed in that same chapter. Having these areas represented was so important in order to have the contrast between these areas and the oft-televised areas with hypermilitarized confrontations. The point was to get a "cross-section" of the United States with both cities and towns, both majority-white and majority-nonwhite areas, represented.[1]

---

[1] New York, New York, and Portland, Oregon, are the two biggest omissions that I highly recommend future studies investigate further, as they both include some crucial 2020 uprising timeline events. See the appendix for more on sample protest locations.

In terms of gender and race, another priority was to have a fairly even split between men and women as well as between Blacks and whites. Again, there are many more books about 2020 yet to be written, and another would most certainly focus more on people of color who were not Black—individuals such as Asian Americans, Latinx, and Native Americans, who study participants observed were a welcome and unprecedented sight in 2020 more so than before. BLM is a Black-led movement, and one of the key contentions about 2020 was the unprecedented level of white involvement, so a focus primarily on these two groups allows this work to stay focused on its major research questions. The interview sample ended up with sixteen white-identified, thirteen Black-identified, and one Native American person, and the gender split was fourteen men and sixteen women (notes on gender and race identification in the appendix). The ages of all the participants are listed in the appendix, but they range from eighteen to seventy. A majority of the sample were under the age of forty—twelve interviewees were in the eighteen-to-twenty-nine age group, eight were in their thirties, and ten were age forty or older (five in their forties, four in their fifties, and one who was seventy).

Another note about the timing of these interviews is that they took place between May and December 2021. As subsequent chapters will review in greater detail, there is some nationally representative survey data available indicating that a sizable proportion—one-fifth to one-quarter—of all 2020 racial justice uprising participants were not in support of Black Lives Matter (Gause and Arora 2021; O'Brien 2021). If I collected my sample at actual protest sites during 2020, certainly I would have picked up some of those more "fringe" participants. However, mid- to late-2021 volunteers for this study likely do not include people who were at this fringe level of engagement with the antiracist objectives of the 2020 uprising. Again, a broader sample like that would have been the basis for a much different study. So the over-one-year-later timing of these interviews indicates at least a surface-level commitment and willingness to volunteer uncompensated time to discuss antiracist activities well after the uprising's widespread popularity has faded from its peak.

There are many more characteristics of these participants that will emerge in more detail in the subsequent pages of this book. Every individual had a unique story to tell, and it was certainly an honor that they gave of their time, totally voluntarily with no compensation, to speak with me via Zoom (video) interviews that usually lasted somewhere between thirty minutes and a little over an hour per interview. Only the written audio transcript was retained from these interviews due to confidentiality purposes, although some participants did ask to be identified by name. For consistency of readability in the manuscript, I only use a rendering of the first name, whether they are actual or pseudonyms, but the appendix denotes with a note those respondents who are using actual names rather than pseudonyms. In the case of clergy, all are professionally accustomed to speaking of their work publicly and asked specifically for their real names to be used, and I add the dignitary "Rev." or "Rabbi" before their first name in the book in those cases.

I personally also participated in several uprising events at the Williamsburg, Virginia, location along with my family. At times during interviews, I did disclose that information about myself when relevant, and I also interviewed a few personal contacts who were present during the events. However, the bulk of the interviews were persons unknown to me, referred to me by friends and colleagues who were aware of my research project and the study qualifications. During interviews, I asked questions about participants' previous protest activities, if any, and what motivated them to come out to demonstrations. I asked them about what they observed in their settings, particularly concentrating on law enforcement, and any other participants. I also asked them about any patterns they noticed in age, race, or other visible demographics of who was participating. As noted in the concluding chapter, I also asked them what their objectives were in participating, if they felt those objectives had been achieved, and if not, what needed to happen next.

I used an approach known as "active interviewing," which asserts that each interview is a socially created product; in dramaturgical fashion, it is a performance accomplished by the two actors—the interviewee and the interviewer (Holstein and Gubrium 1995). As such, we would not expect another interviewer, another context (i.e., face-to-face instead of Zoom), a different date, a different time to produce the same interview data, even with the same research subject/interviewee. This challenges the more positivistic approach that assumes there is one singular "truth" to be obtained from the interviewee as vessel, and it is my job as the interviewer to extract that truth out of them—that is not at all the case here. Rather, we are engaged together in cocreating meaning during our interview interaction, and the result of that collaboration becomes my data. This approach means that I cannot somehow "contaminate" the data by telling my interviewee about my own protest activities or by selectively disclosing (without naming names) what other interviewees have said. In fact, these maneuvers can even be considered rapport-building strategies. Interviewees are active agents, and in my experience, they are not at all swayed to make something up just to approximate another person's experience. For example, I may probe during an interview, "Some participants reported seeing officers using tear gas or pepper spray. Did you notice any of that where you were?" Interviewees are typically completely willing to say, "No, I did not see that where I was," as opposed to some notion of "leading the witness" by discussing others' experiences. Thus, the active interview approach I used included an "interview guide" that, although it had a list of questions, I did add unscheduled probes to in strategic ways depending on the interviewee. In other words, I did not always "stick to the script," and not everyone got 100 percent the same questions in the same order. This is also known as a semistructured interview process (Berg and Lune 2012). In this way, I could tailor the questions to each participant, maximizing the ease of interaction flow between us.

Besides the observational evidence collected through my intermittent level of small-town protest participation, I also traveled to two larger sized U.S. cities (Richmond, Virginia, and Columbus, Ohio) in August 2020 to gather photos and take field notes at various uprising settings. While this evidence is featured most prominently in chapter 5, it also comes up slightly in other areas. Richmond's Monument Avenue was a site of Confederate monument toppling during that period—with Robert E. Lee's statue transformed into a memorial for decades of police killing victims, and a community garden and recreational as well as artistic and gathering space. This has all now been removed. Columbus's downtown near City Hall was also transformed for many blocks of nothing but boarded up businesses—even thriving corporate locations such as high-rise banks like Citibank and Chase had their entire ground-floor levels covered with plywood. Artists had transformed nearly every plywood stretch with various themes, not unlike those in Los Angeles, reported in Cappelli's (2020) Advances in Applied Sociology article. Being physically present in these spaces was much different from seeing it in pictures and allowed me to more fully appreciate this beautiful solidarity.

In the chapters that follow, I have organized this evidence in ways that will best address my research questions: (1) What motivated people to come out for racial justice despite a deadly viral pandemic raging on? (2) What was distinctive about participants' uprising experiences—either in comparison to prior racial justice movements or, if it was their first time, in comparison to their expectations of what they thought would happen there? (3) Did participants feel that their presence as part of this unprecedented, herculean effort accomplished anything—did they achieve what they set out to do? If not, what is the work that is left? As a result of these project focal points, I begin with chapter 2 exploring the questions of how was the 2020 uprising similar to prior racial justice events and how was it different, distinctive, unique from before? Answering these questions entails splitting up interview participants into groups/cohorts depending on their level of prior protest experience. Yet one of the biggest answers to this question of what was distinctive (and not) about the 2020 uprising lies in a deeper investigation into crowd control, which I take up in chapter 3—how were law enforcement engaged in protecting citizens' First Amendment rights to protest? How were they engaged in repression, intimidation, harassment, neglect, and even violence? What other nonstate actors became involved in the uprising in ways that did not support, even undermined, the Black Lives Matter movement? Next, chapter 4 examines how varied the participants were in terms of demographic backgrounds and what drove them to participate—mothers/parents had different reasons than did whites than did people of color—but in keeping with the claim of 2020 being unprecedented, this chapter also examines what might have made this crowd look different than prior protests (e.g., ages, racial/ethnic diversity). Chapter 5 probes the broad "uprising" classification in greater depth—what was happening besides just protest marches? Here, we see evidence of candlelight vigils, spoken word performance, visual art on plywood boards, mutual aid networks, yoga/meditation, monument toppling, consciousness raising, and supporting each other's mental health needs collectively (sharing grief is much different than processing it alone). While some of this is not new (e.g., mutual aid has been going on for decades as part of social movements), some of it became a historical marker of 2020's distinctiveness, such as plywood art.

Finally, as chapter 6 brings the book to a close, we examine the crucial question, what is next? Because of the diversity and different starting points of the various uprising participants, there are various levels of antiracist awareness. So although most interview participants suggest individual-level solutions, and even a good proportion of them also suggest intermediate-level solutions that would reorganize the justice system and create greater accountability at the organizational level beyond just bias training and "bad apples" approach, it is very few who endorse solutions that would attack systemic racism beyond the justice system—in education, housing, economy, politics, and beyond. This helps identify why this latest "peak" in racial justice interest was short-lived. It was an antiracist racial project that did many things—created a space to share collective grief and learn more about one another, provided mutual aid needs for the community, toppled monuments, got rid of racist symbols, and so much more. But it fell way short of its leaders' broader goals for a more racially just world. So there is still more work to do.

CHAPTER 2

Similar but Different

Something Old, Something New

> Darnella [Frazier] responded to a question from a Minneapolis Star-Tribune reporter about why she took the video with a simple answer: "It was like a natural instinct, honestly. The world needed to see what I was seeing. Stuff like this happens in silence too many times." Thanks to her, there would be no silence around George Floyd's death.
>
> —Museum of the Courageous, Class of 2021

There are many claims that the racial justice uprising of 2020 was unprecedented, yet at the same time, much about it was not unfamiliar. As Black Lives Matter activist Sarah L. Chevolleau in Staffordshire, England, put it, the killing of George Floyd "sent shock waves" around the world, leading to an awakening of folks "from all walks of life," but "for the vast majority of Black people across the globe, this was not news. This has been our reality from the day that we were born" (Chevolleau 2020, 142). Indeed, well before 2020, many people of color were already experiencing "a pandemic of racism" in which racism was killing Black people at rates similar to the coronavirus (Disparte and Tilleman 2020). Police killing civilians without much repercussion was hardly new either. Between 2013 and 2019 alone, there were 7,663 civilians killed by police in the United States, with only ninety-five of those (1.2 percent) even charged with a crime, and only forty-eight convicted (Disparte and Tilleman 2020). Known to some as the "first wave" of the Black Lives Matter movement, this mid- to late-2010s decade of social justice activism—beginning with the murders of Trayvon Martin, Michael Brown, and Freddie Gray, among others—gave way to thousands of protests and demonstrations and had been compared to its predecessor, the 1960s U.S. civil rights movement (Tillery 2021). Plenty racial justice activists who had been busy well before 2020 saw this latest surge as just another wave of what they had already been doing before.

Yet it was also hard to ignore some prominent differences from what transpired previously. As historian Peniel Joseph noted in a 2020 PBS News Hour segment,

> So in 1963, for example, there's a 10-week period in the spring of 1963 where we have over 700 racial justice demonstrations, we have almost 15,000 people arrested. In this year alone [2020], we have had over 7,000 separate anti-racist, social justice demonstrations in over 2,400 different locations.... So, this is unprecedented. (Nawaz 2020)

Scholars have concluded that the 2020 racial justice uprisings were not only unprecedented in sheer numbers but also in terms of their spread. It was not just limited to large cities, not just limited to a particular city affected by a killing, not even limited to the United States but worldwide. The racial/ethnic diversity of the crowds, as well as the day-to-day perseverance of events, was also unprecedented (Fisher 2020). Estimates are that between 7,500 and 10,000 demonstrations occurred, involving about 10 percent of the U.S. population and also supported by more in terms of public opinion than the first wave (Nawaz 2020; Tillery 2021). Whereas some were continuing on a long-standing trajectory of social justice activism, for many others it was their first foray, and of course the temporary suspension of many regularly scheduled activities (e.g., work, school, public gatherings) freed up more people than usual to participate.

Many felt so passionate about participating that it was really their first time breaking quarantine (other than going to the grocery store) since March 2020 when they emerged from their homes by the summer to attend a racial justice event. Some survey data suggest that some of those who came out (15–20 percent) were not even necessarily aligned with Black Lives Matter movement goals specifically but were frustrated by government response to various aspects of the coronavirus pandemic (Gause and Arora 2021). It did seem that more people were paying attention to racial injustice than usual due to the pandemic, especially white people. So although the police killings were not new, the pandemic heightened both the awareness and the involvement. "African Americans have felt the triple threats of COVID-19, job loss, and killings; this has forced all Americans to see a new reality" (Lindeen 2020). The Black Lives Matter movement found itself with more allies than ever before (Tillery 2021).

In this chapter, I explore the reasons participants gave for participating in the 2020 racial justice uprising. Thirteen of thirty interviewees were protesting for the very first time in an official way, but a good chunk of those individuals felt aligned with #BLM for some time. The other half (a little over half) of the interview sample had been active with the first wave of BLM and/or even years or decades before that, and this was simply an extension of what they had done before. Although I was initially curious about participants' decision-making process to weigh risks of contracting COVID-19 against participating in the uprising, this was basically a nonissue for most. If anything, most were more afraid of law enforcement violence against them than the virus itself. Most felt that the pandemic was certainly a factor, but many credited previous BLM organizing in immediate years prior as well as the gripping video footage captured by Darnella Frazier of the George Floyd murder for the uptick in numbers and involvement from years past. And some were particularly moved by the international attention and solidarity with the movement.

"This Is Not New": Participants over Forty

One of the most popular chants during the 2020 uprisings was "Say their names." This version of the chant is gender inclusive, but its origin, "Say her name," was part of the first-wave BLM organizing. Coined by the African American Policy Forum, it was meant to amplify the names of women who have also been lost to police violence (Fondren 2020), but there are over five thousand names of victims of police shootings in the United States between 2015 and 2022, and 95 percent of those were men, with Black Americans killed at nearly twice the rate of white Americans (Tate, Jenkins, and Rich 2022). "Say their names" was part of a consciousness-raising effort by organizers to emphasize that killings like George Floyd and Breonna Taylor in 2020 were unfortunately not new. Much of the sample recognized this ongoing pattern, whether it was their first time participating in direct action in 2020 or not. Some participants recalled being outraged by the killings of Michael Brown, Eric Garner, Tamir Rice, and Sandra Bland—particularly those who were in their twenties—but did not feel they had an in-person outlet in which to show their dissatisfaction by marching until 2020. Others who were in older age groups mentioned names such as Rodney King (who was not killed but severely beaten on tape and officers all acquitted) and Amadou Diallo—cases of police brutality against Black men that went back to the 1990s and early 2000s. So, for many I spoke with, the uprisings of 2020 were not a new awakening necessarily but another chapter in an ongoing saga of racist violence in their lifetimes.

Of the thirteen first-time protesters in the sample, none were over the age of forty. So all ten of the forty-and-over interview participants had seen this before, had protested racial injustice before. When we get to the conclusion chapter, we will see that older and veteran protesters were most likely to describe solutions that went beyond the criminal justice system. So it is not surprising, then, that several of the older participants, when thinking back to their first protest, often mentioned demonstrations that were not about police killings specifically. Helen, a forty-four-year-old African American woman in Williamsburg, Virginia, is part of a military family and recalled that her involvement began with a group of concerned parents, protesting racial profiling of children while shopping:

> When my children were younger . . . 2010-ish, around that time was actually my first time actively getting involved but not so much in the level of seeing African American men and women being murdered but more so the injustice of harassment. Actually being arrested or even followed in a mall. There was a situation at a local mall where we lived where teenagers were being targeted in certain stores, so group of moms . . . shadowed standing outside of the stores, but also writing letters to the companies making them informed on what were the practices that were happening, that they may not have realized had racial undertones.

Direct action included making a presence outside stores as well as letter-writing campaign. Jim Bear, a forty-four-year-old Native American man in Minneapolis, dated his involvement in racial justice back to the 1990s when the Super Bowl was in town and the opponent was the team known at the time as the Washington Redskins.

> Well, I would say it was either in January of 1991 or 1992. . . . And the Super Bowl was being held here in Minneapolis, and the Washington Redskins were playing in the Super Bowl and there was protests around the stadium. American Indians protesting the use of the term "redskins" in professional sports and in Native mascots and I was quite young at the time. I was a sophomore, or maybe a junior in high school, so I was fifteen or sixteen years old and made my way down there to be part of that. And so that sort of is like the earliest memory of any kind of direct action kind of protest or racial justice.

Jim Bear's early involvement foreshadowed his eventual lifetime of seeing the connectedness between symbolic violence and actual violence, along with the connection between Black and Native Americans' fight against racism and white supremacy in all its various forms.

Besides the institution of criminal justice, it is government, politics, education, economy, and many other structures that are implicated in worldwide white supremacy. Carly, a forty-nine-year-old white woman in Columbus, Ohio, dated her earliest activist involvement back to her twenties protesting against the Ku Klux Klan as well as the Iraq War—one such demonstration was televised to the point where it reached Iraqi women, and she received supportive feedback from across the globe that made her feel her actions had been impactful. But her cadre of supporters had been built through local groups like Anti-Racist Action and Noise Not Nazis, who made it a point to show up wherever the Klan did.

> I can think of some of the very earliest ones were in the early '90s going to Klan rallies and so the Klan would come to Columbus or sometimes kind of small towns in Ohio and they get a permit and the police would be there to protect them. . . . There would be a whole line of police with their shields like guarding the Klan and then further out from that . . . the protesters were all supposed to be in the fenced-in area, and so it was very weird to be sure because it was like as clear state support of the Klan and then the protesters are the ones they're causing trouble. . . . Noise Not Nazis . . . it was an offshoot of this group . . . Anti Racist Action . . . so, then, while the Klan was speaking, we had just like buckets and some people had real drums, but it's mostly pots and pans and drums to just drown out the message of the Klan, and so that was the noise-making thing, and so, when we were in Columbus doing that, there were way more protesters than there were Klans people, and it felt safe in terms of we knew that we weren't going to be harmed by white supremacy and stuff like that. But then when we would go to small towns, it was fairly sketchy because there were more supporters than there were protesters. . . . And this was before social media, of course, so we would give flyers out to people that we had written with just information about racism.

Carly's observation is echoed in subsequent chapters by other participants—that typically, there is a clear organization and boundary between white supremacists and counterprotesters at such events. Yet in 2020, it was instead chaos. A recurring critique is that law enforcement was not doing enough in 2020 to quell white supremacist violence toward protesters, and white supremacists were not restricted to any particular areas—they operated more vigilante style at times, without the cover of a specifically marked group that had a permit to be there. A first-time participant in 2020 may not have realized that these clearly opposing forces could have nevertheless been organized in a way that did not incite harm.

Kelli, a forty-four-year-old African American woman in Richmond, Virginia, also had participated in racial justice protests for decades, beginning as an undergraduate student at the University of Virginia in Charlottesville, but continuing onward as she moved to Richmond for graduate school, then settling there as a business owner. Like other older participants, Kelli's prior protest involvement was not directly about police violence but rather other forms of institutional racism in her immediate communities where she lived and worked. For example, "going to UVA in the '90s," she was involved in sit-ins at the "president's doors" being one of few Black students at a predominantly white university, where students had to fight for multicultural spaces, so they just created them, although not without resistance. ("You would be in an uproar if there was a white student alliance. You would be in an uproar if there was a white student eating time!") From her early days, Kelli was protesting to be a fully respected participant as an African American in majority-white space. Kelli also saw protest as a dialogue between African Americans and whites, even as a teach-in ("We had to kind of like show them") about forms of racism whites did not recognize or acknowledge at first. This work continued as she moved from Charlottesville to Richmond.

> I will say when I got to Richmond, in the late '90s early 2000s, really the racial issues were here; we were still considered the capital of the Confederacy. No recognition to all of the Black culture that was started right here in Richmond.... I think what protected Richmond was the fact that the politicians were Black, so we didn't really get to the streets at that time the way that we probably needed to with the fact that we were living in a very schizophrenia city that celebrates the Confederate life but does not celebrate Black legacy, right? So I'm trying to think that even with like Trayvon Martin, some of the first murders that were in hands of other people that were racially motivated because you know all of them have not been police driven. For the most part, the energy in Richmond . . . they were fighting very small things; they were fighting public transportation, housing, any quality education, education system, and the food deserts to food disparity. So again, it wasn't on a police killing standpoint in Richmond.

Economic and environmental equity are important components of fighting for racial justice for Kelli. But that did not preclude her from also standing up in the case of unarmed African American civilians being murdered, as she also mentioned Trayvon Martin here. And she does point out Martin was not killed by police.

Likewise, Rev. TM, a fifty-three-year-old white man in Minneapolis, had been doing progressive organizing a long time in different parts of the United States, to the point where he recognized 2020 as but a new chapter in that long trajectory of work:

> I've been doing this a long time, my first was probably in high school or college, thirty, forty years ago—it feels like I've been doing this my whole life. I've been to school of the Americas watch. I've been arrested many times in D.C. . . . I did train at the King Center highlander school. And I've been training people around civil disobedience stuff for a long time so. Please yeah, this is not my first protest or it's not really even a protest; I wouldn't call it that. I think that the Iraq War, that was protesting. I think this was a different feel; it was really a call

> to solidarity, I understand, in my own life I used to be a young energetic activist and now I'm really called to be in support and solidarity of young activists.... I gotta say I love being in Minneapolis; it's a diverse community of activist leaders and we got to know each other over the years at different events. Certainly Jamar Clark's killing, Philando Castille, we been in this police reform talk and abolition talk for a long time. And a lot of us participated in the Standing Rock solidarity events around... the Dakota Access Pipeline. And so the Indigenous leaders are present in a powerful way in Minneapolis, and I did not experience that a lot when I was on the East Coast and doing protesting and those events, but it's certainly a very noticeable leadership presence here is the Indigenous leaders. And I think they bring a different spirit to that work as well.

As with other participants from this age group, Rev. TM had memories of involvements going back to the 1990s but also pinpointed several more recent (pre-2020) events from the BLM first-wave period—Jamar Clark was killed by Minneapolis police near the end of 2015, and Philando Castile was killed by police in Saint Louis, Missouri, in the summer of 2016, which was the same year that the protests of the Dakota Access Pipeline at Standing Rock began. As a spiritual leader, he saw great potential in what he perceived as a new moral foundation of the movement.

> I think the moral fusion work of the Poor People's Campaign is interspersed in a lot of what is going on... speaking in moral and just language—it's much more than pro and against language.... We're building another future, another way of being, so that that language is different. Some of the chants are the same, "Hey hey, ho ho," but there is a sense of evolving of the movement—not there's any one movement but a combination of movements.... When Trump was elected and that was a powerful statement about this is not the world we want to live in and how do we change that for the better.... The primary narrative is we're in a very unjust system that treats some people differently than other people, based on the color of their skin and their economic background and we can do better.... It's a punishment system versus a restorative system, and in the faith world, the restorative system is deep in our bones, and so we've tried to live into that.

To hear Rev. TM describe it, 2020 was hardly an exceptional moment but rather the culmination of ongoing work to bring different social justice movements together, advocating for a more equitable world—made even more imperative by the Trump presidency.

Also in Minneapolis, Rabbi M, a fifty-one-year-old white man, had a history of racial justice activism dating back to the 1990s and was part of the first-wave BLM protests as well.

> I'm not sure where to begin, maybe thirty years ago and I was in high school or college, so I've been involved for a long time. I was arrested when I was in seminary in New York after Amadou Diallo was shot and killed by police officers. . . . I have been involved . . . in terms of housing stuff and getting ordinances changed about spitting and lurking and loitering and affordable housing. And was very involved when Jamar Clark was killed here. And went to Ferguson, with a group of clergy, interfaith clergy, there after Mike Brown Jr. was murdered. And then was helping with their rallies after Charlottesville here, and after the Pittsburgh shooting, and so I have been to these rodeos before, as they say.

The rabbi drew a direct link between the killing of Amadou Diallo by NYPD in 1999, to work on affordable housing and excessive policing (loitering ordinances), to the 2015 Clark killing mentioned above (as well as the 2014 Michael Brown killing in Ferguson), and even to other events of the past five years that were racist-motivated hate crimes/killings by civilians, not police (Charlottesville and Pittsburgh). Like the others of his generation, he did not see racial justice organizing as limited to policing or criminal justice, but it was obviously a recurring, unrelenting drumbeat along with the other racism-related problems.

The oldest respondent in the sample, Bill, a seventy-year-old white man and retired state senator from California, had an impressive record of racial justice work going back to the 1960s.

> My involvement in direct action goes pretty far back. I grew up in Southern California. . . . I went to Berkeley fall of '69 and was very active in anti-war movement . . . '69 through '72. And then went to work with the United Farm Workers Union—first as a volunteer during the strike in 1973, where three thousand workers were arrested, two were killed. . . . And then became a lawyer, with UFW legal department, representing victims of picket line violence, farmworker picketers who were attacked by grower agents and teamsters. So a lot of confrontational politics through the '70s. . . . During my time in Berkeley and as a law student in San Francisco was also involved as an ally, with the Black Panther Party and worked in raising funding for the George Jackson clinic in Oakland during the breakfast programs the food distribution programs, health. And I think it's important to cite that work of the Black Panther Party because a lot of what I think younger generation feel was new with the Black Lives Matter movement, I believe, have roots that go back to the civil rights movement of the '60s and before and in the Black Panther Party brought it to new level of militancy in the late '60s early '70s. I worked as a law student on the San Quentin Six trial were six inmates in the adjustment Center at San Quentin were charged with conspiracy murder. . . . That trial was the longest criminal trial in the history of California

and the longest jury deliberation in the history of California. It led to the acquittal of five of the six. . . . But again, that intersected with the work of the Black Panther Party—Huey Newton, Bobby Seale, Erica Huggins. And that was kind of part of the culture that we were living in as white activist allies of the Black liberation movement of those days.

Bill perceived an affinity between the Black Panther Party work he witnessed in the 1960s and the more modern Black Lives Matter movement. As a lawyer, he was involved not only with injustice in the criminal justice system but also with labor law and immigration law as it affected farmworkers in California. Like many over-forty participants in the uprising, unfortunately much of the injustices of that particular year was not unprecedented to them compared to all else they had seen. What was more unique was the type of involvement that occurred as part of the uprising. But the events that precipitated it were unfortunately not all that different in their estimation.

"Enough Is Enough": Millennial and Gen Z BLM from First to Second Wave

While the Black Lives Matter movement emerged to highlight a type of violence of unarmed Black civilians that was unfortunately hardly new, what it did do was capitalize on new media and technology to galvanize public outrage about such incidents. Of the under-forty part of the sample, the majority (n = 13) were first-time protesters, but seven were not. Most of those seven were part of the first wave of Black Lives Matter; however, even among the thirteen who did not attend a demonstration, they were still actively following what was occurring, participating in "hashtag activism" (Reynolds and Mayweather 2017). Black Lives Matter is one of the three most popular hashtags on all of Twitter (Tillery 2021). While Twitter can be used to share information about locations of protests, petitions, and other direct action events, it is also an important site for community building (Edrington and Lee 2018) as well as "scaling up"—forging coalitions with other constituencies and creating internal movement strength (Mundt, Ross, and Burnett 2018). Social media was also an important tool for publicizing news about harms against African Americans and other people of color when the mainstream media was not sharing widely—for example, Michael Brown's murder in Ferguson, Missouri, first broke on Twitter before it ever hit the mainstream media, which for this and many other reasons Cobbina (2019, 102) describes social media as a "game changer" for the Black Lives Matter movement. This all occurred in the mid- to late 2010s during the first wave of Black Lives Matter, well before the 2020 uprising.

Several protesters in their twenties and thirties were out in the streets during that first wave also; so not unlike participants over forty above, this was not new to them either. Nicole, a twenty-seven-year-old African American woman whose 2020 participation was in D.C., dates her first participation back to 2015 after the Michael Brown killing in Ferguson, Missouri. She did not go to Missouri, but her hometown in Virginia had a march up the interstate highway that she participated in, and social media was important in organizing that event.

> So I have participated prior, I'm not sure if you recall, when people were marching on '64. I was a part of that, and I believe it was in 2015. [Interviewer: Michael Brown?] Yes. So this area they had did a walk and I was a part of that. I think it was after the [Brown] shooting, not the [Darren Wilson] verdict, yeah. . . . Someone had made a post on Facebook and was like, hey, we're going to march, to protest injustice, . . . time, place, we're going to meet at— . . . and we walked all the way through on the actual interstate, yes! [Interviewer: Wow, like up the shoulder or . . .] Yeah, on the shoulder and a little bit in the middle, but I didn't go as far as the interstate because I had the baby with me, so I just turned off after that. But we were in the street, in the middle of the street, I went [street names], so we definitely did that!

Nicole felt so passionate in 2015 that she traversed a slightly dangerous protest route with kids in a stroller in order to participate. Her generation came of age when the Trayvon Martin murder occurred, the incident often credited with the birth of the Black Lives Matter movement. Even though she did not march when Trayvon Martin was killed, that was a formative event for developing her consciousness about racial injustice.

> I was in the twelfth grade when Trayvon Martin was killed, and I remember we had a little bit of something at school, but you know, not too much, but yes, I think I would consider that [2015] my first time really you know rallying and trying to . . . [Interviewer: But would you say that the Trayvon Martin was your first kind of, like, awareness as far as that goes or . . .] Yes, I remember it being so huge. I also remember our class like erupting in an argument because of my twelfth-grade teacher, she would have us do what's called current news Friday—so every Friday class would be nothing, but you brought in a mail article like an article from the mail and you sit in a circle and discuss it. . . . I want to say almost everybody that was Black brought in that as their article, and so, but the class wasn't all Black, so you know all Black people don't feel the same, so on top of other races that had their opinion about it and then Blacks too that had their opinion about it, it turned into a big to-do, like she had to like get security to come to class down

it gotten very tense and people were feeling some type of way, a lot of emotions were in the in the room. I remember that.

The fact that the teacher felt she had to call security during a routine classroom discussion about this injustice demonstrates how contentious the issue became, shaping an impactful memory for Nicole. Nicole's memory is an important reminder that for 2020 participants about to turn thirty, they were still in high school when Trayvon Martin's murder occurred and thus young when the Michael Brown killing happened less than two years later. These young adults have been watching a steady stream of unjust killings where justice often is not achieved for the victim and victim's families, and 2020 may have been nearly one of the first times to participate in organized actions about such injustices as independent adults.

Hood Scholar, a thirty-eight-year-old Black man whose 2020 participation was in Minneapolis, not only traveled there but also traveled to Ferguson in 2014 for the protests after the Michael Brown killing. Then he organized protest in his hometown in 2015 after former officer Darren Wilson was acquitted (would not be charged) for the murder. However, Hood Scholar had a much longer history in progressive antiracist organizing because his mother was a community organizer, so he really started as a child and was involved with an impressive list of actions, including paid employment with DART, a faith-based social justice community organizing group. So by the time the first wave of the Black Lives Matter movement began, this was not new to him, and from his perspective, BLM is just one of many components of the larger international Black freedom struggle. Hood Scholar has two master's degrees as well as a PhD, so he spent most of that decade as a graduate student at two different universities in Virginia. Here, he recalled some of his involvements from 2014:

> Of course 2014 that's when Mike Brown died, right? Mike Brown, I was in my first year . . . going to grad school and I had been following that killing. . . . For a while, I was in Ferguson. October, I met the people who are organizing a rally. He [was] pretty much expecting Darren Wilson was not going to be found guilty. . . . So whenever we expected that to happen, let's have protest and direct action all around the country. So pretty much what happened was we had organized in cities, and we put it on social media—Tumblr, Facebook, Twitter—and said, look, if you want to protest in response to this . . . so I was the one organizing this in Williamsburg. And so . . . we had well over two hundred people, and people were saying like that was the biggest protest that's seen in Williamsburg's history, so I would say . . . I've been doing this for years, work on it, then the most recent recognizable example would be in November, somewhere around late 2014 where we planned a large mass of protests against the verdict.

Hood Scholar explained that by going to Ferguson when the killing first happened, he connected to the organizing infrastructure that was building there. Since local organizers anticipated a not-guilty verdict and public outrage, they were mobilizing to be ready to protest around the country whenever that happened. Social media was a crucial part of building and expanding that base.

Others from the twenties and thirties age group were watching and following closely from the first wave but did not have the impetus to be involved in direct action until 2020. Sometimes it was because they perceived that protest events were more localized depending on where a particular act of racial violence had occurred, or they thought their city or town was not big enough to host protests (before 2020). In some cases, it was almost as if they were holding their breath hoping the justice system would deliver justice; but as the successive rush of stories kept ending in no indictment, no guilty verdict, they finally decided with 2020 that "enough is enough." This was the case with Jordan, a twenty-six-year-old Black/mixed man participating for his first time in Atlanta in 2020.

> I think at first I didn't fully understand in ways to help, as I did, now I feel as though . . . I really didn't want to get in the way of other individuals on before that . . . like other than the Michael Brown protests, and a little bit of the Trayvon Martin protests also weren't as global, the protests seemed more regional like with Trayvon I felt like was more in the middle, in the South, because it was in Florida, I was living in Virginia at the time, the same thing with Michael Brown because that was in the Midwest or was in Missouri that's kind of in the middle of the country. For George Floyd, I felt like it also because . . . you could just see the video and just the amount of rising, and also, I guess the compilation of other racial incidents had also kind of compounded. . . . We have things like Sandra Bland, Ahmaud Arbery, Breonna Taylor. . . . You had Philando Castille, you have all these other individuals. For me, the one that was really impactful was Tamir Rice, and then you go on and you have Jamar Clark. Here, you have Alton Sterling, Rayshard Brooks later . . . on the other side of the city that I live in. So I think it was just a combination of all of these things that just continue . . . and some point, I feel, like any individual is going to have to stand up and say, "Enough is enough."

The sudden upsurge in attendance for the 2020 uprising might lead one to believe that so many people did not care before that moment. But in actuality, even a "first-time protester" in 2020 might have been a social media activist or contributing to the discourse about racial injustice well before that moment. Indeed, this steady unyielding trickle of racial injustice is what led them to finally say, "Enough is enough," leading with their feet in 2020.

Nicole Carney's (2016) analysis of tweets after the tragic deaths of Eric Garner and Michael Brown in 2014 demonstrates how even when people were not marching in the streets necessarily, Twitter users (particularly youth of color) used linguistic strategies and logical arguments to shape the discourse about race and racism. For example, they would actively challenge others who posted "All lives matter" with arguments like, "Why would we say, 'but all cancers matter' when we are focusing on breast cancer right now?" and in so doing, attempt to expose rhetorical fallacies of people who were resistant to the movement. Thus, particularly younger participants may have felt they were part of the first wave of Black Lives Matter of the mid- to late 2010s in some way, even if they are categorized as a "first time" 2020 protester, depending on the extent to which they engaged in such related activities. As Jordan stated above, at first he didn't understand all the ways to help, but nevertheless he was building his consciousness along the way. A similar trajectory was expressed by Blake, a twenty-one-year-old white man protesting in Williamsburg, Virginia. He was of a lower class background than most of the whites growing up at his high school, so he gravitated more toward friends from minoritized groups in his childhood, which gave him insights into the realities of racism. Like several in the sample expressed, direct action demonstration opportunities seemed largely limited to bigger cities before 2020.

> So actually, marches in 2020 were my first actual marches that I attended—growing up in suburban Williamsburg, things aren't exactly as publicized when it comes to inequity of any kind; people try to create the bubble, so I hadn't had the opportunity to attend any other protests or marches or anything. . . . Growing up in a family that was much lower class for being in the Williamsburg area, all my friends growing up were Black or Hispanic or colored people [sic]. I didn't have probably any friends or people that I associated with that were like non, not of color until I was probably in the second or third grade so, and even still, then my best friends have all been people of the Black community. . . . I've been doing my research for a long time on the social injustice and racial injustice and all that and reading more about true African American history and all that not just the stuff that they put in history classes. But seeing the news clips of George Floyd and all that and just all of the carryover of every single news story I've read about it, seeing that there was something in my hometown that people were standing up for it, just I knew I had to be there.

My estimation is that most people who were willing to participate in this study one year or more later, even as "first-time protesters," were developing a racial consciousness and becoming antiracist long before their actual participation in the uprising. This seems equally true of white and African American first-time protesters in the sample.

African American children experience racial socialization much earlier than white children do (e.g., Rivas-Drake, Hughes, and Way 2009; Hagerman 2013). While Blake above describes a somewhat atypical experience for a suburban white childhood, both RJ and Tucker—twenty-nine-year-old African American men in the D.C./Maryland area—were not learning about racism from doing their own "research" or from their friends as Blake was but rather within their own families and communities. So even though 2020 was their first time protesting, again it was not like they had just opened their eyes. As RJ explained when I asked, "Did you find yourself in situations prior to this one where you had stood up about racial injustice or was this your first time doing so?":

> Not in a direct manner, I think my upbringing and childhood experiences definitely were brought to attention but more so to my parents, and my parents then took whatever necessary procedures... to make sure that what I felt in my childhood upbringing was not right, and it was brought to other people's attention that it should not have gone that way, or should have been handled in a better way.

Indeed, RJ's parents modeled for him how to advocate for himself when he was treated unjustly. Even though he felt being a minor limited his ability to speak out on his own in those situations, this was another form of building racial consciousness that one does not remain silent in the face of racism. Like Jordan above, RJ felt even though he was not fully aware as a young person to fully comprehend what the exact action steps would be (how to "vote with his feet"), he still understood that racism was ubiquitous and should not go unchallenged.

Tucker was well aware of being surrounded by racism in his community years before the 2020 uprising, and again, this was not limited to criminal justice or policing.

> It was like a bubbling up thing, you know?... When I got to high school, it was 2010; it was stuff... you can put it as hate crimes—like people spray-paint the N-word on school buildings and stuff like that, hanging, like leaving like prop nooses around stuff like that... not my high school but just high schools in the area.

Intimidating actions directed at African Americans, such as public displays of a hanging noose and graffiti "N-word," which Tucker consistently described with plural nouns, indicating that such graphic blatant threats happened so regularly that there was not one particular event that stood out, were a part of his youth. Tucker described his community's awareness level as "bubbling up" in advance of

2020—and as Jordan put it, "enough is enough." As we shall see in subsequent chapters, several African American participants including Tucker felt that it was important to continue struggles that the ancestors waged against racism. It was not so much that they expected any grand achievements to come from the 2020 uprising, but rather, they felt a moral sense of duty to their elders to stand up and voice their opposition to injustice to continue the work of prior generations out of respect and gratitude for the work that came before them. A coronavirus pandemic—although it placed the world on a temporary standstill—was evidently just one more obstacle on a par with many others the ancestors had seen before.

COVID-19 Pandemic: Worth the Risk

Although the 2020 racial justice uprisings were in many ways not new in terms of the racial injustice protesters were responding to, one thing new about protesting this time were the health risks of COVID-19 especially when no vaccine was yet available. This elevated health risk resulted in closures of many kinds, seemingly indefinitely—schools and many businesses deemed not "essential." Leisure, entertainment, and other activities outside the home were few and far between, so in the summer of 2020, television consumption increased, and news topped the list of what people were watching, as they struggled to stay informed on how to keep themselves and their families safe, with knowledge shifting each time more became known about this novel coronavirus (Fitzgerald 2020). Even as large gatherings were considered high risk to become "superspreader" events (for transmission of the deadly COVID-19), these protesters agreed that their moral convictions on how inhumane this racial injustice was superseded any health concerns they may have had.

While participants of multiple racial backgrounds expressed the sentiment that this historical moment was too important to sit out, it was African Americans especially who emphasized they faced other risks to their lives that were at least equal to, if not more threatening than, COVID-19. In fact, as whites feared they might contract coronavirus even if they took every precaution to protect themselves, some African Americans expressed that maybe now whites would understand how they feel all the time, unable to protect themselves from racist violence. They characterized the virus as merely one of but many other threats they were constantly warding off. As Hood Scholar, a thirty-eight-year-old Black man who traveled to Minneapolis to protest, explained it, Black people were dying regardless.

> We're dying, so talk about which way you want it, right? I'd rather go out during a fight instead of being inside, right? That's what we say, "We outside," instead of

being inside. . . . Black people, many of us have reached a point where it was so hard, okay, inside was a problem, if that makes sense. Recently, we've seen a number of killings . . . so staying inside for over a year right . . . humans were made for interaction. It's like, this isn't the way we were designed as human beings. So if you are alone, you're literally alone in your apartment in your in your place where you're staying all by yourself. Like that's inhumane completely, right? . . . If you're by yourself, if you have no other people, then the stressors of being inside begin to build up. Yeah, so I reached a point where it was like basically an unsophisticated and best way to say this is damned if I do, damned if I don't. . . . And I'm saying this not new for us, right? This is just our normal—it's equal outside. . . . My hope is that concern about coming outside has helped the world see how it is for the way it is for Black people on a regular basis.

This veteran activist summarized it succinctly: "Damned if I do, damned if I don't"—pick your poison. It is a false characterization to say it was any safer inside than outside for Black people, and to stay inside, alone with that fear, is arguably worse, in his view—akin to solitary confinement. When framed in this light, it is indeed a white privilege when one's biggest fear coming outside is contracting coronavirus. It is also a privilege to view home as a safe haven.

Other African Americans agreed that the virus was no greater concern than any other compared to the racism they face in the everyday public square. Sharon, a thirty-nine-year-old Black/Panamanian woman protesting in Williamsburg, Virginia, put it this way:

> It was imperative for me to go because my state is a Black person in America is far more in peril in terms of what could happen; you're talking to somebody that's been put in jail because they were Black in Virginia Beach, when I was with a white girl who had drugs on her and did not a single night in jail, so I felt like the color of my skin was much more of a cause for concern, especially with what we were getting from the people in terms of the violence. So yeah, I really did not, I felt it was more necessary for me to be present and be there.

Whether it was the risk of contracting the virus or the risk of being arrested at a protest, Sharon felt she already lived through threats of that level with the everyday racism faced by African Americans—while white Americans were often exempted from such concerns. Whether they are African Americans or even some other people of color in the United States, especially urban areas, COVID-19 death rates were really only on a par with the same risks they faced from other, much longer existing threats. For example, in San Francisco (which is one of many U.S. cities where whites are less than half the population), where the highest racial-ethnic group proportions are Hispanic and Asian Americans, the deaths from drug overdoses in 2020 were still higher than COVID-19 deaths (Cowan 2022). Structural racism in the form of lack of access to basic lifesaving services has been an active threat far outlasting any specific pathogen.

Tucker, a twenty-nine-year-old African American man in Columbia, Maryland, insisted that "social justice" was much more a prominent concern for him because he viewed the virus as a new and likely temporary threat, whereas the threat of racist violence is something he and his ancestors had to contend with for multiple generations.

> I can say social justice was more on my mind in the forefront than probably health and safety protocols. It's a pandemic going on, but still people, the problems prepandemic are still ramping right now, so it was more of those problems were on people's minds then than the pandemic and staying socially distant. But I mean, I have my mask going out there, and my little sister, she had hers on there too. It's a different experience and I wasn't really in close proximity.... We still are outside. Oh no, it's kind of like a play-by-ear thing and just everybody's temperament and judgment on it is different, so but mine's was—I wasn't—I was really more focused on the cause than the pandemic at the time.

Many participants took solace in the fact that they were outdoors, even if sometimes in close proximity to each other, and most mentioned wearing their masks. Tucker emphasized racism existed before the pandemic and continued to go on during/afterward. From this perspective, the coronavirus pandemic—deadly as it had been—was but a small blip on the radar screen compared to the deadliness of racist violence without justice prevailing. To Tucker, this was a much more pressing concern in the grand scheme of things.

Likewise, RJ, a twenty-nine-year-old African American man participating in Washington, D.C., saw "violence in the street" as just another risk not unlike the virus, especially due to his youthful age, even in the absence of a vaccine.

> We just decided to go out even with the pandemic taking place. Part of that too, I think, is that we're younger; this is before the vaccines and stuff, of course, but we just felt like we're young, we're in good health. At the end of the day, when you're going out to protest, even if it's 2020, 1960—you're going out willing to potentially have something happen to you, whether it's COVID, whether it's violence in the street—you're putting yourself out there, you know what you're signing up for. So I was prepared for the best- and worst-case scenario of the pandemic or just being, dealing with some of the legal, law enforcement type of things too, so

it's a calculated risk. You have to know when you're making those decisions, you have to live with whatever could potentially happen, and I was willing to do that.

As an African American man, he compared this moment to the 1960s from his grandparents' generation—violence, getting arrested, needing a lawyer or bail money—all of these were risks on a par with, if not above, contracting coronavirus in his estimation. RJ described this as a "calculated risk" he was willing to take because of how important it was to him to be part of the experience.

Even if they were not African American, others still evaluated law enforcement violence, and arrests were more serious risks associated with participating in the protests than COVID-19. For example, Michelle, a twenty-four-year-old white woman and first-time protester in Dallas, Texas, mentioned that her family's concern about her participating was not even as much health related as it was about her physical safety.

> I was completely on lockdown, I believe. No one was really leaving their houses unless it was to go to work or maybe get food from a to-go restaurant; it was not normal to be going out into the club atmosphere, or the bar scene, or anything like that. And then when the protests started arising, especially in Texas, in general, I definitely wanted to go, but I was kind of hesitant, not only because of COVID but also because my family was a little scared that something might happen between me and the police and that I might get arrested or might get hurt, and it was never any fear of what people at the protests might do; it's always fear of police. And so I kind of just took it upon myself, and let's just like—I can't listen to y'all; I have to do something! I decided to go to the protests.

For some people, the protests were the first time leaving their homes for anything other than essential tasks. The moral imperative to take a stand for their values and against injustice superseded those fears ultimately. But law enforcement was perceived as more of a threat than coronavirus transmission for some. Also, again her youthful age may be a factor as the family she describes as fearful is likely older.

Similarly, Isabel, a twenty-year-old white woman who protested in Aurora and Denver, Colorado, was rarely leaving her house other than essential work and studying in the summer of 2020. Like many, she described taking every precaution and masking up even though it was outdoors, and she had seen the devastating effects of the virus firsthand.

> Yeah, it was really unique because I have always been very safe about COVID because during the time, I was in school for health care—health care allied position—and so I was in the hospitals, and I was seeing COVID firsthand. Before

going to these protests, I was inside all the time unless I was doing school stuff and unless I was in the hospital. And so it was a big decision for myself to be like weighing the pros and cons or more, so I was thinking this is so important to me and I feel like this is something that needs to be done. So I just decided to take every precaution—I double-masked, I tried to stay away from super-big groups. They were all outside, so that was great, but yeah, I felt like even though COVID also was something that I was really safe and passionate about and wanted to make sure I had that under control. I think the protests—definitely, it was like the only thing that brought me out of the house during that time. So that kind of shows how much it meant to me because I never did anything else.

During this same period, former president Trump and other Republican-leaning groups were holding rallies as an election loomed, and many among these groups felt it was a sign of weakness to wear masks. In contrast, nearly everyone in this sample, whether or not they expressed concern about the virus as a primary threat, reported wearing masks themselves and observed masking consistently among others throughout the duration of the protests. Isabel herself recalled being double-masked, noting it was a priority of event organizers that copious masking be the public face of the uprisings. She heard repeated reminders on megaphones to stay masked "because they wanted everyone to be safe," but also "when it was shown on the media, they didn't want people to have a reason to say they should stop, so I think that was a big reason for that." As we shall see in the next chapter on law enforcement and violence, attempts to quell and shut down the protesting were frequent. Moreover, some recalled police officers without masks, which they perceived as showing disrespect for human life and disregard for the health and safety of the protesters. So in contrast to those who would not mask, it was intentional that the public face of the uprising showed respect for human life in all ways, including protection from contamination by the virus. Several others agreed that the consistent masking they saw at uprising events dissipated any major fears they had about coronavirus being a concern for them.

While the next chapter outlines law enforcement intimidation tactics in more depth, briefly here let us note that threat assessment is relative. The risk of transmission of COVID-19 brought a new element to fear in 2020, but participants considered this on balance with other more long-standing threats that were also perhaps amped up more than usual. Law enforcement does not always show up in riot gear to protests. So, being an essential worker and already coming into contact with people in public during the pandemic at least was a known risk for some, compared to the threat of violence, which seemed relatively more unpredictable, for someone like Patrice, for example. Patrice is a nineteen-year-old woman who identifies as Black-white biracial and participated in both Troy and Detroit, Michigan. Whereas some came outside their homes for the first time in order to protest, Patrice already was exposing herself more than she wanted to due to work.

> I was a full-time student, but our classes were online, and then I was also working full time as a manager at the local Chipotle, and so I was an essential worker and I was still going to work and being in person. And so that was something that made me ambivalent towards going out, especially in the beginning, because I was around so many people that didn't want to like go out and potentially like risk anything. But also, I was living in Detroit at the time, and so once these protests started, they did have a curfew.... So I was just scared to like be downtown and like if the police started to do anything because they were like being violent against protesters ... it was pretty scary because you could see them all lined up outside, they had on protest riot gear, and so it was literally like, very much I'm scared.

Patrice brought up the police presence in response to my question about what people did to feel safe and protected against the virus. As a person of color living and working in an urban center, it is instructive that she characterized law enforcement violence as more of a perceived threat to her own well-being that the coronavirus.

Thus, COVID-19 was certainly an additional risk factor to be contended with during the uprisings. But on the whole, most participants described this threat as more within their own control by having masks, hand sanitizer, and social distancing and being outdoors. In fact, many were quite impressed with the level of cleanliness, sanitary procedures, and structure provided at the uprising events. As we shall see in the next section, a by-product of the coronavirus pandemic lockdown was the increased attention on media coverage, which many believed also increased awareness and concern about racial injustice. So even though the threat of COVID-19 was a new wrinkle added to the movement for racial justice, creating more death and destruction in its path, it also provided certain opportunities.

Movement Proliferation: Can No Longer Look Away

There was a sense among many of those I interviewed that these uprisings were a uniquely historic moment in the movement. Unfortunately, much about the killings of Ahmaud Arbery, Breonna Taylor, and George Floyd were not new, but the timing and context in which they occurred heightened the sense of community outrage. Calling it the moment of a nexus of a "triple threat," professor of peace and conflict resolution studies Ellen Lindeen wrote, "African Americans have felt the triple threats of COVID-19, job loss, and killings; this has forced all Americans to see a new reality" (Lindeen 2020). The way the pandemic disproportionately impacted people of color, while still also affecting white Americans, did add to the "different from before" perception among many in this sample as well. What was different from before included the sheer numbers of people protesting, which created a spillover effect—meaning, the demonstrations were not limited to larger, urban centers but also spread to other regions and worldwide. By early June 2020, over forty nations around the world had protests (what NBC News called "George Floyd protests" but also called by other names) in solidarity with the movement (Smith, Wu, and Murphy 2020). The shutdown of many usual activities meant more people around the world were paying attention, along with a disturbing video to accompany the outrage. Not unlike the way the television exposed the United States globally in the 1960s for not living up to its democratic ideals, with video footage of dogs and water hoses being unleashed on African Americans—or even the powerful image of Emmett Till's open casket funeral as depicted in *Jet* and *Chicago Defender,* or the video of Michael Brown's body lying in Ferguson for over four minutes before police moved him (Cobbina 2019)—the video captured by Darnella Frazier of Derek Chauvin kneeling on George Floyd's neck for eight minutes and forty-six seconds ignited worldwide attention. Several participants, particularly in Minneapolis but not exclusively, credited this young woman who was not even yet an adult at the time of the murder, with being a crucial catalyst of the 2020 uprising due to her video. Indeed, Frazier even earned an honorary Pulitzer for her act of bravery, without which journalists emphasized there would be no case (Hernandez 2021). It was most often these three factors—the video, the captive audience/greater awareness, and the proliferation of available protest sites—that protesters identified as what made 2020 different than before.

The COVID-19 pandemic thus was not enough in and of itself to be an independent source of the uprising, but it did create the context and backdrop for the amplification of the racial justice movement due to the way society responded to the viral threat. It created a certain stillness to make the pain of racism all the more audible when it too would not disappear. The "crushing weight" of the video evidence in a society already grieving so many other losses, in a political climate devoid of acknowledgment of injustice, became the breaking point in many people's minds (Bebernes 2020). "Ongoing aftershock," "flash point moment," "tipping point," and "perfect storm" are but a small sampling of some of the different ways participants described this constellation of factors crystallizing together in the uprisings of 2020. As Jim Bear, a forty-four-year-old Native American spiritual leader in Minneapolis, eloquently described it, the "whole world" was watching.

> That video that was released Derek Chauvin kneeling on George Floyd's neck was so egregious. There was no way to justify that killing. The whole world saw that he was in custody, he was not a threat, he was not actively resisting. It was just so egregious.... I think here in Minneapolis there was just this sense that this is larger than this case, that it's larger than the city of Minneapolis. I'm too young to have been around for the civil rights era of the mid-'60s, but I talked to some of the elders who were there, and they say like there was just this sense, whether it was in Montgomery or Nashville or Selma, wherever—there's just a sense of this is larger than our moment here. And you want to be able to tell your kids and grandkids that you were on the right side of history.... If I'm ever asked, I don't want to say, no, I didn't participate; I wasn't there.

Jim Bear explained that early on in Minneapolis, they had the sense that this case was going to be a global focal point—both because it so *typified* so much of what the first-wave BLM, and even the civil rights movement of the 1960s, stood for but also because it was *atypical* by having video evidence of a clearly detained and nonresisting victim. It is worth noting that police officers' role is not to determine guilt or innocence in the first place. Nevertheless, many people of color carry a collective memory and understanding of the circumstances under which officers are often exonerated by the legal system if there is even a slightest shred of an officer perhaps feeling "threatened" in the line of duty (Cobbina 2019). So Jim Bear felt it was not only the availability of a video but a video that clearly showed that George Floyd "was not a threat, he was not actively resisting," held the ingredients of a "moment" crucial for the world to see.

Add that video to the global health crisis that hit the world in 2020, and there was just the captive audience that needed to see it—an audience already feeling quite vulnerable and confronting its humanity, even regardless of race. As Jim Bear went on to put it,

> I look back and I wonder would this have been what it was without the pandemic. I have a friend who said—she said, the pandemic caused all of us to encounter our own mortality and our own humanity in a way that we have never had to before. And then, when we see a public lynching in which that humanity is not taken into account—I mean, no one can speculate with any accuracy, like if there was no pandemic would this movement have been larger, or if there was no pandemic, would this movement really not have gained the traction that it did.

> Because I really think that the pandemic did cause us to encounter our own humanity in a way that, certainly for generations, we haven't.

This is where Derrick Bell's interest convergence gets illustrated. As Jim Bear put it, this "public lynching" is something that perhaps at another time would draw greater empathy from people of color than whites, given past evidence. Yet at this moment, due to the pandemic, "all of us" regardless of race are confronting the fragility of humanity and feeling vulnerable to threats that feel beyond one's control. Thus, it is not simply just that everyone was stuck at home watching the same TV channel but even more that they are all watching it while feeling afraid and vulnerable to a collective risk of death like nothing many of them had felt before.

Another component of the video that Rev. TM, a fifty-three-year-old white man from Minneapolis, highlighted as adding to the uniqueness of the moment was the audio from the bystanders that further amplified both the atrocity of Derek Chauvin's horrific act and the police force's implication in it.

> But the catalyst, the tipping point of watching that video and so many people did—millions of people watched that around the country, around the world. It was an archetypal viewing. It affected the culture in a way that, wow, this is not a unique situation, this is not an anomaly, this happens and this happens without a lot of protest and thought. And what you heard in the background, we all heard it again at the trial, where the people of George Floyd Square saying, "Stop! Can you hear him? He's struggling. Stop!" and all you could hear is their voices. You never heard nothing from authority saying, hey, maybe we should do this, or maybe we should do that. One time, there's one place, where the officer says, "Hey, you should turn him on his side," and that's it—everything else is from the people. And that cry for justice from the people who are watching affected everybody, certainly affected me and I've been doing this forever.

Rev. TM described the video as not just an exposure of police murder but also an exposure of a "cry for justice from the people" that went unheeded by any of the officers sworn to protect them. When he stated, "This is not a unique situation," he felt the video demonstrated Chauvin is not just a bad apple but rather, much broader, a failure of an entire community to recognize someone's suffering and stop it before it became fatal. This further highlights the collective vulnerability that Jim Bear referenced above—the world heard "the people" screaming do something, yet the cry went unheard.

To the degree to which this 2020 antiracist racial project achieved something in its symbolic elements, it was fueled by some level of empathy that seemed greater than before. Leaders like Rev. TM, Jim Bear, and others in the older generation understood that BLM—in both its first (2014–2015) and second (2020) wave—was a youth-led movement because of its various technology tactics that became so crucial in gaining a critical mass of support. Rev. TM expounded on these aspects as he further reflected on the power of Darnella Frazier's video:

> I've said her name, before, Darnella Frazier I think is a hero, and should be given a Medal of Honor. By being brave enough to take that video, I think she, her actions did more than anybody else to highlight this and I think that video speaks for itself, it would be hard for a jury not to convict—looking at the face of Chauvin and in the inaction of the officers around him. And how scared George Floyd was—he was a scared, vulnerable big man, but he was he was very scared. And if you can't have empathy for that level of fear, it's just—you can't be in public service. And I think the jury saw that, right? Without more videos like that, I don't see any change happening. I don't think the justice system would have done justice if it were not for that video. So, and she is at those protests. She's a humble amazing twenty-year-old young woman who is just—such courage and strength in her presence, it's amazing.

This combination of empathy and bravery in Frazier's act is further accentuated knowing that merely calmly questioning why an officer is doing something can result in death for African Americans at the hands of police (Cobbina 2019). Certainly, the ubiquity of technology and social media has facilitated the public awareness of many cases of racist police brutality in recent years, but just because everyone has a camera in their hand today doesn't mean that every unjust killing is exposed. It took a split-second decision in a highly traumatic situation by a young woman (still a child at the time) known in her community for her willingness to help others to bring this public lynching to light. Those both within the Minneapolis community and around the world understood the power of this crucial piece of evidence.

It was not just participants from Minneapolis in the sample who heralded Frazier's video as the tipping point. Bill, the seventy-year-old white man in California quoted earlier in this chapter, felt that the 2020 uprising brought some much needed legislative change in his state, which he was proud to have been a part of helping to create. As big as these changes were, and certainly long in coming, Bill nevertheless referred back to this video as one crucial catalyst.

> Old habits die hard—and as long as police investigate their own members after use of force, that track record has resulted in a high percentage of police investigating their own finding it to be justifiable use of force. I think the key is to

separate the investigative body from the agency that employs that police officer, whether it's independent citizen commissions in California . . . a reform in California again brought to the forum by the rash of police killings in greater public attention, but I absolutely believe that the response to the George Floyd killing the fact that it was caught on video in all of its horror, definitely not only sparked the uprising, not just nationally but globally; it also had to influence the climate that his trial took place in, the climate that those jurors lived in, and reflected appropriately, and jurors exercised appropriate responsibilities in evaluation of the evidence to reach a conviction. But that case, unfortunately—not every police killing results in a nine-minute video tape or an international outpouring of outrage. So I think the hard work still lies ahead, but each step of progress is just that—it's a step in the right direction.

As other veteran protesters have echoed, what happened to George Floyd was sadly not uncommon, but what helped the case stand out was the video being seen "not just nationally but globally." Those who have been in these struggles to make legal changes for a long while could not help but take notice that things started moving in certain areas as a result of more people paying attention due to this video.

Nate, a twenty-eight-year-old African American man participating in Monterey, California, primarily, also traveled to Los Angeles and other locations for a total of more than forty-five events, more than anyone else in the sample. The 2020 uprising was his "first time" participation, but like most others of his generation, he had been paying close attention, especially to first-wave BLM activities. Nate also referenced the video as an important catalyst for the global attention compared with prior similar tragedies.

> All the people that were seeing what's happening to us—because people mimic the United States so much—internationally, we're a beacon for a lot of things. So . . . for some reason, when it happened for Trayvon Martin and Michael Brown, when it happened for them, for some reason there was no beacon international; there was no coverage like it was with George Floyd, and I think it's because people were—one, stuck at home, watching TV—whether it's five six news or CNN or whatever it may be for you . . . they were seeing a person kneeling on a person's neck for as long as it was, and the person saying I can't breathe—and people were literally just watching not doing anything. And we saw the power cops held and how cops are not trying to tell other cops—were not trying to stop it, or say, hey, maybe we should stop this—like that that hit the hearts, I believe, of Caucasian brothers and sisters.

The point is, African Americans and people of color already knew this was happening, with Trayvon Martin, Michael Brown, and others. Like Rev. TM above, Nate pointed out it was not only the horrific murderous actions of Chauvin but also the inaction of other officers and their complicity, captured on the video, that also made an impact on the "hearts" of whites. It was hard not to be moved by that video no matter who you were or where you were. And more people were "stuck at home" due to the COVID-19 pandemic lockdown, so more people were watching than typically would.

It was not only the action (of the murder) but the inaction (of other officers) that became the national and global wakeup call. Jordan, a biracial, Black-identified twenty-six-year-old in Atlanta quoted earlier in this chapter saying "Enough is enough," like Nate was a first-time protester in 2020 but also was paying close attention during the first wave. Jordan explained that another reason why people across the nation could no longer look away in 2020 was because by now, they had also learned that various individual local cases from the first wave had not been resolved to the side of justice for families of the victims. Whereas the previous cases were often treated as local matters, this moment felt more national and even international.

> You know, after these incidents happened, the court cases are drawn out, and they just don't go and take these guys immediately into custody.... I think another issue was that all the wrong verdicts that led up to George ... we wanted to see that, we wanted to see the police officer prosecuted. And I think that was another thing that compelled it; it was like more of like okay, we were upset before, but now like this is clearly it! We have to get an answer for this; we can't beat around the bush anymore—I think that's also what probably compelled me and probably a lot of people who probably this is their first time. I think they probably were expecting the American justice system to pan out for these other individuals, and then it didn't. I think that was like for me that was the big thing was like it was all the individuals before, and especially like I said was Tamir Rice. With him, I think that really impacted me and I knew like as soon as if I could help I would it then George fully happened that next May and that's when I saw an opportunity to get involved.... Because we're all told, if you're wrong, you're given your day in court and justice will prevail, but ... only things going to go so wrong so many times before you can start that debate after justice.

This quote is reminiscent of a realization similar to that which writer Ta'Nehisi Coates describes in his *Between the World and Me*, when his young son reacts tearfully to the Darren Wilson verdict in the Michael Brown killing—up until that moment of his life, he had faith that the justice system would prevail and then he was deflated at the result. Coates relates that he had a similar letdown coming-of-age moment in his own youth when a college classmate was killed by police. As Cobbina (2019) wrote in her analysis of the Ferguson and Baltimore first-wave BLM protests, African Americans and other victimized communities carry the weight of "vicarious victimization" knowing they are targets of possible abuses of power that will never be acknowledged or vindicated, even if it has not happened to them personally. Because race is a socially constructed group membership, all who are marked by society as such end up being vulnerable in that regard, whether or not their own individual actions justify the harassment. Jordan expressed some hindsight reflections on previous cases, in effect implicating society and bystanders for not standing up sooner. He explained learning with past unjust killings that if the public waits on the justice system to decide, the opportunity to register one's resistance aloud has past. So instead, they must stand up as soon as it happens, objecting with their full might. *The 2020 uprisings were occurring before a verdict, before even an indictment, rather than after.* Coming off the heels of so many other letdowns after the fact, protesters like Jordan jumped in hoping they could steer things in a new and different direction than the others. And many had a local opportunity to do so, even if they did not live in a city where the latest incident had occurred. So bystanders become not only people who stand and do nothing during a killing but people who stand and do nothing afterward to demand accountability—no matter where they are.

The World Was Watching

Nothing was entirely new, but certain elements combined to create this "flash point" moment for racial justice, this opportune time to at least partially right things, after so much had gone wrong before. Veterans in racial justice movements in this sample, especially those over forty, had a history of protesting racism in its various forms, not limited to killings of unarmed civilians by police. But younger 2020 newcomers were not completely green or naive either. They followed the first wave of BLM, through the murders of Trayvon Martin, Michael Brown, Eric Garner, Tamir Rice, Sandra Bland, Freddie Gray, Philando Castille, and so many others. Even if they did not see an opportunity in their own communities to protest at the times of those killings, many were engaging in "hashtag activism" prior to 2020. So when opportunities arose for them to step up and say, "No, not again" and "Enough is enough," this time not even a global pandemic was going to keep them from participating. Veteran protesters were certainly taken aback by the sudden wave of interest by so many new faces, but they had ways of making sense of it. The fact that life was in a sudden upheaval for many who had never experienced that degree of powerlessness before, coupled with the powerful video of George Floyd's killing taken by Darnella Frazier, were all additional elements tugging at people's heartstrings, compelling them to act.

On May 15, 2020, when George Floyd was still alive, UC Berkeley geographer Brandi Summers published an essay in the *New York Times* titled "What Black America Knows about Quarantine." Summers began by describing the horrific hate crime that killed Ahmaud Arbery on February 23, 2020, while he went for a Sunday morning run and explained that while white Americans were protesting having to temporarily quarantine due to COVID-19 in 2020, African Americans like Arbery have always lacked full freedom of movement in a racist, white supremacist society. Summers drew that circle of connection between whites and African Americans, imploring now perhaps whites could have but a tiny bit of empathy for the conditions under which African Americans have had to exist under their entire lives. Even though it became a stretch to equate mask-wearing to slavery as some conservative protesters did, what some analysts hoped was that through this experience of temporary inconvenience imposed on *all* (not just one particular group as in the case of anti-Black racism), whites might develop empathy for the everyday conditions that racist hypersurveillance and social control creates for people of color, whether or not there was a global pandemic. It was after a stretch of months of living through conditions under which no end was in sight, feeling powerless and vulnerable, that the world then witnessed a video of an African American man—powerless and vulnerable, despite his size and stature—being killed by police while many stood by and watched, also powerless to stop it. It was similar yet also different this time.

The racial perception gap (between whites and people of color) of believing racism is a serious problem narrowed temporarily in 2020, mainly due to a large jump in the proportion of white Americans who believed racism was a serious problem. "Never before" had polling experts seen such results, some upward of 25-point percentage jump (Russonello 2020). If it felt different on the ground to the activists who observed it seemed more people cared this time, especially whites, their suspicions were not unfounded. Moreover, the protests in solidarity all around the world—in over forty countries—only provided further confirmation of the magnitude of support for racial justice during 2020, especially summer (Smith, Wu, and Murphy 2020). Whether it was South Africa, Colombia, Indonesia, as a South African journalist put it, "there is a George Floyd in every country" (Westerman, Benk, and Greene 2020). These participants' feeling that "the world was watching" was well grounded in the evidence. Many more were watching than usual and willing to speak out as never before.

By fall of that same year, however, this level of interest about racial justice, particularly among whites, already dropped back down. For example, a Pew Research poll found as high as 60 percent of whites supported the Black Lives Matter movement in June 2020, but only 40 percent supported it a short three months later by September, while for African Americans, support remained consistently well above 85 percent for both periods (Thomas and Horowitz 2020). An analysis of tweets between the two periods also demonstrated that negative Twitter activity about African Americans decreased between May 26 and June 30, 2020, while positive Twitter activity about African Americans increased, returning to an "equilibrium" after June ended (Nguyen et al. 2021). This confirms other data-driven observations that racial attitudes generally stay stable over time, usually returning to previous levels after temporary peaks during atypical events (O'Brien 2021). An NPR poll taken at the end of August 2020 revealed that only 30 percent of whites agreed they took actions to better understand racism since the death of George Floyd—this was lower than any other racial/ethnic group in the poll—and whites were also least likely to have attended a protest or rally (only 7 percent had done so, compared with 13 percent of Blacks, 11 percent of Latinos, and 8 percent of Asian Americans) (Florido and Penaloza 2020). Some evidence suggests that this elevated dissatisfaction with the status quo got channeled into the presidential election by the fall of 2020—more supporters of BLM switched their party affiliation to Democrat due to dissatisfaction with Trump's handling of this and other crises (Mutz 2022). Energies dissipated, transferring to other areas before long. The interest convergence faded before the year was out. But at least for a season, the world was watching.

Sociologist Patricia Fernandez-Kelly wrote in June 2020 that there were both "proximate causes" and "deep causes" of this racial justice uprising. She also identified Frazier's video as an important catalyst during the time of isolation but stressed the more deeply rooted structural inequalities as equally contributing factors that were hardly new or novel. What Fernandez-Kelly (2020) evaluated as the novel and more unique component was that more than the usual folks were caring.

> The protestors clamoring for justice and the radical overhaul of systems of law and order both in the United States and elsewhere constitute the most diverse political constituency ever—they represent multiple nationalities, generations, races, and education levels. Empathy drives them to the streets overpowering

fears of the pandemic. What fueled public protest was the universal sentiment that bonds humans together despite differences of condition or appearance—a capacity to feel the suffering of others as if it were personal. That too should be a subject of sociological interest.

Empathy overpowered fear—or as respondent Nate quoted in this chapter put it, this moment "hit the hearts" of "Caucasian brothers and sisters." Rev. TM of Minneapolis quoted in this chapter also remarked that whites got "out of their heads and moved into a deeper personal experience." It was a temporary overlap of concentric circles, of many different constituencies that coalesced into this historic moment. But ultimately, momentum was difficult to sustain for many reasons—one important one being that many may have been compelled by these "proximate causes," but far fewer were driven by these "deep causes" or even understood or desired to address such deeply embedded roots of the problem.

Moreover, as ACLED data and other participants' testimonies indicate, the proliferation of protest locations during 2020 resulted in events in small-town and suburban outlying areas. Whereas previously, residents of places like Williamsburg, Virginia; Monterey, California; or Rutherford County, North Carolina, would travel to a larger nearby city if they wanted to participate in a protest, now they could participate in an event in their own hometowns, where racism in public spaces and confrontations between law enforcement and the public can look quite different than in large urban centers. When a police killing occurs in Ferguson, Missouri, or in Baltimore, Maryland, and residents of the city emerge to protest that killing, they are encountering the same police force on the protest streets that perpetrated the killing in the first place. It is easy to draw a direct line of connection between the militaristic police force encountering protesters and the police force that kills unarmed civilians. As we shall see in the next chapter, when protesters encountered inconsistent and divergent law enforcement tactics during uprising events, depending on where they were or even what day or hour of the day they attended, it became more difficult to coalesce around a coherent, clear diagnosis of the problem. Thus, uprising participants may have been united in their outrage at the killing of George Floyd—and even the killing of other unarmed African American civilians—but they were far less united in their understandings of what caused the killing(s) and thus what the logical solution(s) to the problem would be. Let us next examine the various forms of resistance this temporarily united coalition of protesters across the nation confronted depending on their geographic positions and social locations.

CHAPTER 3

Protect and Serve

But for Whom?

> I definitely seen a big police presence out there, and you know, they didn't look like they were there to keep our safety; they just looked like they were there to keep the town safety. . . . I never really feel like the police are there to protect me.
>
> —Tucker, Maryland

> One of the critiques of the police was that they allowed a lot of property damage to take place . . . agent provocateurs, promoting the violence and the property damage to distract from the message of the Black Lives movement rallies.
>
> —Bill, California

Two defining moments of the 1990s were the brutal beating of Rodney King by the Los Angeles Police Department (LAPD) on camera with the subsequent acquittal of the officers responsible, and the acquittal of OJ Simpson for the killing of his wife, Nicole Brown Simpson. Although both events took place in California, the world watched carefully, and passionate debates ensued, often fracturing along racial lines, about the criminal justice system and its propensity to deliver justice fairly regardless of race. Many white Americans were taken aback, both by the rioting after acquittal of the (LAPD) in the Rodney King case and the rejoicing after the not-guilty verdict for OJ Simpson. Their "frame assumption" (Feagin 2020) was challenged when it suddenly occurred to whites that not every American entrusts the justice system to mete out justice fairly across racial lines.

This "racial divide" in perceptions of fairness of the criminal justice system continues to be the subject of discussion in popular media (e.g., Howard 2016; Lee,

Schuppe, and Petulla 2017) as well as social science research (e.g., Fine, Rowan, and Simmons 2019; Hurwitz and Peffley 2005; Weitzer and Tuch 2002). Although evidence is clear that arrest and sentencing outcomes are unequal and discriminatory based on class and race, most everyday persons are not well schooled on this scientific evidence, instead basing their perceptions of the fairness (or lack thereof) of the U.S. criminal justice system on their own frame of reference as well as media representations (Callanan and Rosenberger 2011). In short, the divide looks something like this: whites are more likely to believe the justice system renders fair outcomes and that law enforcement is there to protect their interests, while Black and Latino people are less likely to trust the criminal justice system to be fair and more likely to fear its agents as a threat to their well-being. And these perceptions align with the typical treatment each group is more likely to receive from the justice system, unfortunately. However, whites are more likely to base their beliefs on media rather than actual experiences with law enforcement (Callanan and Rosenberger 2011), thus leading them to believe, against all evidence, that police treatment of people of color is fair as well.

As protesters ventured out into the public square to protest racial injustice, especially within law enforcement, these different vantage points inevitably impacted what people expected to experience when participating in the 2020 uprisings. Some hoped the racial divide was finally beginning to close as more people of diverse backgrounds showed up to these events, but as other chapters have shown, it is important to emphasize that these events continued to be majority people of color, even as white presence may have increased. As I indicate in my closing chapter on what needs to happen next, some participants mainly viewed Derek Chauvin (murderer of George Floyd) as a "bad apple" and were marching to demand greater accountability in deadly use-of-force cases, while others sought more widespread reform across policing and even abolishment of police altogether. But among study participants, these differing perspectives were not as simple as a racial divide between Black and white people. Rather, one's local environment (urban/suburban), whether they were a first-time or longtime protester, and if their local police department had a notoriously contentious reputation or not, all were among factors influencing protesters' experiences and perceptions of law enforcement engagement during uprising events.

Intimidating People, Protecting Property

The 2020 uprisings occurred just three years after a white counterprotester, Heather Heyer, was killed by a white supremacist who drove into the crowd in Charlottesville, Virginia, with intent to harm. A 2017 independent investigation of law enforcement during that incident revealed the Charlottesville police "failed to protect the public"—in short, they underestimated the "Unite the Right" rally by not perceiving its participants as a threat (Andone and Johnston 2017). Then-president Trump added fuel to the fire with his statement that there were "good people on both sides" in Charlottesville, which can be clearly contrasted with his critical statements of Black Lives Matter protesters in the summer of 2020—describing them as "thugs" and "terrorists" needing "law and order" (Beer 2021). ACLED's analysis of over ten thousand protests between May and December 2020 found that law enforcement used force in 51 percent of Black Lives Matter protests but in only 34 percent of right-wing demonstrations (Kishi, Stall, and Jones 2020). Clearly, who the protesters are and what they stand for matter as law enforcement mobilizes and prepares for these events.

How law enforcement conducted themselves during the 2020 racial justice uprisings communicated clear messages to participants about institutional priorities. The question of who or what is law enforcement protecting was vociferously answered by the posture of those present—whether they were facing the protesters or the onlookers, whether they had on riot gear, whether it was local and/or federal officers. One consistent theme across locations was a sense that the law enforcement priority was to protect property more than people. Most protesters attended with the understanding that they might end up being targets of law enforcement. As we have seen in earlier chapters, they saw police violence to be more of a threat to their own health and safety than the coronavirus. However, even when they did not become actual targets of law enforcement themselves, several respondents took note of law enforcement dress, gear, positioning, and activities during the events in which they participated, as they felt this spoke volumes about why and for whom they were there. Particularly interesting was the fact that protesters who had attended other protests in the past noticed a marked difference between law enforcement behavior for 2020 racial justice marches and ones they participated in before. This perception is also corroborated by ACLED data.

Abby, for instance, was an eighteen-year-old white woman protesting in Nashville, Tennessee, who had participated in several other "left-leaning" political actions before the 2020 racial justice events. Like others of her generation, Abby marched for climate justice, women's rights (post–Trump inauguration in 2017), and LGBT Pride Parade events with police presence. Yet she had never seen it quite like this. She noted that in a smaller suburban outlying town of Franklin, she attended a vigil to honor the victims of police brutality, where law enforcement was not threatening and imposing the way they were in the city of Nashville. Importantly, the governor had also conveniently (for him and supporters) made it illegal to protest on the grounds of the state capitol.

> The police were much more peaceful in majority of the [past] protests or even just marches, like stood alongside us like the LGBT and the Pride parades . . . making sure the counterprotesters couldn't get out of their little box they had them confined to. . . . Whereas like in counter-response, to the Black Lives Matter movement, like the second past curfew had been hit, people are struck [with] tear gas, rubber bullets, and it was really bad. . . . The police had much more of a violent response to Black Lives Matter protest than any of the other events. Once our governor put in the mandate, saying that you can't protest in the capitol, things got very violent—there was [sic] videos of police hitting people with the batons and spraying tear gas right into like people's eyes, like directly. It was very violent, very scary, and in my personal opinion, this leading violence was not justified.

In prior protests she attended, Abby found law enforcement was doing the type of job they should have been doing in Charlottesville—making sure counterprotesters were "confined" to their designated "boxes" and not interacting with the demonstrators, essentially protecting them. However, with the 2020 racial justice protests, the governor's orders entailed an altogether different stance. In Abby's assessment, the difference was they were a Black Lives Matter group. This is an important point for anyone who misunderstands police violence as a case of isolated "bad apples." These are the same law enforcement individuals attending different events in different locations, but protection of the capitol property was ordered by the executive branch of government, apparently by any means necessary—tear gas, rubber bullets, and most disturbingly, turning off the fountain so no one could use it to wash their eyes out after being hit with the chemical weapon. The intent was to do harm, as directed by the governor, but only in the more racially diverse urban area of the state house.

Policies, practices, and procedures matter, sending a clear message as to whose lives are more valued. Rev. Lane, a thirty-eight-year-old white woman serving a congregation in Rochester, New York, noticed that officers weren't wearing masks (indicating disrespect) and even arrested a medic—clearly there to address wounds inflicted by police (such as from rubber bullets, pepper bullets, and tear gas).

> One of the issues there was that none of the cops wear masks during this pandemic every all the protesters wearing masks and the cops were not, which was, which was concerning . . . to have cops kind of surrounding an area like that created a really unwelcoming atmosphere. . . . I will also say that they arrested at least

one of our medics in the midst of trying to take care of people they arrested her and took her to Canandaigua which is forty minutes outside of Rochester where one of my colleagues had to go and pick her up when she was discharged from police custody and bring her back. Oh yeah, bad move.

These actions did not indicate a desire to protect people from harm—quite the opposite.

Hood Scholar, a thirty-eight-year-old Black man protesting in Minneapolis (the city where George Floyd was killed), likewise found police violence arbitrary and clearly aimed at protecting property and removing protest activity, whether or not protesters broke any laws. He shared,

> I'm not aware of anyone who got killed. I did see a nurse whose full face, she got hit in the face by rubber bullet. This a nurse! . . . So there's literally like a medic pass you have to wear. . . . You can clearly identify them as medics, and a police officer would know if she was wearing this thing. Right? It makes no sense at all! Yep. . . . So they had they had a variety of things, they had rubber bullets, tear gas, or something stronger than rubber bullets because . . . I know somebody whose car got shot, and like rubber bullets don't leave marks in cars. Right, so it left some type of I guess indentation. . . . And like basically what they did, they activated all the law enforcement from everywhere, so you got the local law enforcement, and then they will pull all police officers from other local districts, you have state law enforcement, you have National Guard. . . . Like the person who arrested me, he was just like a highway patrol. . . . Basically, I got arrested because they arrested close to two hundred people. . . . [I'm] telling the cop I did nothing wrong, I'm peacefully protesting, and you're arresting me. . . . The police officer told me, he said that it was either the government, the governor wanted to do something to try to stop the town from burning. . . . So let's just start arresting people because, really, they don't know what to do.

This was the only study participant who was arrested during protest and also the only interviewee who traveled to Minneapolis (a few others traveled to other cities than their residence for purpose of protest, sometimes also because they were sheltering in place due to the pandemic, away from their typical residence). However, Hood Scholar is a longtime organizer who also traveled to Ferguson in 2015 after the police killing of Michael Brown. So he did attend the protest prepared to encounter resistance. However, what he did not expect was just how disorganized the law enforcement activities were, often not making logical sense from a tactical standpoint, other than the fact that they were just given orders to make arbitrary arrests to reduce the flow of protesters on the roads. He also noted "rubber bullets" are quite harmful and cause major facial injuries as evidenced by them leaving indentations in vehicles on impact.

Yet his major point, concurring with Abby, is that often police are simply following orders from higher up. The government instituted a curfew, and the public messaging implied the intent of law and order, but Hood Scholar emphasized that most arrests were of people neither breaking curfew nor doing anything other than peacefully protesting. So more than likely, the curfew was an attempt to quell traffic to lessen the negative impact on "business and capital." He did not observe that anyone was being protected by these activities, only harmed—and the only thing being protected was the inanimate objects of stores and property.

While tear gassing, rubber bullets, and arrests are more active law enforcement tactics, simply a "show of force" or lack of action to protect racial justice protesters from antagonism and harassment also sends a message of whom police are there to protect and whose lives are more valued. As Patrice, a twenty-two-year-old Black biracial woman protesting in Detroit, Michigan, recalled, she did not feel the police were there to protect her.

> Yeah, so it was the [police] headquarters, so it's like a pretty big building . . . [with] fences around it. . . . So that's where we started; that was right on the outside of those fences, and so they [police] were like lined up across the whole width of the building and they were in their riot gear . . . and some of them had those shields. And I'm not sure exactly what they have, but it was definitely very like bulky gear that they had on. And so it did make me uncomfortable that they were just standing there like that. And it was also kind of scary for us to be so close to it, but also as well that these people are like no, we want to make it known to you that we're serious about this.

How law enforcement dresses matters. There is even some evidence that police coming to events in paramilitary-style riot gear can exacerbate violence rather than quell it (Schrader 2020; Stott et al. 2008). Patrice felt intimidated simply by what the officers wore, without any actions necessarily taken yet. Like Abby above, Patrice also attended multiple protest events in both city and suburb, noting that this heightened riot response that was in Detroit (a majority-Black city) was not present at the student-organized event in nearby Troy.

RJ, a twenty-nine-year-old Black man protesting in Washington, D.C., also commented on the riot gear worn by law enforcement at the event he attended. He described it as "militarized" and completely unnecessary—"we're humans, we're . . . not soldiers, we're not insurgents. I don't know what else to call it, but you see everyday people, doctors, lawyers, students, hospital workers, the everyday person out protesting for common understanding. . . . So why did they need to feel like they have to have shields and helmets and all that stuff? It's beyond me!" RJ was indignant and offended as he did not feel the police response matched the crowd gathered there—not only was it overdone but in fact dehumanizing. He said, "You would think that we were preparing for a war battle or something; it's like, that's not what it was."

Right up the road from RJ in Columbia, Maryland, was Tucker, also an African American twenty-nine-year-old man protesting for his first time in 2020. Unlike D.C., though, the Columbia police did not have on riot gear. Nevertheless, Tucker did not feel that the police were there to protect the protesters, and their presence definitely put him on edge.

> I definitely seen a big police presence out there, and they didn't look like they were there to keep our safety; they just looked like they were there to keep the town safety. If anybody got out of line, they wanted to correct them. . . . When I'm observing them, it didn't look like they were watching the protests. . . . And no riot gear. Just the places that they were sitting and how they were observing you could tell you, okay, if we need to step in, we will. And it's just people, they're not normal civilians, so some of the lines get drawn and people can have just not that same reality because what they do for work impacts people's lives, and then . . . whenever you do something over and over and over just becomes a habit, it just becomes nature, so it's their job. . . . The lines just kind of blurred for them, not being a regular civilian and then having to having the authority to tell others civilians, then you can't do this, and they can cause bodily harm. So I mean me personally, I never really feel like the police are there to protect me, so when I seen them there . . . I just have to stay on my side and they're on their side, and I know how I gotta move and act accordingly.

Even without riot gear, Tucker got the clear sense that police were there to "protect the town" from protesters. Tucker explained that even though police are technically civilians like him, once they take this job, he believes their personal ethics and their job training blur, and that coupled with authority to "cause bodily harm" can be a deadly combination, making them altogether unpredictable. Although Tucker felt this way long before 2020, the police presence at the uprising event he attended did nothing to alter or redeem those perceptions.

Having attended many protests in his lifetime, Rabbi M, a fifty-one-year-old white man in Minneapolis, was struck by uniformed officers governing themselves in ways that did anything *but* deescalate.

> I definitely saw the tension. . . . Some of the police officers did not seem to have the energy of trying to deescalate and people were riled up, and with good rea-

son, and it was a pandemic, it was another murder of an unarmed Black man, it was all of these things. And they didn't seem to be interested in deescalating the situation and so were using provocative language and stances and were coming in riot gear.

Again, we see that riot gear, the stances, and profane language when addressing protesters had the opposite effect of keeping the peace. Another Minneapolis respondent, Justin, also a white man, age fifty-six, with a long history of protest, was dismayed that the professional code of conduct was completely lacking for the officers there.

> The police were by and large rude and not helpful. And it was deeply disturbing to see them to drive past the precinct in my neighborhood and see it. I've traveled into the world to help try to address issues of violence, and countries like El Salvador and in other places, and to see to see the city and the police stations boarded up with razor wire, the same way that you might expect, in it in a war-torn country was very disturbing. . . . It was very clear that the officers . . . did not have good control over their emotional state, that they were very amped up on adrenaline. And while, on one hand, I understand why the situation felt like a threat to them, on the other hand, actually expect law enforcement officers have enough training to control their emotions. . . . We don't make good decisions when we're ramped up on anger or anxiety, and I felt they fell far below a professional standard of how I should be held accountable, with an agitated student or parishioner. I thought they were very agitated and walking around with their hands on their guns and just things that I felt like really escalated the tensions. . . . They were clearly protecting buildings; it was not the crowds. . . . I did feel the officers were a threat to my safety and the safety of people around them. . . . It would have been better to leave the city alone than to be present there.

Several protesters echoed Justin's sentiment that the police presence at the uprisings reminded them of a country other than the United States and that the police were the biggest public safety threat.

Sharon, a thirty-nine-year-old Black/Latina woman who was a leader of dozens of protests in Williamsburg, Virginia, had many interactions with local police over her weeks of 2020 organizing. Sharon was a rather unique respondent due to not only the sheer number of protests she attended and led but also because before 2020, she had never been involved with racial justice organizing. Her father worked in law enforcement, and so the combination of that insider knowledge as well as the closeness with which she worked with the local force ensuring the streets were blocked off each evening for the events led to a more close-up view of law enforcement activities than most of the others in this study. In short, Sharon was overwhelmingly disappointed with her experience of law enforcement during the events and did not feel the police were there to protect her.

> I was raised by law enforcement, federal law enforcement, so that's a social contract I understood since I was a kid. . . . He didn't put on a uniform like the cops put on, but he put on a uniform. Right, so it's hurtful, it's disappointing, it's counterproductive, and I'm solution-oriented. Anything that gets me further away from the solution, I'm irritated. So it's very irritating to also see how police treats some of the protesters. . . . I'll never forget the two youngest officers—one was a female, the other was a male—both of them are white, were talking to me, and they have their hands on their weapons. . . . They were resting their hands on their gun belts. And it's like the most comfortable place within the rest of hands was on their weapons and we had a very direct conversation about that; we had to tell them, Excuse me, unless you want the type of reaction that you're going to get . . . you might not want to put your hands on your weapon. And I said . . . if that's the most comfortable place for you to put your hands in, somebody's training you wrong.

Sharon stated these officers striking the threatening pose were white and young. With her "somebody's training you wrong" statement, Sharon's emphasis is on leadership, as opposed to individual bad apples. This menacing pose could be easily outlawed or at the very least highly discouraged at the organizational level. The fact that the officers did not find it problematic indicates the priorities of the department.

Yet far more troubling for Sharon was not this particular incident but rather the time when an onlooker assaulted her while marching by throwing a beer on her. This eventually resulted in a lawsuit which she won; however, Sharon was not near as affronted by her actual assaulter as she was by the fact that law enforcement did not do their job to protect her from the abuse. During the interview, though, in true leader/organizer fashion, Sharon spent much more time discussing the overall neglect of the officers throughout the entire protest season, making her own assault but a tiny morsel of the entire problem. Sharon was much more animated when discussing other protest participants and how police failed to take adequate steps to protect them from harm. When asked whether her protest experiences met with her expectations, Sharon replied,

> No, I expected that protesters would always be kept safe, no matter what. Because we're exercising our rights. We have the right, given to us by the Constitution to do what we're doing, so you would expect it, anybody that uphold any laws in the United States of America would be behind that. So when you're . . . almost

getting hit by a car, when you're seeing cars drive through protest—I'm talking when traffic has been stopped by police. And you see cars, because they just don't agree and they're pissed they were daring stop traffic because we're doing an 8 minute and 46 second lay-down and they have to sit there and watch it. You're watching cars drive through and you're wondering . . . why is it that, when traffic is stopped? . . . People would point and yell at officers, "You need to go give him a ticket!" . . . You're patrolling us like we're doing something wrong.

Due to not feeling protected from onlookers and opposition, this town of Williamsburg, Virginia, developed its own lay security team whose job was to monitor vehicles that kept returning to the protest site like they might have wanted to do harm to the protesters. They hoped to work with law enforcement to locate some of these individuals and be more proactive to prevent harm from occurring, but Sharon was disappointed by their standoff approach.

Blake, a twenty-one-year-old white man who was part of that lay security team, also briefly mentioned the neglect by the officers, agreeing with Sharon's assessment that not enough was done. Given that across the country, protesters were being hit with tear gas and rubber bullets, Blake felt that local law enforcement was mostly cooperative in his area, relative to elsewhere. However, he noted they could have done much more to protect protesters from harm. He stated, "Police officers sort of turned a blind eye as outsiders threw drinks and stuff at our protest group and then acted like they didn't see it. But there was nothing as far as the law enforcement acting in their own merit like belligerently or violently towards us." Taken together, what these observations indicate is whether law enforcement are the active aggressors toward the protesters, whether they show up with riot gear, whether they just stand there eyeing the protesters as if they are the problem, in many cases participants interpreted a clear message that the police were not there to protect their First Amendment rights, not there to protect them from harm. Like the 2017 Charlottesville report concluded, law enforcement agencies may underestimate external threats to protesters' safety while they are too focused on policing the planned components of events.

Because most interviewees saw media coverage of police violence against protesters in various parts of the United States before they even participated themselves, the bar was low. If they did not get arrested, tear gassed, or otherwise confronted by law enforcement, they were relieved. Some interviewees did report even being pleasantly surprised by law enforcement cooperation with protesters, but this was largely in whiter, more suburban or small-town areas. As Faith, an eighteen-year-old Black biracial woman protesting in Williamsburg, Virginia, explained,

> I felt very comforted by the way that the law enforcement was acting because they were directing us and some of them stood with, kneeled with us and—even though you could tell they probably didn't want to—some of them were all trying to protect us from the general public, instead of trying to keep the protesters from what we're doing. . . . I think I feel like the group worked very well with law enforcement so they're very prepared and they weren't like bamboozled by protesters just showing up like they knew everything else going on today and knew what to do, and they were trying, most of them were trying back off the general public and stuff if, especially if people tried to like mess with us, you get through, and we were yelling and stuff they kind of blocked off traffic. They were better than I expected and had been seeing. [Interviewer: So you felt protected by the law enforcement at your protest?] I guess. [Interviewer: Okay, or what would be a more accurate word?] More like comfortable, less terrified. It's not protected, but it was— [Interviewer: Like, no, I don't want to put words in your mouth.] Then I would say, like comfort, not threatened, not as worried as I would have been in other parts of the country like Ohio or California. Seeing videos like of big-city protests and the cops being dirty and rude.

Here, Faith settled on "comfortable, less terrified" for her assessment, mainly relative to what she saw in other bigger cities. But interestingly, she attributed that more to the protesters' transparency and communication with law enforcement, forewarning them about their 8 minute 46 second lay-down in the intersection where they would need traffic blocked. The fact that police did block traffic as requested, without launching an offensive toward protesters, is something that Faith took comfort in, compared to the possible alternatives.

Faith also mentioned police taking a knee with protesters ("even though you could tell they probably didn't want to"). A larger public conversation took place in 2020 on whether it was appropriate or productive/worthwhile for law enforcement officials to engage in this performative gesture. Some African American police officers, for example, shared that they too have been racially profiled and discriminated against, agreeing with protesters that reform is needed (McCammon 2020). Officer Carmella Means in Chicago even received a six-month suspension from the Fraternal Order of Police due to kneeling with her fist up in front of headquarters, which the union stated violates their policies (Sweeney 2021). However, some find the gesture to amount to nothing more than a "charm offensive" to pacify crowds in a moment, that is at best relatively meaningless and patronizing and hurtful at worst, particularly since Derek Chauvin was also in a kneeling position on George Floyd's neck when he killed Floyd. As scholar-activists Ruth Wilson Gilmore and Craig Gilmore explained, the charm-offensive approach aims at "mitigating 'perceived bias' and shifting perceptions of biased police activity, not changing those biased activities themselves" (Byrne 2020). Several activists and organizers criticized these gestures as mere "optics," as sometimes only minutes before or after the kneeling photo op, the same officer could be spotted engaging in menacing behavior toward unarmed peaceful civilians.

Whether kneeling, in riot gear, or on the offensive (or not), the general consensus was that police were not there to protect protesters. This was especially true in larger, urban centers where the majority of the population was not white. One notable exception was shared by William, a fifty-three-year-old white man protesting in Rutherford County, North Carolina. Although he described the protest crowd as half to two-thirds African American and organized by the local Black Lives Matter—hardly an all-white event—the small size and rural environs of the town is part of what William attributed as to why law enforcement did not have a menacing or imposing presence at the protests. But perhaps most crucial of all was this force's organizational leadership.

> We had seen footage of some of these [violent police-protester interactions], but because of the kind of community we live in, we were not concerned about that. I'm inside a rural area that the town's drawn into . . . small town, small police forces that have relations—in our time here, there's been a history of constructive relationships. And there really has been no history of issues between communities of color and [town name] police were there and were really positive in their relations with protesters—in fact, before the event, they sent in the chief to address his employees that they were committed to what we were doing. I mentioned, they were there, they were not conspicuous, they were simply officers on foot to who were there in a way that they would have been present for other kinds of public events. . . . One expectation that we had [that] did not materialize and we were glad about that was the expectation that there would likely be counter-protesters. And that there could be problematic altercations between counter-protesters and protesters, they did not show up. There may have been one person who dropped by us and kinda honked horn loudly and discussed what they were saying, but many more people drove by and gave us thumbs-up out of window. And so that that turned out to be a very positive thing.

Unlike others who noted differences between how police carried themselves at the 2020 racial justice uprisings versus other events, William noted that in his town, the police presence for the 2020 Black Lives Matter march was no different than it would have been for other public gatherings. Importantly, William credited proactive leadership on the part of the town's police chief. Although it is unclear how William knew what the chief stated to his police force, he felt law enforcement had clear directives to be supportive of the protesters. This yet again underscores a rejection of the "bad apples" or individual actors approach to racist policing. Institutions and policies can and do shape individual actions. Consciously proactive tactical choices on the part of the force leadership as well as executive branch of government are what drives law enforcement practices—for better or for worse.

Ideally, the U.S. Justice Department can investigate local police departments and find them in violation of civil rights. Just in 2021 alone, the U.S. Justice Department announced it was investigating several departments, including Phoenix, Mount Vernon, Minneapolis, and Louisville. Rev. David, a forty-eight-year-old white man in Kentucky, who is both clergy leadership and army reservist, found himself defending one of the Unitarian Universalist congregations he serves from the "kettling" technique used by law enforcement because he knew that it was illegal. He was asked to go to Louisville for this work around September 2020, when the decision to not indict the officers who murdered Breonna Taylor was to be announced and the National Guard was sent in anticipation of riots.

> Our congregation in downtown Louisville made the commitment to offer sanctuary to people that were directly involved in the actions protesting Breonna's murder and, in doing so, opening up the sanctuary providing a space for protesters to rest, recover, to get medical assistance, to sleep. The police decided that they wish to use the kettling technique. . . . It's a tactic by police using in anti-protest movements, where police will surround a space and prevent anyone from leaving. . . . And then arrest them, or just prevent them, or if they try to leave, they get arrested, they get harassed, or there's all kinds of different aspects. So in the case of Louisville, the police surrounded one of our congregations and would not let anyone leave. It happened over multiple nights, in which case I got in my car and drove to Louisville to be the denomination saying to the national authority saying to the local police department and political authorities, this is not okay; you cannot get to surround a religious institution that is offering sanctuary and prevent anyone from leaving and providing that level of intimidation. . . . What I saw of the police presence seemed really large to me. I've served overseas for the military and it felt like a couple of other countries that I've been in including El Salvador and a couple other places, and the level of police, the armed nature of police and the control of blocks, I've seen that in Latin America.

Over and over, we see accounts of intimidation. Intimidation is not the decision of a bad apple; it is an institutionalized practice, ordered by leadership because it is a coordinated effort. Years later, the Justice Department is still investigating and untangling all the human rights violations that took place during the 2020 racial justice uprisings at the hands of police departments. Far from protecting protesters' First Amendment rights, they instead came more interested in protecting property and intimidating everyday citizens. Yet if you did not emerge from your home during this time and relied solely on media to tell you what was going on in the streets in 2020, you might have been led to believe that the police were simply restoring order. Rather, we find that in many places, it was the police who were inciting the chaos.

Unannounced Raids and Media Spin

Over 95 percent of the racial justice demonstrations occurring between May and August 2020 were peaceful and nonviolent (Garth 2021). However, as noted above, for the 5 percent or less that resulted in violence and chaos, it was all over the news and social media, giving the impression that it occurred more often than it actually did. Several protesters in larger metropolitan urban centers witnessed confrontations between protesters and law enforcement, reviewed in the previous section. Additionally, though, several participants witnessed mass acts of tear gassing of protesters that they found particularly troubling—not only because of how arbitrarily and suddenly it happened but also due to the incorrect and misleading information implying the police violence was somehow necessary or provoked when it was not. This pattern emerged almost identically whether the city was north, south, east, or west. Again, we see the coordinated efforts between law enforcement and executive branch as far as the messaging sent to the masses. The pandemic lockdown further contributed to the ease of misleading the public. Many people were still not venturing out of their homes except for necessities during this time, so they were left apt to believe whatever public statements government officials made about why they deemed tear gassing protesters necessary at certain events. Several protesters were quite critical of how what they saw with their own eyes on the ground became twisted in the media to make it look like protesters had been aggressors when in reality it was law enforcement that had done so.

Monica, a thirty-three-year-old white woman, attended her very first (and turned out to be her only) protest in Tampa, Florida, when her gathering was tear gassed. This experience made quite an impression on her.

> We were in an intersection . . . listening very carefully to the organizers; they were giving us instructions and they asked us to please kneel to show that we were nonviolent, didn't want any kind of confrontation, so we did, and I remember being on my knees and somebody threw a water bottle in the air. . . . And there was no warning, no nothing; they just started firing [tear gas]. . . .The police [got] . . . on a megaphone and said that the protest was no longer lawful and we needed to

> disperse.... There is a boy that got really badly burned with some tear gas and people were like pouring milk all over him and stuff.... It was then that I learned what it's like to be scared of police, so it was eye opening.

What floored her after experiencing all this was that the order of events reported in the media afterward was completely backward from how it happened. The police made it appear that they had first given instructions to disperse, before the tear gas, but Monica knew that is not the order in which it occurred.

> I did not expect it to go the way that it did at the end. I was pretty shocked by that because we weren't doing anything wrong. I kept thinking back what did we, what were we even doing? We were doing nothing, just standing there. People were playing music and talking, and then all of a sudden, it looked like a war zone, so that I will admit I was not expecting that.... There was no like warning like "Disperse or we will begin doing X, Y, and Z." That's not at all what happened, and the way they reported in the news was that they did do that—which was not I have on video, that that's not what happened. So they did not report it correctly, and I do remember very clearly, they did not speak a word; they were completely silent and only then did somebody—after people were running and they had deployed tear gas and other things—that they tell us, "This is no longer lawful. Please disperse." And if they came and said something first and gave us the chance to move, then okay, but they didn't do that. That's not what was going on.

It is concerning that law enforcement was directed to deploy chemical weapons in such a haphazard manner. In the chaos, Monica's primary objective was to move to safety, so she and her husband caught an Uber and left immediately while the hubbub continued. But even in that short time, she observed two different people who needed first aid. In these cases, not only are law enforcement not protecting citizens, but they are inflicting wounds onto a nonviolent crowd of people. Moreover, those at home watching the news are misled into believing that protesters were not following orders and the tear gas was required.

Janay, a twenty-eight-year-old African American woman who attended over a dozen protests in the Atlanta area, witnessed a similar tear gas deployment at one of the events she attended downtown. Likewise, the official story told afterward was misleading for those not at the scene.

> We were at the CNN Center and it was transcribed as people broke into the CNN Center, but what really happened was, everybody was protesting around the CNN Center speaking with the police chief and then they gave us thirty seconds to get off the sidewalk, and obviously with that many people that wasn't a possibility. I remember seeing like an older lady that was sitting there are signs around her

> walker, and she couldn't get up and move fast enough, so police literally just drag her out of the street, probably like a seventy-five-year-old white lady, and she was just protesting, but [how is] she physically going to get up? . . . Thankfully, I was only tear gassed twice. One time I went to the capitol and they had like rubber bullets. . . . And they would like rubber bullet and like shoot different people to kind of get them to go away. But that only happened thankfully once. It was very heartbreaking to see.

Like Monica, Janay was also upset that the media mischaracterized protesters as provoking police tear gas when in her experience that just was not accurate. The CNN Building was the only place to get away from the danger of the chemical weapon in their eyes and face; with a crowd that tightly packed, there was no other place to seek shelter or safety. Entering the building for shelter from the attack came after the police violence, not before. So to characterize it as a "break-in" to the building was highly misleading. In the next chapter, we will hear more from Janay about how uplifting she felt her overall protest experience was, so miscasting the uprising as destructive, when her experience was nothing but constructive, felt like a betrayal.

> Here in Atlanta on the first day, they showed us like the protesters were breaking into the CNN building; that wasn't the case. The reason why people broke into the CNN building was because we were being tear gassed and we're being forced off the street and we had nowhere to go. And there were people, down to their children, like, I saw five-year-old just crying because their mom's like covered into your eyes and there was no escape because you're on a four-way street. And the street is no bigger than I mean probably the size of like an average bedroom. And you have thousands of people standing there and no one has anywhere to go, and they have dropped it on all four intersections. So the only were to go into this one building that you can't get into. But then when you watch on the news: "Oh, they're violent; they're destroying things; they're looting." . . . I protested like I said fourteen times and I did not hurt a single soul, if anything, made friends, ran into friends. I kept walking like I would follow police protocols of continuous walking. I was home by curfew. But rain or shine, I was still out there, speaking for what I just felt was right for me and the people that I love and care about. And I have brothers and sisters and uncles, aunts all that and I would hate being a people of color to look on the news and George would be my uncle and I have lost him because something as simple as a hate crime. And the news described it that way; they just described it as people are just being violent, barbaric, and that was not the case.

In a recent analysis of the 2020 Los Angeles uprisings that characterizes them as an extension of the 1992 protests in the same city, Hanna Garth (2021, 101) writes that the dynamic between police violence and media justification was similar: "The local news media focused on the looters, insinuating that police force against the protestors was acceptable; the language of 'looting' and 'rioting' was used to delegitimise protests in which all Americans have the right to engage, and to cast protestors as violent and unruly, so justifying even more police violence against them." Janay's quote above epitomizes that delegitimization, and she pinpointed the attempt to cast protesters as "barbaric" to dehumanize them, but Janay pushed back on that by naming family members and imagining George Floyd was her uncle, asserting she is also human and has a right to speak out when she is being dehumanized.

Sally, a thirty-six-year-old white woman protesting in Louisville, Kentucky, expressed similar outrage at the media's mischaracterization of the events, which she experienced as "peaceful" until police came.

> And then we would do marches in the evening. There was one evening I was down there that got pretty intense. We were basically having a standoff with the LMPD [Louisville Metro Police Department] and there was a lot of tear gas, rubber bullets, and things like that.... Honestly, they were the LMPD were the ones that were causing the aggression and causing inciting the—I don't even I don't want to call it violence, because there were it wasn't violent per se, but the violence was on part of the LMPD on their force.... It was so disheartening to see people in this city, and the way that they address protest, they address it like protesters are rioters and we're problematic and we're the ones causing the problems. Which, in fact, I mean every time I was down there, it was so peaceful—I was offered hot dogs, pizza, water. Times we were just sitting there talking with the community. And when they would come, theLMPD was so out of control; they were up on buildings standing guard with—like there were so many protesters that had lasers pointed at them.

The next chapter explores more of this unexpected joy found in community, but here, Sally briefly evoked that ("hot dogs, pizza, water") as she attempted to contrast what she experienced at the protest location with the "rioter" stereotype. Sally identified law enforcement as the aggressors, not the protesters. Sally carefully chose her words to not say "violence" mainly because she wanted to make it clear that any altercation was not two-sided, and if there was any show of aggression or force at all, it was solely on the part of police, not protesters.

Likewise, Rev. TM, a fifty-three-year-old white man in Minneapolis, juxtaposed people of color standing in grief, hugging and supporting each other, with the militaristic assault of those peaceful persons by police. The National Guard was sent to Minneapolis after the summer uprising was over; it was during the Derek Chauvin trial along with the Daunte Wright killing.

> And the presence of National Guard really was poorly executed . . . just because you had one thousand or more troops and tanks marching through peaceful neighborhoods . . . it was just weird. It did not feel like it was the purpose they wanted to have right. But in the Daunte Wright thing was just was over the top, and during the trial because there was now who knows it's second-guessing what would have happened if the jury had said that Chauvin you know wasn't guilty of murder, what would have happened, but the level of barrier in tanks and militarization there was an armed military person on every corner in the city. I took my kid, my thirteen-year-old out to Brooklyn Center and that was a traumatic event for her to look at the levels of police barriers, the hundreds of officers in riot gear. And people on the other side of that hugging and singing and praying and there was just no violence there. And in the end, to look at the other side and just all of the military presence. And then obviously at a certain time at night, the National Guard would come in come through with tanks and tear gas and disperse the crowd, with no provocation, is something I'd never experienced before; it was really over the top, and it did not bode well for this generation of people and mostly young Black activists, they have any trust in military or police, it was really not helpful. That's a generational mistake, I think that our military in Minneapolis—I don't know what happened other parts of the country. But it was a generational mistake, I think they're going to be feeling those effects for a long time. And if you can imagine, families, kids, dogs, you know even just people sitting in that grief and being assaulted like that, by military vehicles felt like things I'd seen in the news from other countries. You know, it felt like a Tiananmen Square moment; now, I mean, that's its own drama right. But that's what it felt like to just be present and then to have that level of military presence come at you.

If the military and law enforcement really want to recruit a diverse force, they just made it look very uninviting. If a thirteen-year-old daughter is traumatized simply by looking at the spectacle, imagine the Black families hit with the tear gas while grieving. A community while awaiting some semblance of justice for one murder (George Floyd) becomes the site for yet another killing of an unarmed Black man (Daunte Wright). Both media and law enforcement corroborated the misleading picture that protesters instigated the violence.

Also in Minneapolis, Jim Bear, a forty-four-year-old Native American man, emphasized that protesters themselves were not only nonviolent but were essentially "begging" anyone who was caught up in the gathering not to do anything even as slight as tossing a water bottle because they understood how easily provoked the law enforcement violence was.

> For context . . . the Court Hennepin County courthouse where Derek Chauvin was on trial is seven blocks from where I am here in my office. Yeah, so for a while, even coming into the office, every day you're driving by, every intersection is blocked off by National Guard. Large vehicles at our clergy marches, which were very peaceful. I mean, they were protests, yes, and then there were marches, but no one was getting out of hand, nothing like that, but had overwhelming police presence National Guard was there kind of just watching everything. At Brooklyn Center for the Daunte Wright's protests, the police presence there surrounding the police station was just ridiculously out of hand, officers on the roofs, big giant National Guard vehicles everywhere, this huge presence and I think the police escalated things so violently, and quickly, that it was absolutely unnecessary, there's thousands of people on one side of a barricade. And like a water bottle a half-empty water bottle gets thrown and then also here come the rubber bullets, here come the tear gas, right. All of this so just got escalated way out of hand and the reality is that within the protest groups there were people within the protesters that are actively trying to put down any form of escalation that would come from our side of the barricade, so if someone threw a water bottle, they were quickly surrounded by people, security people, saying, hey, we're not doing that because you're putting everybody at risk, here you putting everybody at risk. . . . It was very, very surprising to see the level of that was mobilized as quickly as it was.

Concurring with the previous interviewee, these gatherings in Minneapolis that occurred almost one year after the George Floyd murder were equally as contentious as others from 2020. However, in both cases, a common theme was the people gathered were peaceful, and ultimately the people were really the deescalators, while agents of the state were the provocateurs, if anything.

When these government agents wanted to put forth the story that the protesters were the ones provoking or necessitating violent responses, Rev. Lane, a thirty-eight-year-old white woman in Rochester, New York, explained that it was video footage from the people, not the press, that set the story correct.

> Oh God, we also learned a lot about media; we learned so much about media coverage and the ways that the media was going to cover these things in the ways that they weren't. . . . We had people in the movement who had press passes who were denied access to our local police union's press conferences. . . . Same here in

Rochester, very same that folks were saying that the police officers were shooting pepper bullets were throwing water bottles at the cops. And like people will be like, "I was there. I didn't see anything like that!" And also not covering ways that police officers use military tactics against our own people, against the people that they're here to serve, like all of the video footage of that came from the people; it did not come from the press.

Interestingly, Rev. Lane noted that the police tried to keep reporters from attending their union meetings, so we see the institutionalized practices of information control that extend well beyond the protest sites. With accurate information restricted from the press, they may end up reporting only what the police tell them, which clearly does not always match up with what people on the ground are seeing. Again, at a time when many people were still not leaving their homes, with no way to observe alternative, firsthand information, the mainstream press did not always capture the full story; and when it was in error, it was often to paint police in a more favorable light than what actually happened. This is how social media helped with live streams from protest sites, sharing more accurate information for those not present.

Isabel, a twenty-year-old white woman protesting in the Denver and Aurora areas of Colorado, described a tear gas attack by police on peaceful protesters after she left an event site at the Aurora Police Department. This one was more difficult for police messaging to twist in the media because videos had already gone viral that made the attack look quite unprovoked. The only thing they were able to do was correct the record in some of the local press that the substance sprayed on protesters was pepper spray and not tear gas (Cinone 2020). But regardless, it was not pleasant and an unnecessary assault on a peaceful, nonviolent assembly.

> So the first protests, I went to the really big one downtown [Denver] was very peaceful and their goal was to not interact with law enforcement at all. So that was the first one, and then, as more started happening, I feel like when they would announce them, post flyers on Facebook or Instagram, it would be they would be clear about what their goals were, if they were trying not to interact with law enforcement at all, or if, [you should] come prepared wear goggles for tear gas, they were very communicative about it. The first one I went to was very peaceful and then there were a few like the one in Aurora with Aurora police department, where it was a little scary, I brought goggles and I made sure I was safe because I didn't want to get hurt either, I don't want to get tear gassed.... There was one specific protest I went to that it kind of went viral after this happened, but it was for Elijah McClain. And I had left, I was there for a few hours in the day, and right when I left, I looked online and there was a bunch of violin players

outside the police department and the cops came out and started tear gassing the violin players. And it was like out of a movie; you can probably find the video online somewhere, but it was crazy because these people are just playing violin and the cops are marching towards them with tear gas. Wow, it was crazy, and I wasn't there for that, but I had just been there and I had just left in time. So yeah, that was probably the craziest thing that had happened.

Again, we see a common theme of police as the aggressors in the tear gas incidents. About a year and a half later, in November 2021, the McClain family won a $15 million lawsuit against the Aurora Police Department for causing their son's death (Franklin 2021). This incident occurred before George Floyd's and before Breonna Taylor's murders. But because Elijah McClain played the violin, some protest events utilized the musical instrument as a way to humanize the victim, and apparently the Aurora Police Department felt particularly affronted by this public rebuke of their force's tactics.

As Isabel explained, her region of the United States is a reverse from the typical pattern whereby the center city protest police were more militarized, while the suburbs, towns, and outlying areas had whiter crowds and a relatively less menacing law enforcement presence. In Colorado, Denver is the center city but only 10 percent Black, and Isabel did not witness any police aggression toward protesters there. In contrast, she stated that Aurora is well known for being one of the "most corrupt" police forces in the nation, and it has a slightly higher percentage of people of color than the city of Denver itself. Denver is majority white(55 percent), while in Aurora whites are in the minority (45 percent), and apparently the racial threat hypothesis is real there in terms of police response. A Denver Post analysis of local police "use of force" data found that both Denver and Aurora have African Americans overrepresented in the number of citizens they use force against—in Denver, Blacks made up 27 percent of all police use-of-force incidents in 2019, for example, even though they are only 10 percent of the population. While this is more than doubly disproportionate and concerning enough, Aurora police far outpace this discrepancy—nearly half of all Aurora's use-of-force incidents that same year were on African Americans (Schmelzer 2020). Given this long-standing pattern in Aurora, Isabel was not surprised and came prepared with safety goggles whenever she attended events there, as local organizers advised. Video and social media have greatly assisted these situations where police spokespersons attempt to minimize or deny when unprovoked law enforcement violence occurs. While one police quote mentioned that "smoke" was used to clear the area around the police department, once media websites posted video footage from the protest site stating tear gas was used, police had to retract their previous statement, admitting it was pepper spray (Cinone 2020). This suggests that without cell phone cameras and press websites with video capability, police would continue to attempt to mislead the public about whether use of force on protesters was necessary, provoked, or deserved.

Nate, a twenty-eight-year-old African American man who protested in various areas of Monterey County as well as Los Angeles, agreed with Isabel that whiter areas were met with friendlier and nonviolent police presence than more racially diverse areas, even within the same greater metropolitan area. Nate was part of a "near miss" rubber bullet situation where the police threatened to shoot, but the citizens were able to talk them down.

> I was about to get shot by rubber bullets. . . . I have to send you photos, so it was it was a powerful moment. We were locking arms one of his name's John was there I think he's running for state assembly or something or something, but he was like a city council member, he was there, he was one of those people pushing defund police, and all this other stuff. Here we are locked arms, and I'm thinking in my head, oh man, they're about to shoot us like, hey, there's this young guy was a young officer who was leading him, he came up, and I wasn't even the person being the voice, I was just marching with two people at this point, and he said, "You don't want to go to jail today, son. I don't want have to shoot you," and all these younger white folks that were marching with us walked in front of us and made a shield, a body shield for us and that's the first time I had ever seen that before. And this young lady formed a specific role to stand in front of all these Black and brown folks and babies. "If they're shooting them, they're going to shoot us first," and that was, well, it was so surreal for me. And I just was telling this officer, "I love babies, we have babies in strollers, don't shoot your bullets that rubber whatnot, you don't shoot at these kids, or these elder older folks." . . . Eventually, [name] elder of the African America Queen of the Seaside California African American Community, she's very into the policy scene there. She was angry, she was like, "Are you really going to shoot all of us? You already knew we were doing this. What's going on?" . . . And yeah, that that was probably the most surreal moment for me where because there were some communities where literally the cops were riding on bikes like Monterey where a lot more white folks and very high-income place to live, where they were literally riding a bicycle with people . . . when I would be marching in the Black and brown communities folks for literally have military gear prepared or something else, it was it was really interesting to march in a white community than in march with the Black and brown folks on different things.

Note the audacity of putting children and elderly in line of fire that we have seen in other accounts. Nate attended more protests than anyone else in the sample. The year 2020 was his very first time protesting, as was not uncommon for people of his generation, but he dived right in! As a result of the high number (he estimated about forty-five) of events he attended in a variety of settings, he was able to compare the different police reactions depending on the demographics of the various communities. Nate contrasted the riot gear for the Seaside community with the bike-riding friendliness of the Monterey department. He was the only respondent to also share photo evidence, and the contrast of the two police stances was a powerful visual to see! This inconsistency of police in general (even within the same department and community) is a theme explored more in the next section.

Outside Agitators, Inconsistent Law Enforcement

Due to limited or misleading information in the media, protesters often reported a discrepancy between their initial expectations and what they experienced once in the protest setting with respect to law enforcement use of force. Most especially, 2020 protests often involved a variety of actors, not always aligned with the same goals. The media can report a "Black Lives Matter" protest, but plenty of 2020 racial justice events were not sponsored by a BLM organization, and some people who attended were not even antiracists. As earlier chapters noted, the pandemic lockdown created a relatively unique situation where there were no longer bars, pubs, other venues open where people could gather to blow off steam. As a result, some protest-goers hitched their wagons to events whose goals they may not have fully understood or supported. In particular, there was a daytime/nighttime change in the crowds gathered for the summer 2020 events reported especially during the early weeks of June—with the nighttime crowd sometimes attracting the ire of law enforcement. This flow in and out of different types of people, sometimes at cross-purposes, created confusion in reports of incidents at protests: "Despite the media focus on looting and vandalism, however, there is little evidence to suggest that demonstrators have engaged in widespread violence. In some cases where demonstrations did turn violent, there are reports of agents provocateurs—or infiltrators—instigating the violence" (Kishi and Jones 2020, 5). Sometimes these "agents provocateurs" were solo actors, but others were affiliated with organizations.

Many U.S. cities instituted nighttime curfews during early June 2020. Participants overwhelmingly reported that curfews were enforced sporadically at best. Selective curfew enforcement only added to the overall confusion participants experienced. From a social control perspective, constantly changing up whether a law is enforced (i.e., by using intermittent "crackdowns" in areas where violations were previously overlooked) can be seen as effective in deterring incidents (Sherman 1990). However, this unpredictability in police violence at protests was very destabilizing to individuals who only came to peacefully protest. Intermittent reinforcement, in short, is advantageous to those who seek to abuse power and control but traumatizing to those it targets, as behavioral psychology has shown (Carnell 2012). Indeed, those attending multiple protests at the same location found no rhyme or reason in when police violence occurred versus when it did not. Other analysis revealed that "government response to the demonstrations was not uniform" (Kishi and Jones 2020, 6)—the same police officer that posed for a photo op taking a knee with a protester could be seen beating another protester around the corner.

Janay, the twenty-eight-year-old African American woman who described the CNN Building incident in Atlanta above, found law enforcement engaging in friendly conversation with protesters one minute, then unleashing tear gas the next, with no clear reason for the change.

> It was weird. . . . Everybody was talking to the chief [former chief Erica Shields]; she was standing in the middle, she was taking questions there, it was live, it was very really calm. And then, with like the flip of a dime, it was like were aggressive and there's tanks and like you'll look at the police officers in the tank and they're waving tear gas and like laughing. And thinking it's funny and it's like we're literally fighting for our lives and we're having a conversation with you and everything's totally fine and dandy and then, okay, it's okay to harm us. Well, you don't want to be harmed either, so what makes you better than anyone else and harming people?

Later in this interview, Janay traced a direct line from former president Trump's leadership to how police conducted themselves—as if the rules apply to everyone else but themselves. Without consistent accountability on all sides and consistent practices of security measures, it is difficult to respect that leadership. It also is unreasonable for authority figures to expect compliance when they are not consistently following their own procedures.

Sally, the thirty-six-year-old white woman protesting in Louisville, Kentucky, agreed that police procedures were inconsistent across different protest days, with no clear reason for the change.

> So it was really strange. Sometimes we would go down there to Injustice Square Park and we would all just be hanging out . . . having hot dogs and water and then getting ready for our march, and there would be no police presence. And then there were other times we would go down there, and there was a very heavy police

> presence just the one night in particular that I was there, say it was like a Tuesday or Wednesday night and but there was no really rhyme or reason for the presence, whether they would be down there or not honestly. So yeah, it was really hit or miss; sometimes there wouldn't be a presence and then sometimes there, it would be bad.... And there wasn't a reason for it like there was no reason why they might be there on Monday night and not be there on Tuesday night.... And so, there was a curfew. To say whether or not like, you know, police will use what they want, when they want, how they want, so if they wanted to, enact the curfew, then they when they a lot of times they use that to disperse us at Injustice Square Park. Yeah, so a lot of times they use it just to disperse us at the end of the evening. [Interviewer: What time?] I think it was I felt like it was eleven.... [Interviewer: Your memory, they only use that at certain times?] Pretty much.

Sally's report on the inconsistencies of police presence as well as the inconsistent ways curfew laws were used was not uncommon. Several other major U.S. cities instituted a nightly curfew during the height of the 2020 racial justice uprisings. For example, Los Angeles had a 6:00 p.m. curfew and Santa Monica had a 4:00 p.m. curfew, from May 31 to June 4, 2020 (Garth 2021). However, several observed that these curfews did not do much. As Rev. Lane in Rochester put it, "They had a curfew of 9:00 p.m. I can't remember how long it lasted; it was like on and off like it would be on some days and not on other days. So it was hard to keep track of what's going on for or when it was on or when it was off."

One of the most orderly, consistent impressions of the curfew came in an interview with Jordan, a twenty-six-year-old Black/biracial man who had recently moved to the Atlanta area and attended one protest there. He stated that they got a universal alert on their cell phones and the National Guard came through public areas like shopping malls where people were eating to remind them of the upcoming closure and the need to return home.

> The curfew was at 9:00 p.m., that's when the National Guard would come in, and ... the only time you could be outside was if you are going to work or something. Or you couldn't be outside or else you're arrested.... You got an alert on your phone that like it went off like an amber alert alarm thirty minutes before that says the curfew be in effect and 9:00 p.m. and everybody knew. It was on the news the governor had declared a state of emergency and everything so. Everybody kind of already thought about it ... [when] George Floyd happened, it was Memorial Day weekend, it was a four-day weekend, so we were in Atlanta, June was like the first day of Pride in midtown is like right in the middle of the heart of Atlanta, and we were there at eight thirty and we saw like the National Guard walking down there like, "Hey, you know, trying to finish up your meals every-

thing, and you know get out of here by forty-five, that's when we're going to start shutting things down," and then we were already gone before eight forty-three already finished or not. But yeah, you can like literally see on like on the interstate like where they're like blocking traffic and everything.

Jordan's account—peacefully notified of curfew while not even at a protest but simply eating dinner—depicts a much more universal curfew enforcement than most other participants'. For most, they saw protest activity occurring after curfew, but rather the curfew was a tool officers kept in their back pocket in case they opted to use it, often in arbitrary manner.

Rabbi M, a fifty-one-year-old white man in Minneapolis, observed notable chaos and inconsistency more than usual in the local police presence, so it took the governor coming in to restore order.

> I've been to many, many, many, many protests before and, not always, but much of the time, law enforcement is present, but sort of silent and stoic and they stand there and whatever. And here there was just it was like nobody was in charge exactly. And so there were some officers who were just standing there hanging out by their cars and there were some who were just driving through yelling things and there were some who were like they're in riot gear. The tanks didn't come until the verdict, the trial, but . . . I mean, it felt like there was nobody in charge. Half the cops were super aggressive and half were like just gone, like they just weren't there. They just didn't show up to work, and like I have no idea what's going on with the mayor, he was completely MIA. The governor was trying, I think, to navigate his way through a complicated situation, I think, finally had to show up to be the grown-up in town.

As we have seen, it is leadership ordering officers to mount their offensives but leadership also allowing chaos and inconsistency to prevail. Curfews were meant to restore order, but if inconsistently enforced, only as a repressive social control tool, they do not do much to provide order or stability.

Some felt curfews just made matters worse. Kelli, a forty-five-year-old African American business owner participating in Richmond, Virginia, observed protests from a variety of angles—as a participant in the crowd, as a business owner protecting her business, and then opening that business as a safe space and shelter for protesters. She also live streamed the protests so others who were not attending could better understand why they occurred. Kelli noted the content of the chanting lyrics changed from daytime to nighttime, exemplifying the difference in crowds assembled before and after curfew time, as well as on different nights, depending on which group was organizing the event.

"Say their names," like that that was the focus . . . no, Friday night I spoke, let me think Friday night's focus was "say their name, say their names, Black lives matter," right. Saturday night's focus was and, if I can be blunt "F-12" . . . that's all they kept saying. . . . It was all about racist bleep bleep bleep bleep and Sunday night unfortunately that's when the Boogaloo Bois and the other ones that weren't really there for Black Lives Matter, the ones that will be disruptive came into town, and it was less chanting, it was just chaos, at that point. [Interviewer: Wow. So what is this group, and where did they come from?] So, supposedly, there are these organizations and I don't want to be quoted on their exact names, I know one is called the Boogaloo Bois, and these are the guys I also was told—again, I'm sorry, I want to make sure you do the correct citation and research on this, but in Charlottesville with the tiki torches, that group so they're known to wear the Hawaiian shirts and I think the camouflage pants, I think, but they're very distinctive and they will mingle in with the protesters and cause the drama and chaos. And they're more so also are anti-government people, so they get into the conversations from a different angle . . . they're not necessarily there for the Black Lives Matter movement, but they are there to drum up the drama. And a lot of the videos that are recorded you'll see random white faces breaking the windows of these places, and then all of the Black bodies rolling it, so of course it looks like, Oh, the Black people were the ones looting and starting the chaos, so even though someone else broke the window, so it could look like you were the ones that we would want you know doing it. . . . See, also remember, we got a curfew; I don't know if that happened [elsewhere] too. [Interviewer: It did.] And that was just like the dumbest thing to ever instate. Because it was like, oh, we're on a curfew; everybody come outside! It had me; it was almost the reverse effect.

Kelli distinguished between protesters and rioters, the latter of which were not even about ending racism, seeming more anti-government altogether. These outside agitator groups, or "agents provocateurs," often traveled into the protest areas from elsewhere. The "Boogaloo Bois" that Kelli tied to the Charlottesville white supremacist attack has also been identified as a factor behind the January 6 insurrection at the U.S. Capitol building. They are known to recruit former members of the military due to their tactical weapons experience, and one of their plans in 2020 was to attend racial justice protests and evoke an outsized government response, aiming to incite destruction (Thompson et al. 2021). Kelli attributed the government's decision to institute a curfew to be inadvertently responsible for the conditions that fostered this "chaos" as she called it. In short, the curfew did not really clear the streets; it only partially cleared it, leaving those more willing to risk getting arrested concentrated there.

RJ, a twenty-nine-year-old Black man protesting in Washington, D.C., stated they also had a curfew, but it did not prevent protests from continuing after dark if they continued in a peaceful manner. He echoed Kelli's view that agitators came from outside the area.

> Yes, D.C. definitely had curfews; during that time, I believe it was around 9:00 p.m. as well. I can't remember the exact time, but that sounds right. But even with that, if people were acting accordingly, even if you were out past a curfew quote unquote, you weren't doing anything wrong or harmful to anybody, so most of the time there wasn't any interactions with the police per se. Yes, they will be around, yes, do you try to clear out certain areas, but it was known if the protesters were peaceful, then the law enforcement tended to be peaceful, at least in D.C. Now, other cities we see on national news, that wasn't that way, but in D.C. as far as I saw except for a handful of incidents, but that was more so related to a different type of protesters coming into the city, which I'm sure we can talk about later on; it was a different dynamic amongst them.

Like Jordan in Atlanta, RJ did not see any arbitrary curfew enforcement, but unlike Jordan's experience, RJ saw the D.C. curfew as flexible but sensible. RJ found curfew was more of last resort, used only if citizens first initiated violence. Complicating matters was the fact that "a different type of protester" could show up at any time, bringing the wrath on them all.

In their study of 8,700 demonstrations across 74 countries during May 26 to August 22, 2020, Kishi and Jones (2020) of the U.S. Crisis Monitor counted dozens of car ramming incidents (a major increase from prior years), as well as at least 50 incidents of armed nonstate actors, individuals claiming to "keep the peace" showing up at racial justice demonstrations. One such actor was Kyle Rittenhouse in Kenosha, Wisconsin, in August 2020, whom a jury found not guilty for killing two people and wounding another in such a capacity (Yang and Walters 2021). Due to what already happened in Charlottesville in 2017, many were already keeping a watchful eye out, not only for police violence against them but for onlooker violence like this. As mentioned earlier, some interviewees expected law enforcement's job would be to protect them from these types of injuries while they were protesting, but others were not hopeful about such protection. Protesters encountered both physical and verbal abuse from onlookers who criticized them for what they were doing. One near–car ramming incident occurred in Williamsburg, Virginia, as twenty-one-year-old Blake, a white man working security, recounted:

> On my first day when I was working as a security person, we were blocking off the road so that people could walk across the crosswalk. . . . But we had people in strollers and people who were elderly who were moving quite a bit slower, so

[the light] changed. The police officers had the road blocked behind us, but there were cars sitting at a red light that turned green. Our security people were still in front of the car and the car decided it was going to try to go, us not moving out of the way of the path. One of the passengers of the car decided to get out of the car and start screaming at us for being in his way. [Interviewer: Wow.] So as we move towards the person who was out of the car, I actually almost got punched in the face by this individual because he was so outraged at the fact that we had held him up for one or two minutes. But it was that was the only time things got like violent, or he did. Because of people normally it was people who were being ignorant saying things like, why do you have to do this, like in front of like all these people. . . . And people were just saying all these nasty things all that I can honestly say I do not remember anything in particular. . . . It wasn't nice or understanding. Yeah, people from the community definitely there were some individuals who weren't with it.

As Abby stated earlier, at other protests within recent years of this uprising, law enforcement was more organized, and counterprotesters were "confined to a box," for example. The fact that racial justice protesters were left so open and vulnerable to onlooker violence like this demonstrates governmental priorities. Far from enacting any legislation or executive orders that would protect protesters exercising First Amendment rights, the Department of Homeland Security was busy enacting Protecting American Communities Taskforce (PACT). As a result of this act, by the end of June 2020, federal agents were deployed around the United States to target protests, especially in Portland, Seattle, and Washington, D.C. (Kishi and Jones 2020). Carly, a forty-nine-year-old white woman protesting in Columbus, Ohio, noted that unmarked vans were scooping up protesters, and organizers posted warnings on social media about this law enforcement threat, which tended to intensify at night. Since she had children and "the police tended to escalate their violence later in the day," they only went in daylight.

Taken together, most participants characterized violence as coming either from police and/or onlookers or counterprotesters, not from protesters themselves. Data show that protesters' fears were not unfounded. In a September 2020 analysis of the U.S. Crisis Monitor data, Kishi (2020) reported that five times as many demonstrations in 2020 were met with government engagement than in 2019. There were also five times as many armed nonstate actors in 2020 than there were in 2019, and counterprotesters increased seven times since 2019, expanding to twice as many states in 2020. In other words, the 2020 racial justice uprisings saw greatly intensified police presence as well as intensified civilian resistance that included armed and violent individuals. Many participants perceived this intensification from on the ground as unpredictable and erratic. As noted in chapter 2, even though it was the midst of a global pandemic with no vaccine available and no end in sight, most respondents perceived these law enforcement threats, along with the white supremacist militia threats, to be more of a risk to them than the coronavirus itself.

While a majority of the interview sample was young and for almost half (n = 13) it was their first time protesting, for those who were older and had a long history of racial justice demonstration participation, police repression was not new to them, but the level of white supremacist militia involvement was. This was particularly prominent in Minneapolis and Louisville interviews. Not only were these "outside agitators" causing destruction after the curfew and trying to make it look like it was racial justice protesters (BLM) responsible for the wreckage, but police turning a blind eye to their destructive activities was highly disturbing. Rev. TM, a fifty-three-year-old white male of Minneapolis, said,

> The violence in the evenings, that when there was more burning and looting and those kind of things and rubber bullets and tear gas, I felt like they were not the people who were protesting, the first three days that was my experience. We saw a lot of garbage can kind of fires like that would attract attention and then a block away, there was some other bigger thing like it would somehow the crowd would be moved towards that and then something else happened. There was a lot of boarded-up businesses, obviously. I witnessed a guy run by the crowd I was in with a battery-powered circular saw cutting down the boards on the building so that the glass was exposed. He was not part of the group, dressed all in black. And then disappeared into alleyway... It felt like the group was not engaged in any of that stuff, but the individuals certainly were, so that was my experience.... Yeah, there was a lot of chaos; I mean none of us are prepared for that. I wasn't prepared for the counterprotesters who came through like I said and cut down the wooden stanchions in front of buildings. And it was the only time I was scared was watching a hooded guy come towards me with a circular saw. That's not a weapon I've noticed ... at other events like this.... Within just a couple blocks from my house were from people in trucks, who came by and threw fire incendiaries on buildings and drove away. They weren't people in the neighborhood; they weren't people who were protesting. And so we had quite a bit of property destruction in our neighborhood, but it wasn't anybody who was part of any organized neighborhood action.

This reverend had seen a lot in his decades of involvement, including counterprotesters that did not agree with them but never a circular saw. This willful destruction of property's main purpose was to make the racial justice uprisings look more disruptive and criminal than they actually were. This is why the reverend emphasized that those doing this were not with their group.

Likewise, Jim Bear, a forty-four-year-old Native American man also in Minneapolis, found the white supremacist tactics to be new in all his decades of protesting also.

> This is the first time I've ever been present, where there were active white supremacists who were there, trying to stir it up, to initiate a police response, right? And I think at first I downplayed that because we all heard rumors: "Oh, you know the Boogaloo Bois are rolling into town," . . . but I think I was sort of downplaying that until . . . I saw all these vehicles with the plates that were removed, which is a sign that these are outside agitators that are coming in, and . . . a span of five or six blocks, I must have counted about four or five of these cars that were just left their plates were off, and I'm like, Whoa, holy shit, like they really are coming in! And this is before we had the video of that guy "umbrella man" who was the first one who knocked out the windows at the auto parts store that I think really started then kind of escalated everything from there. . . . Well, maybe it was the morning after, two mornings after, like things started burning and getting set on fire that I went through the neighborhoods and saw all of these abandoned cars . . . and it was like, Wow, this is like those white supremacists are really coming in, so that that surprised me.

Later on in the interview, he also pushed back on the erroneous notion that these were racial justice protesters setting fires, mainly because of the locations of the businesses that were hit—they provided essential services and then communities had to initiate a system of rideshares to get diapers, prescriptions, and so forth as a result. "I mean, these are community resources, and . . . these are not people in this neighborhood that are doing that to themselves." Jim Bear was surprised at the level of audacity required to create these actions: "That's what I what I wasn't suspecting early on as things on unfolded was that we would have active white supremacists who would come in and try to destroy Black neighborhoods and make it look like it's the Black people who are doing it to themselves because they're just too stupid to know that you shouldn't burn down your own pharmacy?" If it was at the level of local rumor mills back then, by January 6, many more had heard of these groups like Proud Boys, Oath Keepers, and Boogaloo Bois and understood they were real threats, from Charlottesville, Virginia, in 2017 to these racial justice uprisings and Stop the Steal rallies in 2020 (Thompson and Fischer 2021).

Even as far as California, interviewees noted these groups' presence, finding it disturbing that police did not intervene more to stop their behavior. Bill, a seventy-year-old white man attending protests in Monterey and Sacramento, stated,

> The National Guard was there for about two weeks, as I recall the curfew started at either 8:00 or 9:00 p.m. at night ... and the National Guard followed. Really, the majority of the nighttime violence went for several days without a lot of police intervention, one of the critiques of the police was that they allowed a lot of property damage to take place, a lot of the peaceful protesters were critical of their suspicion of agents provocateurs—promoting the violence and the property damage to distract from the message of the Black Lives movement rallies. ... That type of violence that was not related to peaceful protest was hard to predict the trajectory that it would go. Some buildings were set on fire. A lot of private cars and small businesses were ransacked ... the violence distracting from the cause of a peaceful protest movement, militant but peaceful. ... As it went from light to darkness is usually when the breakaway groups started the violence and some of that self-proclaimed anarchists who were hell bent on doing as much damage as possible but to the dismay and announcement of activists that had been organizing the protests.

Bill got rather impatient with my questions about this because he was so incensed that they would take our energy away from discussing movement goals. Likewise, in Louisville, Rev. David, a forty-four-year-old white man, reported that police letting white supremacists run rampant at these events was a clear problem.

> These individuals kept walking with their weapons between the two churches back and forth trying to be intimidating, right. They weren't stepping on our church property, but they were walking around trying to be intimidating. ... The police weren't stopping them. And that this area is supposedly an exclusion zone keeping everybody out, but these guys seem to have the ability to walk right past those police checkpoints carrying firearms. ... And there's a high-rise building that's an apartment building next to the church in front of the church and it's got balconies and people were on those boundaries throwing stuff off at protesters, like batteries and coins, and a battery from ten stories up hitting you in the head could kill you, right. I mean, it was making divots, dimples in the concrete and in in the asphalt ... and the police were not stopping them. The police were surrounding the building because the threat was the protesters, not the people throwing stuff at the protesters.

Police neglect of harmful behavior toward protesters has been an ongoing theme, along with white supremacist groups' attempt to sabotage racial justice activists' work. We know that uniformed police officers have been found to be affiliated with white supremacist groups and militia, and these are often treated as isolated "bad apples." Yet systemic willful neglect of these groups' damage to citizens peacefully protesting is a much more institutionalized practice and garners decisively less media attention.

Who Is Protected? Who Is Targeted? Who Decides?

In May 2021, in an eighty-eight-page opinion, U.S. federal judge Algenon L. Marbley ordered Columbus, Ohio, police to stop using all weapon forms of resistance against nonviolent protesters (rubber bullets, tear gas, batons, pepper spray). Judge Marbley's opinion cited Dr. Martin Luther King Jr.'s quote, "Somewhere I read that the greatness of America is the right to protest for rights," invoking the First Amendment rights of press, speech, and assembly (Murphy 2021). Ideally, law enforcement would have protected 2020 racial justice uprising participants exercising their constitutional rights of peaceful protest and assembly. However, in many U.S. cities, law enforcement was, at best, more interested in protecting property and turning a blind eye to those who attacked protesters and, at worst, an aggressive force turning violent against nonviolent protesters. Moreover, executive leaders in government not only ordered these repressive police actions but then issued false statements to the press about their actions and the protesters' behaviors. Yet the same cell phone cameras and social media that exposed police killings like George Floyd, Eric Garner, and Walter Scott as excessive, unwarranted uses of force can now expose misrepresentations of police violence against protesters. Despite reading that people "broke into the CNN building" in Atlanta or that police issued warnings "before" firing tear gas in Tampa, these participants were able to see for themselves that reports of "justification" of police aggression against unarmed civilians can easily be twisted from the truth.

Yet not all participants witnessed police aggression toward protesters. Some were even surprised by the orderliness and respect with which their events were handled. These exceptional cases were more likely to be in outlying suburban areas or small towns with high proportions of white residents and protesters. The findings here underscore that individual actors or "bad apples"—or even "implicit bias" at the individual level—are not the only factor in police use of excessive force and certainly not the most influential. Rather, clear directives from the top down in government are what directs law enforcement activities. During 2020, protest demonstrations overall greatly increased, but in 2019, authorities intervened in only 2 percent of all events, while in 2020, they intervened in 9 percent (more than quadruple the intervention rate), and use of force was at over 5 percent of

Black Lives Matter protests while only 1 percent of others (Kishi and Jones 2020). Chiefs of police take orders from the executive branch of government. They were ordered to send a greater proportion of their force to these events, ordered to take their riot gear and use it. If they had been ordered to protect protesters' First Amendment rights and to protect their safety from armed counterprotesters and car ramming as their primary mission and objective, it is likely these protesters might have had a different experience. Even for those who witnessed police neglect and mistreatment at some point during their 2020 protest experiences, these same persons also witnessed other events where this did not happen. This shows that (a) mistreatment does not have to happen all the time for it to exist and for it to be real, and (b) intermittent punishment and inconsistency is destabilizing and traumatizing because the victim never knows when to trust or let their guard down.

One of the many things 2020 taught us—growing from the groundswell of the post-2013 Black Lives Matter movement and its genius use of social media and technology—is that increasingly, the police narrative will no longer be the hegemonic, dominant, only narrative of what takes place in a public setting where use of force occurs. Using their tried-and-true old tactics of saying, "The protesters started it" and telling the public that the police use of force on protesters was "for the good of community safety" will no longer suffice. Under the Biden administration, the U.S. Justice Department launched investigations of the police departments in Minneapolis, Louisville, Phoenix, and other cities for their unlawful use of force against protesters during 2020 (Wolfe 2021), and we see the condemnation of Columbus Police Department violations by the federal judge cited above. As of this writing, the FBI and the Justice Department continue to prosecute cases related to these egregious actions—for example, in May 2023, a former Louisville Metro Police officer pleaded guilty to firing rounds of foam bullets aimlessly into a crowd of protesters, admitting he had not identified who exactly threw the water bottle that prompted his actions (U.S. Department of Justice 2023). With such a diverse and large group of eyewitnesses during 2020 to the fact that police do not always tell the truth about their "crowd control" actions and whether they are unprovoked or lawful, now the proverbial cat is out of the bag, and perhaps the tide is turning. Yet it remains to be seen whether the degree of accountability occurring subsequently will match the level of overstepping of authority and unnecessarily aggressive tactics that occurred.

It may seem as if some of these demonstrators were stepping into a war zone during an already scary time in the world with a global pandemic. They faced the threat of violence from both law enforcement and onlookers/counterprotesters. Yes, they were making a sacrifice for a greater cause, putting their lives on the line for those who had already died, in hopes of putting a stop to future killings and racism in general. They found their greater cause to be worth that risk. However, they also found togetherness and comfort in shared grief during a time of tremendous isolation. As we will see in the next chapter, protest is driven by emotion (Jasper 2018), and although these protests were not a single unified melody, they combined a variety of voices into a discordant harmony that resounded: enough is enough!

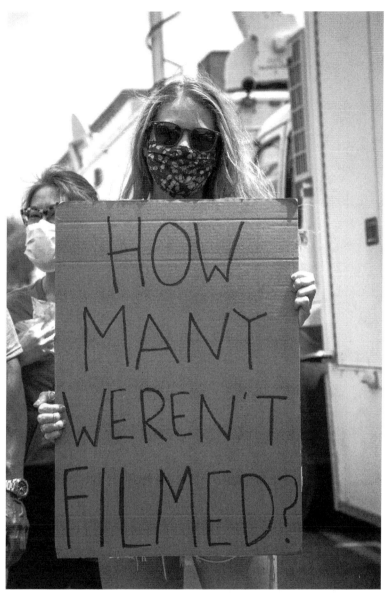

The Unseen, June 4, 2020. A protester holds up a sign outside of George Floyd's memorial service in Minneapolis, Minnesota, questioning how many instances of police brutality were not filmed. Photo credit by E Mackey.

Sitting on Top of the World, May 29, 2020. A group of people sit atop a building that overlooks the area now known as George Floyd Square in Minneapolis, Minnesota. Photo by E Mackey.

Declaration, May 31, 2020. A woman stands at the base of the steps of a federal building in Saint Paul, Minnesota, to declare to police and members of the National Guard that Black lives matter. Photo by E Mackey.

Community, June 13, 2020. During a silent protest in Los Angeles, California, a man holds an image of some of the Black lives that were taken at the hands of police. Photo by E Mackey.

Peppered, August 25, 2020. Two men are shot with PepperBalls by Kenosha Police, after one of the men came too close to the fence and the other rushed to convince him to leave. Photo by E Mackey.

Sweet Serenade, July 18, 2020. A violinist serenades a little girl at a violin vigil held in memory of Elijah McClain in Central Park, New York. Photo by E Mackey.

Breonna, August 28, 2020. Individuals march with a graphic image of Breonna Taylor at the 2020 Commitment March in Washington, D.C. It was the fifty-seventh anniversary of the March on Washington for Jobs and Freedom, where Dr. Martin Luther King Jr. delivered his iconic "I Have A Dream" speech. Photo by E Mackey.

Soledad, 2020. Nathaniel Sawyer (holding megaphone) leads march in Soledad, California. Photo by Rachael Sawyer.

Marina, 2020. Nathaniel Sawyer (kneeling, right, with No Justice No Peace fist T-shirt) leads a march in Marina, California. Photo by Rachael Sawyer.

Black Lives Matter, Williamsburg, 2020. Protesters march on Monticello Avenue in Williamsburg, Virginia. Photo by Latanya Wallace-Conyers.

2nd Place Losers Don't Deserve Monuments, August 4, 2020. Author's son, Kaden O'Brien-James, stands at base of Robert E. Lee monument in Richmond, Virginia, after community space was created and before city removed statue to repurpose the space. Photo by Eileen O'Brien.

CHAPTER 4

Discordant Harmonies

Age, Gender, and Race

> Until the killing of black men, black mothers' sons, becomes as important to the rest of the country as the killing of a white mother's sons, we who believe in freedom cannot rest.[1]
>
> —Ella Baker, 1965, as quoted in Dreier 2014; Patton 2020

Ella Baker's quote above not only speaks to the importance of allies and calls out white privilege but also explores how parenthood and gender interact with who empathizes with racism-imposed trauma and injustice. George Floyd notably cried "Mama" as one of his last words before dying (even though his mother had passed away two years prior), which some took as a call to "mothers everywhere" to do something about this atrocity (Disparte and Tillman 2020; Spalding 2020). Although ideally all citizens should care when human rights are violated, historically it has been rare for whites to do progressive antiracist work (Bonilla-Silva 2017; Feagin 2020; O'Brien 2001). Baker acknowledged this unfortunate racial gap in empathy with her eloquent words.

Likewise, it is not only race but gender, age, and other statuses that have historically complicated people's relationships to racial justice work. It was a Black woman, Ida B. Wells-Barnett, who persistently brought the problem of the lynching of African American men to national attention during the Jim Crow era, yet we often see men as the most notable faces of the twentieth-century civil rights movement—such as Rev. Dr. Martin Luther King Jr. Clearly, Baker's quote above

---

1 The women's singing group Sweet Honey in the Rock shaped this quote into their tune "Ella's Song" (Dreier 2014).

does center "the killing of black men," yet by the twenty-first century, some statistics show that Black women are even more vulnerable when it comes to police violence (Johnson, Gilbert, and Ibrahim 2018; Lisenby 2018). Interestingly, Jermaine McDonald (2016, 149) argues that "The Black Lives Matter Movement has more in common with the decentralized, Ella Baker–supported SNCC [Student Nonviolent Coordinating Committee] of the 1960s than King's SCLC [Southern Christian Leadership Conference]," and it is three Black women who founded the Black Lives Matter (BLM) movement (Opal Tometi, Alicia Garza, and Patrisse Cullors). So although Baker's call begins with Black mothers and sons, it acknowledges we all stand in a particular relationship to Black lives depending on the race, gender, class, and other statuses we are assigned in the social structure and that inevitably shapes our involvement.

The factors about 2020 that created the "perfect storm" discussed in prior chapters are inevitably varied by race, class, gender, and other social statuses. Essential workers were more likely to be people of color, women, and immigrants and on the lower end of the social-class ladder—continuing to have to work as usual during the pandemic, often without sufficient safety protections and without option to work from home or access childcare (McTaggart and O'Brien 2021). White suburban and more affluent populations as well as college students were more likely to be either working from home or able to take time off—perhaps one of several reasons why more whites than usual were reported by some at the protests (Dumas 2020; Patton 2020). Kids were out of school, contributing to wider age spans seen in protest crowds. All these factors increased the diversity in the demographics of participants at these events, but the qualitative data collected for this study allow us to explore what was expected or surprised from the protesters' perspectives, especially from the vantage points of those who reside in these communities and are more intimately familiar with them. Moreover, the relatively even split between those who identify as white and Black in the sample enables us to investigate how protesters' intentions and experiences once in the setting differed by "race"—yet at the same time, these "racialized" experiences are hardly monolithic or uniform within the two groups because many of the other statuses discussed here (whether they are men/women, protested in suburban or urban areas, are younger than most in the crowds, etc.) interact with race in various ways. For those familiar with intersectionality theory, these patterns aren't surprising, so the objective here is not so much to announce the discovery of this diversity as it is to describe it in qualitative detail, documenting how it manifested in this historic moment.

The 2020 uprisings weren't a uniform singular event but rather a stretch of many related events over a concentrated period. These uprisings attracted people's attention for a panoply of reasons—each location had its own character, and even in a single location, the mood shifted over time of day and may be perceived differently based on the social location and personal biography of the participant. The present analysis does not seek to arrive at any singular "truth" about any given protest location but rather to give voice to the multiple realities present during this historic year of uprising. It is notable, for example, that two interviewees who participated at the same location differ on how they describe white involvement at the protest—whether they observed it as uplifting and inspiring, or whether they perceived it as performative and disrespectful. These truths can coexist, and the social locations and personal biographies of each individual can help us make meaning of both perceptions. I also supplement these reported perceptions with secondary data as available for context—for instance, a perception of more white involvement than usual is not the same as a majority-white crowd by any means. Even throughout the diversity of respondent experiences reported here, some consistent patterns do emerge. Whether perfect unison melody or discordant harmony, there is no denying their resounding cry out loud.

Age and Ability

Several participants commented on the presence of children at their events—oft unexpected but always inspiring. While civil rights protest has historically heavily represented youth, particularly college students (Gershon 2020; McAdam 1986, 1990), these 2020 uprisings contained even more reasons to include younger people than usual. Schools were closed—both universities and K–12—due to danger of community spread of COVID-19 with no vaccine, and by this point in the year, public health data indicated older people were less likely to survive the virus. So youth were not only more available with their time but also relatively more willing to emerge into public outdoor gatherings due to the pandemic. Most (twenty) of the interview participants in this study, although not a representative sample, were in their twenties or thirties—only five interviewees were over fifty at the time of their protest activities. But even many of these young adults commented on how impressed they were with the young people who attended. In some cases, marches and demonstrations were designed especially for children, as well as there being parallel events for those who were differently abled or could not "march" in the traditional sense.

In Columbus, Ohio, protests proliferated so much in 2020 that, along with downtown demonstrations near the courthouse, there were neighborhood protests in outlying suburbs. These neighborhood events sometimes had a distinctly youth-led focus. Carly, a white forty-nine-year-old mother of two, was aware of these events through her children—one a teen and one in elementary school. Carly resided in a middle-class suburb called Clintonville, known for more progressive politics than surrounding areas.

> [At] the intersection very close to my house, there are weekly protests, there have been for as long as twenty years or more, like there's always at least a small group of people talking about whatever, but then, certainly in the summer of 2020 they became much, much larger, and the ones in my neighborhood were largely led by youth—high school students and young adults. I went there with my teenager and his girlfriend, and my teenager has been to dozens of protests just through the years because I bring them along ... but he's not one to seek out some type of social justice work really on his own, so I was happy that he really wanted to go, and his girlfriend had never been to a protest at all, so it was her first but and so they made signs and stuff. ... And there's actually a new group "pint-sized protesters" and it's specifically like about children protesters; it's organized by parents, but yeah, it's pretty cool.

Another mom of teenagers, Helen—an African American forty-four-year-old mother of three—is also a high school teacher who recognized students at her local neighborhood protests she attended in the town of Williamsburg, Virginia. She, too, was impressed by the existence of protest events designed especially for youth, noting that when protesting in the past, there weren't as many opportunities for youth, and she commended this unique feature of 2020 organizing.

> In the past it was ... older individuals ... individuals who were at the time my dad's age because they had lived through more things. But summer of 2020, there were protests demonstrations that were created for little kids in the area, so to see four- and five-year-olds, first and second graders I even know, I have a really close friend where her boyfriend—I think his daughter is ten or eleven now. He took her. ... There were things that were created for not only young people but individuals who were also disabled. A way that they could participate—the car demonstrations, where you can ride and honk your horn. Individuals who are willing to send in snacks and fruits and just advertise that it just shows that this is a collective issue; it's not a Black issue, it's not a white issue, it's a collective American issue and that we were willing to find a way for everyone to be involved and have their voices heard as well. So I really think that opened up the possibilities and the need for ways to make things accessible to everyone.

Helen noted here it was not only the presence of younger children but accessible options such as ride in your car and honk your horn, as opposed to getting out and walking, that made 2020 social justice organizing feel more inclusive. Others have noted that many areas of social life (work, school, socializing) also grew more accessible in various ways out of necessity due to the COVID-19 lockdowns and social distancing, indicating that maybe once the threat of the virus subsided, some adaptive strengths could be maintained going forward, with or without a pandemic threat (Ali et al. 2020; Collins 2020). Such inclusion might open up participation beyond not just diverse ages and physical abilities but gender, race, and family status as well.

In some cities where the tenor of protest events shifted from day to night, participants found daytimes to be more family friendly, including a more diverse age range than nights. Jim Bear, a Native American forty-four-year-old man in Minneapolis who has been protesting racial injustice since his teen years at the Super Bowl challenging Native mascots, noted decisively more youth involvement in 2020.

> The crowds were overwhelmingly young people; I would say millennials and younger. At some of these events, it was really interesting to see parents or guardians with young children. I never ever saw children in direct harm or danger, and that is for the most part, like when I saw parents or guardians with young children there, it was during the daytime, it was before curfew, those kind of things, lending their voice. And then as curfew approached, they would leave, obviously, for the safety of their children.

Isabel, a white twenty-three-year-old woman in the Denver and Aurora, Colorado, area, also recalled seeing a strong youth presence but more during the day than at night. She said students would organize midday protests where she would see more families and "young kids," but at night it would be more young adults who "just got off work" and "not as much kids, really no kids" because "I think it was kind of a given that things might get a little scary."

As discussed in the previous chapter, the existence of curfews in many cities during late May–early June 2020 exacerbated the stark difference between the demographics of the daytime-nighttime divide between protests. However, Isabel raises an important point that high school students were not yet tied down to full-time jobs, so could maintain—and even lead and organize—protests during daytime, while the young adults who appeared to be the majority by the prime-time evening hours could not always be there at those earlier times due to work. Youth workers experienced a couple of different prominent labor paths during this early period of the pandemic—they were not only among those most likely to be jobless, but if they were able to retain their jobs, these were jobs least likely to have a remote/work-from-home option, or "essential" work (Gould and Kassa 2020). So both these groups were clearly seen during the protests—the jobless youth organizing during the day and the young adults in the early evening hours as their essential work shifts may have been drawing down.

Like Isabel, Bill, a white seventy-year-old man in both Sacramento and Monterey, contrasted between the safety level of a smaller, more homogenous town and a bigger, more diverse city in terms of police presence and whether or not families found it safer to bring children. And like Jim Bear, Bill is a longtime protester since his first days as a white ally to the Black Panthers in the Bay Area, and he too found the multigenerational presence different than before.

> So at all these events, there was definitely a younger demographic but I say in terms of the solidarity of a lot of families, so parents and children. And sometimes very young children attending and, again, I think, demonstrating the breadth of solidarity and also a sense of safety and security to attend and participate. Despite reporting of other areas like Sacramento where there might have been more fear of violence, if you were taking a family member, but the ones in Monterey County, a lot of young people, a lot of families, parents and kids.

Contrary to the "riot" label that nonparticipants may have placed on these racial justice uprisings, indeed much are more aptly described as family gatherings.

By late May 2020, when the racial justice uprisings were in full swing, the medical science was clear that elderly were more vulnerable to serious illness and death upon contracting the coronavirus (Mueller, McNamara, and Sinclair 2020). So while pandemic health concerns are one reason older adults were less represented at these protests, there is another reason younger adults were in high supply for these events, that is not work related. Several participants felt that this was a "coming of age" moment politically for Gen Z. The 2016 election of Trump may have been the first presidential election in which they were old enough to vote and pay attention. Not only is this the generation most supportive of the Black Lives Matter movement, but they were also in the forefront of other progressive organizing of the most recent decade—for example, the 2018 March for Our Lives anti–gun violence protest after the Marjory Stoneman Douglas High School shooting (D-M. Davis 2020). Several participants from this generation emphasized that their own age peers were key organizers of the uprisings. As Jordan, a twenty-six-year-old African American (biracial) man protesting in the Atlanta area remarked,

> But for a lot of people is probably that I saw was a lot of them were innovative individuals like my age. A lot of millennials Gen Z individually, so those are for

sure, probably their first major protests unless they participated, like the Trump protests probably.

As Jordan notes, for several 2020 protesters it was their second major protest they ever attended in their lives, the first being those related to former president Trump's election and policies. So young, Generation Z already had a blueprint for participation in protest prepandemic—a pandemic was the new part for them, while the protesting was not. As noted in earlier chapters, Jordan's word choice of "innovative" here could refer to the social media infrastructure built by 2013–2015 Black Lives Matter organizers that facilitated getting the word out almost effortlessly to mobilize a wide range of people in 2020 in a relatively rapid amount of time. For Jordan, the word "innovative" and his generation go hand in hand, so it was no question they would be not only heavily involved but leading the way.

Was it the fact that colleges were suddenly closed due to the pandemic that made youth just more freely available to participate? Some of the interview data suggest that idle time is not the only factor. In areas where progressive movement leadership is largely well established, it can be hard for new faces to see where they fit in. Rev. Lane, a thirty-eight-year-old white woman in Rochester, New York, where antiracist organizing has been happening before and after 2020, thought this time, there were more college students.

> And I also saw more college students involved here in Rochester.... We have a couple of universities here and they really keep to themselves.... They do not even come downtown very much. So you had a lot more college kids involved in this than I had seen previously. [Interviewer: Classes were suspended or virtual or things like that, too, so.] I think that helped, and I would also say that I saw I did see a lot more like a multigenerational spread.

At its best, the movement leadership saw potential in the plethora of youthful new faces and sought to empower them to carry the torch into the next generation. Another clergy in the sample, Rev. TM, a fifty-three-year-old white man in Minneapolis, elaborated thus:

> I've been doing this for a long time. It's always been the kind of the same players, whether it's the same Black leaders, the same white leaders, whatever [but this time] it was held by younger, more passionate and newer activist leaders. And it was intentional that I could see that the old-guard people that I was used to be part of standing in the line to get up to the microphone, we weren't doing that. Some of them were, but they were not given the microphone like this is not your time. You know, we want to hear from this family who lives down the street, we want to hear from this young person, we want to hear from this—and I think that

was another super-important piece at least here locally, to hear from and to be impacted not by old voices but by new voices of all kinds of different shapes and sizes and colors. And again, I really believe that's born from what we've learned at Standing Rock, the Indigenous community that brings a[n] egalitarian leadership model and have a matriarchal leadership model. I heard more from more women in this movement than I've ever done ever had before. And that's a powerful thing, and so I hope that continues; I mean, that was different and beautiful.

Along with a diversity of age ranges was more diversity of gender and ethnicities than some had observed previously.

Often, the human mind can be allured toward exceptional events such that we lose sight of the more frequent pattern. Most of those I interviewed observed that, although most protesters tended to be in their twenties and thirties, it was refreshing to see people of other age ranges, even if in the minority, represented. These individuals took heart that it was not just younger folks to care about racism and injustice and also admired that those for whom it might have taken more effort had the courage and conviction to show up to these events. When I asked Faith, an eighteen-year-old African American (biracial) woman, how the age range of prior protests she attended compared to the summer of 2020 (in the town of Williamsburg, Virginia), she responded,

> I would say that in all the original events . . . the age group is primarily young people, like early twenties, so I think that this time, there were even like there was someone in a walker, like there's old, older people are getting out. And . . . middle-aged people who were . . . kind of one minded or one track mind . . . like didn't really open their minds to diversity until they got to a later point in their life, so they were trying to make up for it, but I still think that the age group was more like early twenties to early thirties like that age range.

Most young adults were accustomed to protesting with those around their same age, so it did stand out to them when older people were also in attendance, and the general impression was positive and appreciative of their involvement. Faith was not the only one to recall someone on a walker at her location; Janay, a twenty-eight-year-old African American woman protesting in Atlanta, was quoted in the prior chapter about seeing police "just drag" a "probably like seventy-five-year-old white lady" who had "signs around her walker" when she "couldn't get up and move fast enough" for them. Age became a symbol of vulnerability and indeed even an indictment of a society's values with how it treated its children and its elders. As U.S. vice president Hubert Humphrey stated in 1976, "The ultimate moral test of any government is the way it treats three groups of its citizens. First, those in the dawn of life—our children. Second, those in the shadows of life—our needy, our sick, our handicapped. Third, those in the twilight of life—our elderly" (Editorial Board 2016). Most of the African Americans I spoke with and marched with were especially impressed and excited about non-Blacks and elderly coming out to the protests. As reviewed in chapter 3, many younger participants came out expecting to be targets of police but did not expect to see the elders nor the abuse. That was especially reprehensible in their view. But at the same time, it magnified the urgent need for change.

The African American mother and teacher quoted earlier in this section, Helen, appreciated seeing youth in the lead at these protests, especially framing them as the future leaders of society. Helen repeated the word "empowering" more than once to characterize her feelings thus:

> For me, seeing so many young people, people my youngest daughter's age, my son's age, but the faces of students—college students, high school students—on the forefront. That was not only empowering, but it was also a relief that we're moving in the right direction. This can no longer be a conversation online, a conversation at home; this needs to be a conversation where the community is involved.

Having worked to equip her own children and students with the tools necessary to challenge racism and microaggressions in their educational lives, only to be met with inaction or apathy on the part of older adult administrators, Helen viewed her hometown marches as catharsis for the youth, who finally had a public forum for their concerns. This shifted youth from the disempowering role of individual grievance filer up against a big school or other institution to one of many voices raised in a community voice for change. Youth concerns can tend to be dismissed in a society run primarily by middle-aged to older adults. When Helen stated, "This can no longer be a conversation online, a conversation at home," she was referring to the youth who take to social media with a "vent" post or video about racism they encounter with peers and/or authority figures in their lives, often leaving the situation ultimately not redressed, and the teenager feeling alone. So this made youth involvement in the uprisings a welcome addition and a game changer compared with prior patterns. Knowing that youth who speak out now will become the nation's future leaders indicated to Helen that "we're moving in the right direction" as a society. This observation felt important to her not only as an educator but as a mother herself, an identity to which we turn in more detail in the next section.

"As a Mother": Gender and Parenthood

As the Ella Baker quote at this chapter's opening makes plain, a mother losing her son to police violence is the painful and all-too-common reality that is only the tip of the iceberg of all the injustices addressed by the Black Lives Matter movement. Nevertheless, it is the gut-clenching, heart-wrenching tragedy that wakes the apathetic into paying more attention. The parent/mother and son/man as victim component to this example is worth exploring more from a gender standpoint, especially in terms of how the modern BLM movement broadened this perspective. From the beginning of white supremacy, gender and parenthood have been building blocks of racist ideology—for both framing and counterframing white racism (Feagin 2020). Baker's quote strikes a chord because it challenges the hegemonic symbol of white womanhood and motherhood as virtuous, but as antiracist counterframing from African Americans such as Sojourner Truth has long retorted: "Ain't I a Woman?" Black women can also be mothers, yet their grief at losing a child, their fear for the physical safety and mental well-being of their children is often disregarded in racist framing of parenthood and public safety. The unjust state-sanctioned murder of any child should spark a society's outrage, but in a racist society, racist ideology and framing scrambles to immediately concoct any flimsy defense of the murderer by insinuating that an unarmed child somehow deserved or provoked their fate if they are not white. For example, the supposed innocent virtue of white woman, somehow needing white man's protection even when it includes violence, was used to frame white woman Carolyn Bryant as a victim who needed to be avenged when the fourteen-year-old African American boy Emmett Till was lynched in Mississippi in 1955 for allegedly whistling at her. Till's mother, Mamie Till, was determined to change that narrative, flipping the script of who the innocent victim was by insisting on an open-casket funeral for her son amid her grief. Still living, Bryant (now Dunham) admitted later in life that her story was fabricated, but that of course will not bring back the mother's child (Daniels 2021).

Racism in the United States often includes a gender component, and the racist framing of African American males as predator to be feared and controlled dates back to the end of slavery in the United States, when a caricature made popular by propaganda films like Birth of a Nation served to justify draconian Jim Crow measures of legal segregation and white terrorism. The question "Would you want your daughter to marry one?" explicitly identifies white women as those to be both protected and controlled, while African American men are characterized as desiring to harm white women, as opposed to perhaps wanting equal access to housing, education, and jobs (Vinas-Nelson 2017). The Black male criminal as not only stereotype but ideology has become such a dependable trope that many whites committing crimes have taken to fabricating the "Black man did it" alibi to take the heat off themselves—what legal scholar Katheryn Russell-Brown (2008) calls a "racial hoax." Protests of unjust killings by police often focus on Black male victims—Michael Brown, Tamir Rice, George Floyd, and Eric Garner, just to name a few—but as evidence presented in prior chapters demonstrates, the adultification of Black girls starts early and Black women are also increasingly at risk. "The talk"—once framed as a warning that African American parents passed to their sons—is now deemed necessary for sons as well as daughters (Bouchard 2016).

Themes of gender and parenting emerged in several of these interviews, as for these protesters, being a mother and a parent was one factor compelling them to act despite fears of possibly contracting COVID-19 by participating. Only a minority of the interviewees were parents themselves, which is in large part a function of the age of those who participated (most were in their twenties or early thirties and childless). All those quoted in this section for this theme were between the ages of thirty-nine and fifty-three at the time of the interview, which is the upper end of the age of the total sample. In prior chapters, we explored participants' decision-making processes for weighing the risks of participating in the uprising. However, for the parents in the sample, for nearly all of them, their kids were part of their reasoning for why their participation was desired and necessary. Interestingly and not a planned component of the sample, all of the parents in the sample also have at least one son.

Parents did not always participate with their child, depending on the context. One respondent was pregnant, so her unborn son was participating in utero. The father who traveled to Minneapolis to participate did not bring his children, and one mother who attended several protests was selective about which ones her children would also attend. However, in all cases, standing up to say no to injustice was part of them living out the values with which they also were teaching (or planning to teach) their own children. They saw themselves as fighting to build a better world for their children and their children's peers. Discussions about these decisions often included a gender component—sometimes briefly stated but sometimes consciously and deliberately explained.

Teaching and modeling values is an important part of parenting. One white, fifty-three-year-old man, William, was a parent as well as a minister, who taught theology in Rutherford County, North Carolina. Social justice was a component of the university curriculum where he taught, and both the town and the campus he described as majority African American. These uprisings were not his first time protesting for social justice, and he felt it was important to be an ally to the community of which he is a part. Like several of the parents in the sample, they marched as a family. Interestingly, William briefly brought up being part of a transracial family as one of several reasons he participated.

> We believed that the issue of racial injustice was important enough that it was worth whatever risk may not be taken to assemble publicly at that time. One motivating factor is that we're a transracial family are our son, that is not African American who's Korean, but we have long existed as a transracial family and which one of our members is a person of color.

Another white parent in the sample was also part of an interracial family. Carly, a forty-nine-year-old white woman in Columbus, Ohio, was raising two racially mixed sons of color—one teenager and one six years old at the time of the protests. Carly was more explicit and intentional about describing the teachable moments she wanted to have with her children and also had a much longer history of participating in direct action for racial justice in that community, as she had been active since her twenties, whereas William had just attended one prior protest related to the Trump election a few years prior. Also, the city of Columbus, Ohio, presented far more opportunities for participation than the more rural North Carolina area where William resided. Columbus also included numerous examples of property damage and boarded-up businesses where the plywood had been covered in inspiring images—what Carly described as "resistance art"—that she wanted to show her children when she felt it safe to do so.

In fact, because of Carly's long history of direct actions, she had mostly curtailed her activity to donating and supporting social movements in other ways in her later decades, so it was mainly because of her children that she reactivated herself, ultimately, for what she understood would be a historic moment and important for them to see.

> I have a long history of going to direct action protests, and now that I'm a little bit older, I think most of my energy goes into other types of justice work . . . redirecting my skills in a different direction, but it does feel important to me that my children see the importance of protest and the role that protests can play, and so I do like to take them to some protests and stuff, and I like the energy and I think it's important for there to be a big swelling showing support in the community around different issues. I guess in the summer of 2020, I went with my partner and our then-six-year-old to protests, a couple protests, I think, to at the state house downtown, in Columbus, Ohio, at the state house downtown. And it went well, it was also during COVID, and so we were really cognizant of covid happening, and there were many, many, many, many, many people, so we really

wanted to be sure that we were still able to not distance six feet but distance like fifteen feet, and so the way kind of the area was set up, it did lend itself well to that. We just kind of stayed off to the side and back fifteen feet or so, in masks and everything, of course. But still, if you have signs and you're right there, you're still part of it. So we did that with our youngest, and I feel like that went well. It was during the protests, there was, the businesses downtown were, there were broken windows and graffiti and some things like that, so it was a good opportunity for us to talk to our young child about the role that different types of resistance play out during protests and why someone might do graffiti on a building or break the window and then also talk about outside groups sometimes doing those things and then can blaming protesters for doing that, but then also kind of the legitimate rage that people have that might lead to doing that as well, and so there was a really outside of the protests and the people in the signs and the chants and the discussion.

Carly could have stayed at the smaller youth-led protests closer to her suburban neighborhood, especially since at such smaller events, social distancing would be easier to maintain, but she felt that seeing the downtown, urban protests with more attendees and the property damage and graffiti would be an opportunity to share her values with her children. Carly used the term "legitimate rage" to explain to her children that different types of resistance might happen and why, also raising the possibility that outside groups might be responsible. Also employed in higher education at a community college, Carly emphasized critical-thinking skills, allowing her children to draw their own conclusions while exposing them to a range of possible explanations perhaps not heard in mainstream media. Although she wanted to, along with her family, be a part of a critical mass standing up objecting to racist police violence, based on her age and the coronavirus, if it were not for her children, she likely would have found other ways to support rather than attending directly.

Two other African American mothers in the sample felt their roles as mothers compelled them to participate despite relatively advanced age and health concerns. Both participated in the college town of Williamsburg, Virginia, but from very different prior backgrounds, neither being native to the area. One was a military spouse with all three children young adults, and a longer history of prior direct action (Helen), while the other mother at the time of the interview had her first child, still a baby not yet one, and was carrying him in utero during the uprising (Sharon). Interestingly, Sharon had never participated in direct action for racial justice prior to the 2020 uprisings, yet she quickly catapulted to a leadership role with near-daily protests for months on end. And she asserted she would not have been as involved if it were not for the passion she felt about bringing a new person into the world, especially recently learning that he would be a boy. In fact, she even chose to name him "Justice."

As a visible leader of the protests, Sharon had very different perceptions of law enforcement and the threat of violence at the events than did Helen. An onlooker threw a beer on her during a protest, and in not intervening, she felt that officers were indeed sanctioning the attacker's action. She witnessed other onlooker provocations as well, yet still she felt her time spent in harm's way was ultimately worthwhile.

> There were people that try to drive through us, so I almost got hit by a car last summer, and I found out that I was pregnant right before these protests, so the protest took on a different meaning because I was carrying a child during the process. So I was almost hit by a car; I was almost hit by a motorcycle. Other people were almost hit by cars that tried to drive through. . . . It felt good to be heard . . . but I was just really disheartened by the ugliness that was around it, the people that were threatened that were part of Williamsburg community that were threatened . . . on Facebook . . . the juxtaposition it was there, but we still felt like we had something to say and everybody was just tired, and so from that standpoint, we did exactly what we needed to do, and from that standpoint, we were uber effective.

The protests took on a "different meaning" once she found out she was going to be a mother, and she repeatedly used the word "juxtaposition" to describe the opposing forces of the "ugliness" of people who did not support the protests, and the benefits of participation—both for protesters and for those who were educated by the events. As an organizer, Sharon sought to move the protest locations to more traveled areas to create increased opportunities for dialogue with people who did not understand why they were marching. This strategic move put them more in harm's way, but she felt the benefits of educating the public were worth the increased risk.

Interestingly, Sharon felt that as a woman (and daughter of law enforcement), she was not likely to encounter police brutality herself, even though she is a Black and Latina woman (Black/Panamanian), so she explicitly identified being a parent of a Black son as a game changer for her and her newly activated passion for this injustice. Despite health challenges during her pregnancy, she wanted to stay involved.

> So yeah, there was a lot going on with me, but in the midst of it, I was like, no like I'm carrying a child and I'll be damned if my child is just sitting in a car and

> get shot, like Philando [Castille]. . . . Everything for me kind of changed when I found out that I was pregnant, the likelihood of me, being a victim of police brutality is low; I'm a female that was raised by law enforcement so, but it was just me being pregnant and I was like I'm gonna have a baby, my baby might be out here, and I promise you, y'all might want to try it with somebody else! So let me try to change the system before they bring the wrath on themselves, but messing with my child, I'm a be, yeah.

Though yet unborn, the fear of something happening to the child she would soon be raising highly motivated Sharon to speak out. Although data tell us that neither being a woman nor the child of law enforcement makes one exempt from these abuses of power, it is striking that Sharon's status as expecting mother brought her a bit more in touch with the truth about her being in greater proximity to risk, albeit secondhand (in her perception).

In contrast, Helen, as a parent of older children as well as a high school teacher, came to the protests with a longer experience as a mother, with two daughters as well as a son. During the interview, she described her more recent journey of eye-opening to the fact that not only her son but also her daughters were at risk for racist police violence due to the case of Breonna Taylor.

> So it was really not only a religious, a mother, but also just for my own sake that I decided to . . . when my kids brought it up, I'm hearing their concern. We have to do something. So the first step, let's talk about it. Second step, let's make our posters. Now, let's make sure we have the masks so that we can go out. Let's make sure that we can be as socially distanced as possible, and there were times during the marches where I was thinking, oh my gosh, there's so many people close to me. Oh gee, there is no social distancing; we're arm to arm. We're crying. We are doing all these things, but when I thought about it, this was not just a movement; this is about life, and it superseded my own need for personal security, healthwise, because at the end of the day . . . I would be contradicting myself with the values I have created if I did not stand with them . . . and not just standing with my own children, but I'm standing up and by children that I don't even know, parents who may not have been out there. I felt like I'm standing for all of our Black and brown people in general.

Helen had a much longer history of direct action fighting racism in the various communities in which she lived as a military family, but she said, "It used to be just for my son." It was not until 2020 and the case of Breonna Taylor (who was the same age as her eldest daughter) that she broadened her perspective that she was doing it for all children, not just sons. Despite being older, immunocompromised, and fearful of the virus, she attended many 2020 events with her family because of how passionately she felt about living her values and standing up for her children.

Interestingly, for those with younger children who might be in harm's way, it was mainly the white participants who described this as primarily a teachable moment for their kids, albeit at controlled times and hours. For parents of color I spoke with, especially in larger urban areas where police presence was high, the risk was often described as outweighing the benefits. For example, Jim Bear, a forty-four-year-old Native American man in Minneapolis, explained,

> Weighing heavily in that decision, part of the reason why I don't want to get arrested is I have four young kids. My oldest two, my daughters are now they're now fifteen and thirteen, so they would have been, you know, fourteen and twelve and thereabouts. They're aware; they see what's happening. For them, this time became a moment where protest was something that was righteous and admirable, and it morphed into something that was dangerous because protests are where people get hurt and they get shot by the rubber bullets and where people can die, and you have counterprotesters that are there just to stir shit up. . . . Immediately outside of our dining room window is the entrance ramp for the freeway that goes down into Minneapolis, and so my daughters would sit at our dining room table, and they would count . . . the armor you know from the National Guard. And then they would count the city buses that would come by that were filled with state troopers in their uniform. . . . And it became a traumatizing thing for them to watch as it happens. I remember at that Daunte Wright vigil where they had the curfew of seven o'clock. Seven o'clock came, and we were all still there at that intersection. We had just wrapped up, and I remember, I was literally walking back to my car and my phone rang and I looked at my phone and it was about 7:04, right, so it was four minutes after curfew. And I glanced at my phone and it's one of my daughters and she just says, "Where are you? It's after seven o'clock. And fifteen tanks just drove by." And so yeah, so it was very traumatizing for them.

As a parent of color, one fears for one's children being in harm's way, but children also feared for their parents as they watched their city become occupied by potentially violent elements, particularly in cities like Minneapolis. Here, the violent elements were the agents of the state, along with the white supremacists.

White Protesters: Strength or Liability?

These uprisings were not simply joining hands in racial unity and singing "Kumbaya." Passionate, even angry, calls for justice and accountability coexisted with speakers who boldly called for self-care to heal from trauma and celebrate Black joy. Many white protesters came with clear instructions and understandings that they were to govern themselves accordingly and that expectations for them differed slightly than for protesters of color. Likewise, several whites felt it was their duty to show up precisely because they had privilege, seeing themselves almost as "breakout" representatives, doing something not altogether expected of them. Conversely, many African American participants interviewed felt a certain obligation to continue carrying the torch of the previous generations, having no expectations that any significantly new breakthroughs or changes would occur from prevailing racist patterns. Rather, they sought to stand in community with others who shared the same moral objections as themselves to racist killings and, accustomed to being the racial majority at most protests, were generally pleasantly surprised when encountering anyone who was not African American. These racialized patterns varied by whether the communities were smaller and suburban or larger and urban. Some understandably questioned whether increased white interest was fleeting or a lasting commitment.

A closing interview question for this project asked participants if they had any dos and don'ts advice for others wanting to get involved in direct action demonstrations for racial justice. Although this question was not originally crafted to elicit any race-specific responses, it was striking how many whites answered this question specifically directed at other whites and how they should conduct themselves at protests. Unanimously, whites felt it was important these events were Black led, and they take a supporting role and humble themselves to follow instructions—including standing in front as a buffer between police and protesters. Often, white interviewees took care to distinguish themselves from other white protesters they felt might not have yet understood their role, potentially undermining Black leadership.

Although violent act of terrorists driving vehicles directly into protesters unfortunately happened in many places, like the 2017 event in Charlottesville, Virginia, which resulted in the death of Heather Heyer, interviewees in Virginia expressed a more heightened concern than others about this impending possibility. In Williamsburg, another college town a couple of hours east of Charlottesville in the same state, the protests had an interesting structure. There were those who marched, chanted, and carried signs in the protest, but then there was a lay security detail that also carried signs with messages about racial justice—their signs were not made of posterboard but rather thicker wood that also served as shields meant to protect marchers from onlookers and passers-by. The lay security team was mostly, if not exclusively, white. The security had meetings with organizers and worked with police if they noticed any cars that seemed consistently following or trailing the protesters, they would track license plate and identity information for those vehicles. Blake, a twenty-one-year-old white man marching in Williamsburg, explained why he chose this supporting role in the marches:

> So there was one main thing that was outside of my expectations, and it was something that bothered me . . . given the demographic of Williamsburg; it is a predominantly white Caucasian community, so there were a lot of times where you'd have the people who organized it, which is African American, they were trying to lead chants and stuff from the front of the crowd. And then you'd have some of the more traditional [white] Williamsburg community would try to yell over them to chant and all that and. In my mind, that just felt very wrong, like you aren't going there, isn't to speak for them; it's to give them the room to speak and give them like raise their voices, not raise our own. So that was one thing I did not expect and honestly, quite frankly, bothered me a lot.

His advice to other whites: "Black individuals whose lives are being threatened, don't speak over them or speak for them. Protect them; give them the space to speak on things the way they want to speak on them." Blake felt he was in the proper place for a white person as a supporter and protector rather than a leader. It frustrated and angered him that other whites did not do the same. This group working security provided Helen, a forty-four-year-old African American woman at the same protest location, with an emotional moment when she realized they were there.

> I did cry the first time at a protest when we were marching, and I don't remember the term what they call the individuals, but they were kind of flanking all of the marchers and they had these wooden billboards . . . [saying] "When Black lives are under attack, what do we do? Stand up, fight back!" But to see that those were people who are not Black, flanking us and protecting us and chanting that like that in itself that was, wow, there are people who not only care, but you don't know me [tearfully stated]. And you run over to these older people who are yelling these horrible things and you just up to them to guard us like that. That did something to my soul to see that happen because we know and I know I have friends, where race is something that I can't talk to them about. . . . I just cried. It was just so . . . I did not expect that much power, but to see it and feel it, it superseded my expectations."

Helen was so moved because whites she had once considered "friends" would argue against her when she said her family's lives were under attack, saying, "I don't see color." Yet here were total strangers, white yet able to understand that Black lives were under attack, who provided the empathy that she could not get from her supposed friends.

Although this varied depending on location, several sites had organizers that laid out a specific role for whites during the events, diverging from what was expected of others. Both in Dallas, Texas, and Tampa, Florida, white participants described clear instructions that were given that whites should be in the front of the crowd to take the brunt of the charge from law enforcement, if necessary. As Michelle, a twenty-four-year-old white woman who marched in Dallas, stated,

> The African Americans in the protest were telling the white people to get in the front lines, in case police did decide to use action. They were saying, all the white people to the front, so we did that. . . . And I would suggest, if you are white, to just listen to the African Americans because it's not your protest. You're there to be an ally; you're not there to be front and center, not there to try to make it about you, and so just keep an open mind, have a big heart, and do what they need you to do, not what you think should be done.

Monica, another white woman, age thirty-three who marched in Tampa, saw firsthand the reasoning behind why organizers requested whites be in the front of the crowd. As noted in the prior chapter, as a first-time protester, she got quite the initiation by getting tear gassed that night, so it was the first and last time she went. However, she attended expecting that something like this might occur and was mentally prepared for the possibility. Like Michelle, she felt it was important to follow instructions that were specific to whites.

> Listen to the people who are organizing, don't do anything crazy, don't engage them, listen to what they're saying. Don't speak over people of color who are there if they are trying to speak. If they're trying to chant, that's their time to talk; you just listen. And if they tell you to go up front, I think that that's your own personal choice; if you don't want to put yourself up there, I mean, then, you certainly don't have to. But listen to what they're saying, and if you can find it on yourself to put your body in between, then that's important—I think it's an important gesture that you should make and just be aware that you could get hurt.

The utmost in ally behavior would be to "put your body in between" a person of color being attacked by police (or other onlooker) and the threat. But at minimum, Monica and others stressed that whites should not be trying to speak or lead chants at these actions.

Keep in mind that an artifact of this sample is that these are individuals committed enough to want to discuss their experiences about one year later in a voluntary unpaid interview. This likely distinguishes them from those who were not as committed, unaware of all these unwritten yet important rules. Abby, an eighteen-year-old white woman who marched in Nashville, Tennessee, explained that even though there were no organizers giving explicit instructions of where to stand as a white person, her perception was that most whites should understand their role as ally at these events.

> The whole point of me going was so that people there understood that, as a white ally, I am here to project your voice; I'm not here to silence your voice. And being at least where I was at in the South, it was really important just to be there and to be supportive of people of color. . . . I would say, if you aren't a person of color, don't give your opinion on how people of color should feel; let people of color feel and grieve and process and be angry and listen to them and accept what they're saying because as a white individually, you will never understand that same struggle. And I think that's kind of part of being a good allies, just listening and lifting up their voices. You don't want to silence their voice with your own opinion. I think that's really crucial if you're going to be somebody in these protests as a white human. . . . I think, as a white person, it is safer for us to stand up front, just show that we are supporting, that we also do not support the police. I think it's safer for us because my white skin is like a shield of protection. So we didn't have anything explicitly telling us that a lot of people ended up catching on to us white people being in the front to protect our people behind.

Abby described the importance of amplifying voices of color as well as being out in front as a "shield of protection" that is likely to be safer in interactions with police. At the time of the interview, Abby was living in Los Angeles, so she further contextualized her perspective to emphasize that in the U.S. South, it was especially imperative for whites to protect people of color from potential law enforcement threats, given historical relations with police in that region.

A basic understanding of the different structural positions of whites and people of color in everyday interactions with law enforcement is crucial for white protesters, and if they came only to indicate their outrage for the tip-of-the-iceberg incidents like the George Floyd killing, they may not yet know enough to govern themselves effectively at direct action events. As the previous chapter explained, there are municipalities such as Louisville, Kentucky, and Aurora, Colorado, where police departments can pretty much carry on with impunity, giving little to no justification when using force on protesters and facing no disciplinary repercussions for doing so. White civilians are not likely to bear the brunt of this, but people of color are. As Isabel, a twenty-three-year-old white woman in Colorado, put it,

> If you're coming from a place of privilege . . . for white people, this isn't their reality, so as a white person, I think, for us to be joining this is—step off your ped-

estal, accept criticism from people. Accept if someone says to not do something a certain way, like at the protests [we are told,] "Hey, if you're a white person and you're here, don't incite violence because it's going to come down on us" [people of color], so I think actively listening and from your place of privilege, uplifting others, that's my biggest deal. Yeah, and don't make it about yourself; don't ignore the leaders and the organizers because they're the ones actually doing the work. And just do what you can to help, and don't make it centered around yourself or for your own personal gain.

One concern about white involvement was them participating for their "own personal gain." In earlier months of the pandemic, many schools and workplaces shut down and social media activity intensified, leading some to be concerned that the uprisings became just another cool event to see and be seen at for some. Some interviewees, especially people of color, felt it was a double-edged sword with media attention. On a positive note, more whites than usual were paying attention, but on the flip side, it seemed a popularity contest or fad for some, and those fighting for their very lives would appreciate more than just passing interest in their well-being. As Faith, an eighteen-year-old African American (biracial) woman in Williamsburg, Virginia, reflected,

> I also think it's really bad, but I think that the social media impact was really big because people would want to link to their friends and they saw something, they're like, "Oh, I want to participate in that. I want to do that." So, since there's a big social media aspect to it, like the biggest one there's ever been, I think that that played a key role. And I think that was a good thing, but at the same time, since social media is down now people aren't caring about the rest of the issues, there's still more we have to fix and not everyone gets their justice, so I think that it was helpful but, and it did change the outcome, and that there were more people due to social media and seeing the suffering news and stuff like that. So I think that there's more of an outside force than there typically was, and that was why there was more of a turnout. And people just wanted to join their friends and make it a big thing, take a picture with a sign [and] feel like they did something.

When Isabel mentioned "personal gain" above, this is the kind of "take a picture with a sign and feel like they did something" status-seeking behavior to which Faith referred. Hence the cautious optimism about white involvement. As Kelli, a forty-five-year-old African American woman in Richmond, Virginia, discussed,

> [I saw] maybe three or four five solid non-Black allies before 2020. It was scary to see majority non-Black, brown walking down the street chanting, "Black lives matter"—parts of me were like, "Where you been?" I try to feel the genuineness

> of it. . . . It was something that I never thought that I would ever see. And I had to question the authenticity of it. So yeah, it was a new thing. . . . The best thing that ever happened was the fact that Juneteenth got blown up, right. . . . But you just had your Black Lives Matter sign up on your business, you took that down real quick once doors open. . . . I just sit back and I'm like, just a year ago, oh where's your black square now? . . . Weah, I mean, it's sad. It really is sad, and it's what else was sad is that I own two Black-owned businesses . . . and the amount of money that was thrown our way. And now it started to just— So again, that should just be normal, you should be supporting Black-owned, women-owned community. . . . Why did it take a murder in an eye opener for only twelve months for you not to recognize that your patterns need to change a little? . . . The amount of not knowing what to do with what you know. I think I was more intrigued by my friends that were like, I'm here—whenever there you need to talk, I'm here—not "Explain this to me," like it was my duty to help you understand why you may be racist. So I just think that . . . as it stopped being mainstream and in their faces and at the world open back up, it was easier for you to revert back to your comfort. Because you weren't forced to look at this anymore.

Reflecting now one year after the protests occurred, Kelli distinguished between two different types of white behavior toward her. Those she viewed more positively did not ask her to teach them about racism or try to cut and run without asking much of themselves—rather, they simply told her they would be there for her, asking her what she needed. Eloquently, Kelli described problematic white ally behavior as "not knowing what to do with what you know." So one problem is white people not willing to educate themselves who rely on people of color to do that for them (and worse yet, becoming defensive once learning the information). But another problem is only caring when it's popular, and then "revert back to your comfort" when racial justice is no longer the most popular theme on the internet.

Likewise, another longtime activist, Jim Bear, a forty-four-year-old Native American man and spiritual leader in Minneapolis, was critical of religious leaders in his community showing up to events like George Floyd's funeral and other 2020 demonstrations, particularly when they had been silent all other opportunities for speaking out against police violence, before and since.

> What really surprised me is the number of pastors and clergy from my old denomination and even from my old churches that I know have never ever come out for anything like this, never shown up—were not there when Mr. Clark was killed, was not there when [name unclear] was killed in the protests. And yet here George Floyd gets killed and here they are. I've always been suspicious about that,

like, why now? Is it because they have a sense of this is something bigger than them, and I want to be able to tell my grandkids I was there when we tried to change the world? Or is it is it the fact that it's never been—as far as their career and as far as their standing in community—it's never been safer to come out and protest. And now I don't mean physically safe, but I mean—like we all saw it, we all saw the video, there's no way to justify that, in a way there's really no controversy there, right; this is an act of murder. We don't even have to nuance the word "murder" here, right? . . . Like the politics of their own churches and their own congregations like it's never been safer for them, right? You know when Philando [Castile] got shot and we were all protesting . . . you had the people saying, well, you know the officer said he reached for the gun, so he wasn't complying. Right here with George Floyd, there was no point of debate. You kneel on a guy's neck for nine minutes and it killed them. . . . So I've always been suspicious like of that, like why, why are you here now? . . . I did not see you when Jamar Clark got killed, I did not see you. . . . This is literally the first time I've ever seen you show up for any kind of protest whatsoever. And this is the safest time in terms of your career to do that.

White allies are needed not just in the "safe" times but, most important, in the times when there is more debate and less clarity, when the victim is not squeaky clean but still has the human right to live and go to trial. When they show up for racial justice only at these "safe" times, it is largely performative and likely doing more harm than good (Calendario 2021).

Blake, the twenty-one-year-old white man who was lay security for the protests in Virginia, also expressed his frustration for lack of longevity on the part of some whites, stressing that protest is just one part of the ongoing work needed in the movement. "Just showing up to protest, yes, it's great . . . but if you're not doing the research, doing reading in your own time, working on bettering yourself, actually then you're not really doing as much good as you think you are." Blake was critical of performative allyship: "Don't make it all about you. . . . Don't turn it into some social status thing of, like, oh, I'm going to protest, I'm doing this, I'm doing that, curtain." Blake advised that whites should "not make it all about you." Instead, they should take stock of what the community is already doing and get involved in that. Blake admitted disappointment that he participated for weeks on end continuously, but as weeks went on, he noticed others' participation declining and interest waning.

Ever since Black Lives Matter movement's founding, several major news outlets published editorials from activists regarding white involvement. In Stacey Patton's *Washington Post* article, she quotes Professor Simon Balto (2020) as saying, "I have no problem with white people being out in the streets demonstrating alongside black folks and other people of color so long as they are taking their cues from others and not driving the action." In the same article, Malkia Devich Cyril, founder of Media Justice Center in Oakland, adds that white allies are indeed needed because "blacks cannot win alone," but at the same time, "high-tech capitalism creates a real danger of turning rebellion into spectacle, into sport" (Patton 2020). Whites for whom activism is largely "performative" are not helpful (Candelario 2021). And while Seattle activist Amir Islam shares these concerns about the sincerity of white involvement, from a practical standpoint, "some Black activists are burnt out from marches. . . . It's hard enough to survive let alone get to your own people for a march" (Green 2017). From a sheer numbers standpoint, it seems white involvement may be needed, but the quality of that involvement gives some pause. As Erica Sklar put it, "One of the deep tragedies of race in this country is white people are never told that they don't belong somewhere. So they think they belong everywhere. . . . Sometimes, we as white people have to understand that support means leaving a space" (Green 2017). Most whites in this sample understood that their role should be supportive, not take over, and take initiative to educate themselves beyond just marching for performative purposes. However, regardless of how they racially identified, most participants were certainly aware of and even observed problematic white behavior at these uprisings. This might explain why an open-ended interview question about "dos and don'ts" that could have gone in any direction—from wearing masks for a virus to carrying milk for tear gas—most often went in the direction of "if you're white, don't do this." Clearly, it is a known factor in these circles that whites should tread cautiously in these spaces.

Nate, a twenty-eight-year-old African American man in Monterey, California, attended more events than anyone else in the sample, and 2020 was his first year doing so—from his hometown to Sacramento to Los Angeles—and he eloquently described white involvement as a double-edged sword.

> People of color and Black African Americans have seen this before; we know what's been happening to us. But for a lot of other people, it was like, wow, this I can't believe this and then . . . felt like they had to do something, or even if they want to be part of some kind of popular movement, they still were part of it. . . . I started seeing cliques, I started seeing white people kind of making their own [way], they were advocating for Black and brown folks, but it started becoming like their thing. . . . They want to bring people in, but they want to control it, might be to manage some stuff, and I started seeing political game. . . . A lot of people use it as a platform for political gain. We did see a lot of that, especially

for the people wanting to be politicians and stuff like that, but I also love, it was beautiful, though, also to see white people kind of try to create their own things fighting for ... racial equity. And there were some my Phoenix folks fighting for their kids in cages, you know, and things like that ... and they wanted to get in on this this movement to advocate for it, as I remember ... mentioning names that weren't even African American at times, because sometimes it was in movements with and I was fine with it, and I think that's what is powerful about the civil rights, but is that the surprise kind of opened up a world where the Black lives matter ... but also for women's rights and all these other things, I think that that's the beauty.

The fact that the Black Lives Matter movement (which began well before 2020) was foundationally intersectional and embraced racial justice for all types of people gave rise to a variety of interests. Nate noticed that whites were sometimes more comfortable in spaces where the concern was not only ending racist police violence but ending "kids in cages" and marching for trans lives. As he saw it, whites "making it their thing" could be problematic but also beautiful when it was at its best all inclusive.

Due to the ubiquity of the "whites taking over" problem, some activists of color asked their white colleagues to participate mainly for purposes of intervening in these situations. As Justin, a fifty-six-year-old white man in Minneapolis, stated,

> Some clergy of color who are colleagues said they felt that it would be very helpful to have clergy presence down there as a listening space to listen to folks who might be upset. ... And so that's what I initially went with another colleague that also had a lot of experience, and part of what we went prepared to do is also to talk see if there were there white folks who were being disruptive that we might talk to them. There's a role for white people with other white folks in those moments. ... [To advise them:] You're choosing to join in something that people are doing, and if you don't like how they're doing it, organize your own thing next. But be really respectful of spaces of what people are trying to say and communicate in those spaces and recognize what it is to be part of the community. So there are times that I heard about it, once I saw where people [would] try to reorganize things, [I would say] like this isn't your space, so this isn't actually about you so, [those] moments.

Sometimes whites get overconfident taking risks that would draw the ire of law enforcement during protests, not mindful enough about what deadly consequences those behaviors could have for those people of color present—a "privileged polemics" position (O'Brien 2001). It is to the credit of activists of color that they found diplomatic ways to advise allies accordingly so as not to lose their participation altogether.

Whites should not confuse "come on your best behavior" with "do not come at all." Helen's awestruck emotion that whites she did not even know would stand up for her against racism, when her own so-called white friends would not, was one of the most heartfelt moments of all the interviews. Likewise, Nicole, a twenty-seven-year-old African American woman who protested in Washington, D.C., stated that one of the biggest, pleasant surprises for her was the amount of whites present.

> I know D.C. is a big city, but of course, not as big as all the others that have been televised, so I really wasn't expecting such a mass group of people to be there, and it's funny to say, but I wasn't expecting so many white people there. I wasn't expecting that at all! . . . I [expected an] all-Black event, but it was it was so good to see that [so many] people don't like what they're seeing!

This was not Nicole's first Black Lives Matter protest; she had participated in smaller sized ones in her Newport News/Hampton area of Virginia where she resides in prior years, and these were primarily Black events, so she expected the same in a city like Washington, D.C., where the Black population proportion is equally as high, if not higher. To see so many whites, to Nicole, was a pleasant surprise, that people cared about Black lives besides African Americans only. Put simply, the bar was low, making any presence at all appear impressive. But even if more than expected, it does not mean that that presence was sizable or the majority. Most interviewees felt the demographic makeup of their city or town's protest usually mirrored the demographics of the region itself. In white suburban areas, that is mainly who showed up to the protest, whereas in cities where Blacks are the majority, that was usually the composition of the protests as well. So whether it was a cautious optimism or a more skeptical view, most noted a white presence; but for most, that was not the primary area of concern. Standing up and saying no to racial injustice and abuse was the primary focus, whether or not whites were a part. And although this sample might be united in its opposition to racial injustice, believing that their vocal dissent would result in any true change is an area where they were clearly divided. That difference in perspective is a topic to which we now turn.

Black Pessimism, the Permanence of Racism, Consciousness Raising, and Community

Derrick Bell (1993), considered a founder of critical race theory (CRT), argued that accepting racism is permanent would be the first step to being able to do effective, pragmatic work to curb racism's negative impact on people of color. Afropessimism, while diverging slightly from CRT by centering anti-Black racism specifically, also concurs with this racial realism approach, challenging the notion of inevitable racial progress (Ray et al. 2017; Ray 2022). Although no interviewees spoke in such academic jargon, it nonetheless struck me that these theories might help to explain some differences between Black and white protesters I came across in the interview data. Specifically, when explaining their reasons for participating in the uprising, African Americans were more likely to prioritize the benefits of being in community with others who cared that their lives were being threatened. This focus on community bonding over institutional change challenges the idea of protest as a means to a specific policy end (stopping racist police killings, reversing the trajectory of structural racism)—turning the means into the end. It is not that African American protesters did not want the racist abuse to end; they very much did. It is just that this end objective seemed so out of reach and unrealistic in their estimation that the best they could hope for as a primary goal was standing up and saying no to racism once again, feeling the strength of others who agreed with them. As Ray (2022) put it, paraphrasing Bell, it is the struggle itself that is redemptive.

Take, for example, RJ, a twenty-nine-year-old African American man who marched in Washington, D.C. RJ knew killings like those in 2020 were hardly new. His ancestors fought similar battles, just different names. This was the first time RJ participated in direct action demonstration for racial justice but not the first time he and his family had stood up against racism. As a child, he recalled his parents had to stand up for him, addressing when questionable things happened at school. Now he is a successful professional completing his MBA. For many of his generation, 2020 was one of their first times marching, even as they followed earlier BLM protests and supported and shared. To RJ, he was just continuing to carry the torch for prior generations.

> It was an energy that I never felt before. As my first time protesting, and being that what we're actually protesting for was very much relatable to me—I can be George Floyd, I can be Breonna Taylor, I can be Ahmaud Arbery. I could be any of the lost lives that we've seen over these years decades centuries. So it's a different type of energy; it felt good because... people were standing up for the peo-

> ple that can't literally stand anymore, and I never felt that. And my family's from the South, so my parents were kids in the civil rights era, and my grandparents obviously were the adults, back then. I would have never thought I would have participated anything somewhat similar to that. However, here we are. So my expectations were none; it was just to get out there, just to be around my peers of all backgrounds, all ages, all colors. And just to feel the energy and just feel that like I'm here, I'm here to be heard, to be seen, I'm representing what everyone else is representing for in solidarity and that's when I wanted. Was that expectation per se? No. But that's what ended up happening.

RJ did not have particular expectations but was compelled to be among those showing support and dissatisfaction with continued killing and abuse. However, he did not expect to glean such a positive feeling from the experience, which is what will stay with him.

> It felt good to be around a lot of people in my age range that were very much involved and vocal and wanted to be seen and heard during these times. Because our generation, I think, is a little different from the generations in the past, specifically the civil rights era, the generation where they are very much outspoken and very much willing to risk whatever it took to be heard and seeing that these issues were not good for society as a whole, let alone, some of our minority community, so I felt good about going out. Obviously, is not enjoyable for the sense of what the circumstances were for, but I feel good about my participation.

Enjoyment is not a state of being that one might have taken from media coverage of events that involved tear gas, rubber bullets, and property damage, yet as we have learned in prior chapters, well over 90 percent of uprising events were peaceful and nonviolent. Yes, there was crying, grieving, and anger, but there was also a satisfaction of being together in community, feeling less alone in one's convictions. For many participants, especially African Americans, they felt empowered from the togetherness as well.

Janay, a twenty-eight-year-old African American woman marching in Atlanta, participated in fourteen different marches and also led yoga events in her community, as a place to grieve and heal from the collective trauma of these killings. Like RJ, she evaluated her participation positively because of the relationships she built and things she learned, rather than accomplishing any type of formal political goal necessarily.

> It definitely was one of like the best experiences I've ever had, in the sense of not like it being enjoyable—I definitely shed a lot of tears, it was very heartbreak-

ing—but at the same time, being a woman of color, you don't just wake up and understand like what you're what you've been through or like oppression and things of that nature. And I always make it very clear to my friends ... that I was learning, just like everybody else.... And as I was learning, I was willing to learn with other people, and I was willing to educate people.... A lot of the times, I would go for walks or do the walks with people, and then I wake up the next morning, and it was just bawling from the texts I would get from friends that were just like thank you for letting me go with you, or thank you for like opening my eyes or like I didn't realize how hard things were.... And I could say that I've grown closer to a lot of people. I did lose a lot of people in it, but I grew closer to like my core friends and things of that nature, and their memories I'll cherish forever.

Like RJ, Janay found the term "enjoyable" problematic because of the reason for the gatherings; however, looking back one year later, she evaluated it as a memory she will always cherish and an opportunity to grow closer to people.

Faith, an eighteen-year-old African American (biracial) woman participating in Williamsburg, Virginia, agreed with Janay that these protests were not just public statements but also consciousness-raising events for sharing information as well as grief. Although grief is painful, there was some comfort in sharing it together at a public event as opposed to harboring it in isolation. Faith reflected,

> There's one protest, the news wasn't there, but they were instead giving stories, back stories to all the people.... People were also able to share their personal stories with racism from cops and even in communities, so it made it more personal, though. And sort of like big event, it was more a healing and grieving time where you could feel and touch one another. And other experiences. Yeah, I thought it was kind of eye opening to me because ... you don't realize how many people face that every day, when you see the big things in the media, when someone dies, but there's near-death experiences all the time or unfair circumstances for just existing, well, being a person of color.... I feel I made some sort of impact in just being there to support people because someone, some random person who's saying give them a hug, and that makes them feel better, especially the people who've been locked up for all this time alone. So it was nice to be able to talk to people and hear their stories.... It brought awareness to the cause.

As discussed in other chapters, several participants distinguished between types of demonstrations—some were protest marches, but others were rallies and consciousness-raising events—so I encouraged study participants to count whichever events they wanted as part of their participation. It was especially participants of color who expressed gratitude for events where one "could feel and touch one other," sharing grieving and healing beyond one's immediate family.

As emphasized throughout this text, these were not just "George Floyd protests." As Faith stated above, people of color in attendance had a space to share their own racist incidents with police that were happening every day to them. Although these community events alone would not stop racism from continuing to happen, many participants found comfort in being together to voice their outrage in one collective voice as opposed to being alone.

Charles was a thirty-eight-year-old African American man who attended an event in Columbus, Ohio, after the killing of Casey Goodson, months after the murder of George Floyd. He was traveling for work during the summer protests but hoped to support when able. It struck me that one of Charles's main objectives was to show the Goodson family they were not alone, that someone else cared about their loss. Inherent in this statement is resigned acceptance of the inability of individuals to change the trajectory of racist violence, unfortunately, when the main objective becomes comforting those in the cross fire rather than stopping it. Despite this tragedy, where a young man bringing home a Subway sandwich was shot and killed by the National Guard on his own back porch, after Charles attended the event, he nevertheless came away feeling "good" about being with others who felt the same outrage he did.

> The march was in downtown Columbus and it was large, I got emotional because—it brings water [to my eyes]. But thinking about it, it was so many different types of people, you can look and see they're all types of walks of lives and it's Black, white, brown, just young, old, and that just made me feel so good to see that people realize that this wasn't it wasn't a situation that was right. . . . My expectations were, I expected a big crowd. I did expect something crazy to happen. It didn't happen. It was empowering almost, but it still had a sense of peace; it was nonviolent. And it felt good to have so many different types of people there to support and to just let their voice be heard. It was just powerful; you can just feel it. It was unity, it was unique, I've never experienced in my life.

Like others, Charles felt it was a memory-making moment he will never forget. It felt good—not because someone was killed, but because others, even those who were not a young Black male like him, cared at all that this had happened. People did not just silently accept it; they spoke out. Also, because he had not previously participated in any racial justice direct action events, he was left to imagine what they are like from media sound bites, which are rarely typical representations of the full event. He was expecting "something crazy" to happen, which left him pleasantly surprised that it was nonviolent. Relief turns to satisfaction and even joy when it becomes a space of comfort and "unity."

Nicole's experience was also one that pleased her. Nicole is a twenty-seven-year-old African American woman who traveled to D.C. for this day, which she described not so much as a march but as a collection of many neighborhood-specific events one could experience just by walking through the city, and each stop had a slightly different focus and mood. Like Charles, Nicole was pleasantly surprised to see others besides African Americans at these events since in her Virginia hometown where she had participated in BLM events years prior was largely all-Black gatherings. It made Nicole happy to see different types of people coming together over more than just the matter of one single killing but many issues needing reform in the community, such as poverty and immigrant rights. The consciousness-raising aspect was enlightening to her, especially when she came upon a rally with speakers who emphasized that social justice work is tiring and taxing and that they should not feel bad if they cannot respond to or watch every incident of racial injustice—for their health and well-being.

> I remember when in one of the sections that they're breaking off they were saying how traumatizing it was to continue [seeing] the media—somebody's been shot somebody has been brutalized somebody's been beat on. And then, when the details come down to it, no weapon was found. Maybe there was some attitude or pushback from the other party, but certainly that doesn't mean that someone's life should be taken because they're not being respectful. So . . . of all the little places that we stopped . . . that one resonated with me the most because it is traumatizing to the point that sometimes you don't want to turn on the TV or the news or watch the news there's you feel like it's always something else. I remember after the George Floyd conviction, the next day that girl was murdered, so it was like it wasn't even time to process . . . because the next day, someone is murdered! So I really enjoyed that protest that speaker because she was just talking about how we shouldn't we shouldn't be upset with people who don't really want to keep current on all the killings because it's a lot. Recognizing that they have to take care of themselves, their mental [health] first, and sometimes that's very overwhelming to just be always seeing who was murdered today. . . . So I've never been to something like that, so I didn't really know what to expect other than negative things, but then seeing different keynote speakers . . . it brought so many different aspects to everything, not just the anger in it all.

Like Charles, Nicole found comfort in the diversity of experience she was able to connect with at these events. While she appreciated the spaces for venting anger also, she most liked the consciousness raising with others who felt the same trauma that she did, sharing strategies for coping with it. Like several others above, it fortified her to be less alone in her grief.

Jim Bear, a forty-four-year-old Native American man in Minneapolis, likewise took solace in the way people of color from different backgrounds shared what they had in common at George Floyd Square in a "beautiful intersectionality and solidarity."

> My personal objective I think was to show myself to be in solidarity with all of my Black and brown brothers and sisters and relatives out there. To say that in this struggle for equality, that the liberation of American Indian people is tied up inextricably with the liberation of African American people. Because that's I think one of the beauties, that we've seen in this in this age of the last ten years that we haven't seen in previous social justice racial justice movements, because this intersectionality particularly with American Indian, African American, and I would say Latinx immigrant communities, there's this intersectionality where we are present for each other's causes and needs. So when Jamal was killed in the fourth precinct and North Minneapolis was occupied for days, weeks. And that's a uniquely Black space. However, every single night, you could hear the drums of Indigenous resistance fighters, you could hear those drums there every single night, you could smell our medicines or sage and our sweet grass and stuff in the air, so we were present there. With George Floyd like same thing, you go to that George Floyd Square. . . . I've gone down there and I'm like, hell, there's Paulo dancers here like, you know, and George Floyd Square again, it's uniquely Black space, there's a uniquely Black narrative that's held there, but . . . we have Aztec dancers, you know part of this Latinx community there, and there's this kind of beautiful intersectionality and solidarity that is playing itself out here.

There is healing in sharing grief and feeling less alone in it. Building coalitions across communities to share in that healing despite what differences exist was a powerful experience for many.

As explored more in the next chapter, many noted a collective beauty in uprising spaces. One source of such beauty was a system of mutual aid created by grassroots community, especially in Minneapolis. Both Hood Scholar, a thirty-eight-year-old Black man who traveled there for the uprising, as well as Rabbi M, a fifty-one-year-old white man who lives there, remarked on this. As Rabbi M stated, "There was this incredible kind of makeshift system of mutual aid where people were delivering food and housing supplies." This is hardly the "riot" setting that the cameras and the heavy militaristic police presence would suggest. As Hood Scholar recalled, "There were places I went to where I didn't see any cameras, but a whole lot of work was being done so, for example, in Minneapolis, because of the pandemic and everything, a lot of things that closed . . . affected . . . people's access to the daily needs—food, bread, eggs, toilet paper. So what we were doing was organizing and collected supplies to meet needs . . . making sure that babies had diapers and older folks had their formulas, their prescriptions." People felt pride in their communities coming together to meet collective needs while folks were hurting. The uprisings became a space not only to protest police violence but to celebrate Black lives and provide for one another where institutions failed them.

Justin, a fifty-year-old white man in Minneapolis, described it as a "beautiful uprising."

> The other thing was the role of artists in this. Some people were burning buildings, yes, but many people were painting them, and I don't think I've ever been to such a beautiful uprising before. Never been to such a place where the art played a pivotal role, and even like right down at George Floyd Square like changing the discourse around people's land and space and decorating that with beauty, in the face of death and rage and also the need for community of beauty and to have powerful artwork, some of which was overtly political and so on, but was flowers great and the flourishing of the land down there with the plant. With plants, space for animals and all kinds of things, I've never been just been to a space that so transformed in those ways with so much enthusiasm. . . . There's always been protest artists, but it just seems so much more widespread now people boarded up their buildings and someone quickly painted a mural on it, and that was great. As somebody who studied art, the arts and how that can express things from across communities, I just was blown away with how just how beautiful, profound the city became visually.

Some of the art from the plywood boards of the 2020 uprisings has been collected to be preserved by artists and historians (Fadel 2021). Visual art as well as spoken word and poetry were ways in which collective grief and outrage was expressed. To hear interviewees who had participated in decades' worth of racial justice protest emphasize that the artistic presence was particularly unique about 2020 was moving indeed. Bill, a seventy-year-old white man in Monterey, California, reflected,

> I'd say the pleasant surprise [was] . . . a lot of the program featured young poets and artists. Mostly spoken word, and a little broader inclusion of the artistic community than just straight political speeches. . . . I think it's important to mention the Asian American community organized rally at City Hall that I attended again in solidarity. . . . Monterey County has a rich tradition of Chinese, Japanese, Filipino immigrant communities working in agriculture, working in fishing. And so those communities all have rich histories and stories of discrimination

and oppression and exclusion. And there was increased anti-Asian discrimination as well in the Bay Area especially. . . . I thought of that because that also featured some people that participated more through poetry than just straight political speeches and . . . all those speakers spoke from personal experience, being part of an immigrant community. So . . . there was an intersection of recognition of Black Lives Matter movement in George Floyd's killing.

Similar to Jim Bear, Bill was heartened to see solidarity from other people of color with African Americans and felt that added to the beauty of the uprisings—as not only political but artistic community spaces.

One thing this sample can agree on is that they are traumatized by each and every unjust killing and want it to stop. However, unfortunately, there is some resignation toward its inevitability, given the long historical trajectory of more of the same. Most did not expect their actions to directly result in conviction of offending officers. Indeed, as seen in the concluding chapter, when asked if they felt the conviction of Derek Chauvin (George Floyd's killer) was a hopeful turning of the tide, most predicted this verdict was likely an exceptional result rather than the beginning of greater accountability. So there is indeed a racial realism, or pragmatism, in much of the sample, particularly the African American interviewees. Their expectations were generally not idealistic in the first place, therefore upon experiencing what Durkheim called collective effervescence (Strong 2020) at these protest sites, many participants, especially those identifying as people of color, took some sort of comfort, solace, and even joy in being together. The isolation of the early stages of the pandemic also played a role in this heightened sense of connection.

Protesting: It's Complicated

Jermaine McDonald (2016) summons Ella Baker when he examines the "leaderless" Black Lives Matter movement, advancing the alternative possibility that its relatively looser structure renders it "leaderful" by comparison. Baker understood that for social change to take place, it takes more than just the groups personally affected by the injustice to step forward and express outrage. Yet in building that diverse coalition, obviously not everyone is coming from the same place. This is with or without a global pandemic occurring, further complicating the matter. Those old enough to have had more protest experiences were less likely to come out for a variety of reasons, including health-related concerns. That left a majority of the crowd in their twenties and thirties, and for many, it was their first time using something other than social media to "speak out." Yet being a parent, especially a mother, became a motivating factor for those who were older (forties and fifties) to brave the health risks to come out and live their values, engaging in teachable moments with their children.

Everyday activities unexpectedly canceled due to the pandemic left some in this younger age group with more idle time than usual. This may explain why some inexperienced protesters were in greater prevalence for these uprisings. This novice level of experience led to whites taking over chants led by people of color or lacking understanding of the role they should take. Those who came looking to educate themselves were warmly received. Whereas those whites seeming to attend for a photo-op moment, using the protest as a vehicle for their own self-promotion, were negatively evaluated by many participants, whether white or African American. Other protesters chose to focus on more positive aspects of the racial diversity of the crowds, simply because they expected all-Black gatherings and were impressed that someone else cared enough to show up alongside them. The fact that very young and very old folks were also in attendance, even if in small numbers, seemed impressive to many as well. These interviews also reveal an understated function of public protest—collective bonding and healing, and reduced social isolation. This was valued not just in the context of a pandemic but also in the context of heightened media exposure to collective trauma that mirrored individuals' everyday experiences with racism and police.

These protesters certainly had some manifest, institutional objectives—such as greater accountability of police, restructuring of police departments and their roles, voting rights, reparations, and more—yet with this chapter, we see that the uprising served some latent functions for participants as well. While they may not have come searching for healing or education necessarily, these are just some of the other objectives interviewees gained for themselves and their families, even as some political goals were left unachieved. Feeling empowered enough, buffered by one's community to challenge the ongoing racism one will face in everyday life was an important by-product of these uprisings. This is especially valuable given the clear evidence showing that police violence against unarmed African Americans has mental health impacts on the entire Black community, not just those in the family or immediate vicinity of those killed (Bor et al. 2018; Eichstaedt et al. 2021). Add that to the heightened risk of depression during the 2020 physical distancing and the greater reliance on technology as substitute for social interaction (Collins 2020), and the cathartic effect of participating in the uprisings can be understood from multiple angles. Even though there is much work still to be done, as the subsequent chapters will show, the strength of these qualitative data attest to how valuable, life-giving, and educational it is for protest to happen, even if it gets messy and there is not one unified voice—in fact, perhaps all the better if it is not. Such is the discordant harmony of beautiful solidarity.

CHAPTER 5

Beyond Marching

"A Beautiful Uprising," an Antiracist Racial Project

> Some people were burning buildings, yes, but many people were painting them, and I don't think I've ever been to such a beautiful uprising before.
>
> —Justin

Historians of the U.S. civil rights movement of the 1950s and 1960s remind us that front-line, charismatic leaders such as Rev. Dr. Martin Luther King Jr., Malcolm X, Huey Newton, and so many others were but one component of what made the protest movement successful. The March on Washington for jobs and freedom in 1963 or the 1965 march from Selma to Montgomery are well-known protest marches, with historic speeches given, but the Montgomery bus boycott lasted over a year, requiring much behind-the-scenes coordination. It was not just Rosa Parks getting tired one day and refusing to give up her seat. It was, for example, people like single-mother Georgia Gilmore who cooked food for bake sales that would go to funding the alternative transportation for the boycott (Gingrich 2018). Gilmore may never have given a famous speech, or even marched with a sign, or gotten arrested, but she is considered one of many "unsung heroes" of the movement.

Admittedly, when recruiting subjects for my study, my pitch said something like, "if you marched," I want to hear from you, so it was not until others referred participants to me that I broadened my understanding of what it meant to participate in the uprising. One of my first interview questions was, "About how many protest events did you participate in, where were they, and how did they go?" Not infrequently, interviewees responded that some of the events were not protests exactly. Thus began my reformulation of understanding of this moment in history as "uprising" rather than protest. We know this was certainly not a "race riot," as according to ACLED data, fully 95 percent of all 10,600-plus events in the uprising were peaceful protests, not involving violence (Kishi and Jones 2020). So "riots" is not the best word, but "protests" does not adequately characterize what happened during that stretch of time either. "Protest" suggests an organized march with people holding signs and chanting, traveling a predetermined path for which permits have been issued. While some have argued that writers select their term (protest vs riot) based on their own political slant or vantage point (Waldman 2015), I selected "uprising" because it more readily symbolizes a larger variety of different types of events. It was an uprising of yoga classes, candlelight vigils, consciousness raisings, resistance art, monument toppling, collective grieving, picnics with hot dogs and water, and makeshift networks of mutual aid in communities, just to name a few. To reduce these stretches of days, weeks, even months of various events to a "march" or "protest" shortchanges it. In this chapter, I explore what else happened *besides organized marching* to contribute to the 2020 racial justice uprising.

Although I am undoubtedly missing some aspects, the variety of uprising components that weren't formal protest necessarily—even just among the small group of thirty interviewed here—is so numerous that even reducing them to four broad categories already shortchanges them. Nevertheless, for purposes of this analysis, here I examine these themes: (1) resistance artwork and monument toppling, including creation as well as taking down of art; (2) grief support, candlelight vigils, yoga classes—supporting each other's emotions and mental and spiritual health in community; (3) logistical supports, includes medics, providing bail money and bailing/picking up people from jail, congregations and small businesses providing sanctuary, "protest kits" for sale online, and networks of mutual aid (i.e., water, food, diapers, prescriptions); and (4) extension efforts, such as live streaming of protests to those unable to attend and persuasive conversations with onlookers/nonparticipants off-site. Although these activities are largely "backstage" and unseen (with the exception of the art that is visible after its creation), highlighting these components of this historic moment is crucial because a good proportion of participants' energy went to these "other" activities, not often highlighted in mainstream media. This relative silence may keep other potential participants away if they are unaware of ways to support the movement besides marching in crowds. Let's explore now some lesser seen but nevertheless crucial supporting activities of the uprisings.

Resistance Art and Monument Toppling

Especially longtime/veteran activists remarked on the artwork and spoken word they found more unique about 2020 than other times prior. Last chapter, I quoted Justin about the art in Minneapolis (a "beautiful uprising"), along with Bill about the spoken word and poetry in California, particularly from Asian Americans. Jim Bear noted Native American drumming and dancing in Minneapolis as well. The artistic presence in the uprising took on a variety of dimensions—visual, musical, and community performance based. The word "uprising" especially captures this dimension of the historic moment because whereas protest marching and direct action demonstrations entail copious planning and organization, obtaining permits, security detail, and other components, the artistic components often involved a degree of spontaneity. Much of the artwork happened on wooden plyboards that were erected to protect businesses in the wake of the destruction that we discussed in chapter 3 as unlikely to have been caused by the racial justice protesters themselves. So *these wooden plyboards were makeshift practical solutions to an unanticipated problem that activists were not going to let shut down their movement.* Resistance art, thus, is resistance not only to racism and police violence but resistance to those attempting to water down or tarnish the movement for Black lives by destroying buildings and property. As we reviewed in chapter 3, *these were often white supremacist or anti-government militia groups* causing such destruction, not necessarily antiracists. So to paint uplifting messages in vibrant colors—onto the drab plywood that made it look as if the community were dead and abandoned—was an act of resistance saying, we refuse to go away quietly, and we refuse to let our message be muffled or covered up or silenced.

Carly, quoted in the last chapter about taking her kids to see "resistance art" in Columbus, Ohio, noted that she avoided attending nighttime protests due to safety concerns, but one way to still witness those intense emotions was through this artwork. Cappelli's (2020) analysis of this "visual activism" in the Los Angeles area found the messages to be quite varied, from anger to grief to resilience and even joy. The three frames Cappelli (2020) identified in L.A. graffiti were the "anarchist frame" (i.e., defund police, kill a cop), which often expressed anger; the "pity and fear" frame (i.e., say their names, Am I Next?), exemplifying grief and despair; and the "cathartic frame" (i.e., let equality bloom, love prevails, together we rise, love heals), which was much more hopeful. While some resistance art was temporary—captured by photography but eventually removed—other works became permanent or semipermanent, migrating into gallery spaces or other locations where visitors could continue to take in the moving messages. For example, Leesa Kelly, founder of Memorialize the Movement, has collected over seven hundred plyboards from the Minneapolis area that were decorated with art during 2020 (Fadel 2021). In New York City, the Plywood Project was founded in collaboration with Artists' Rights Society so that the creators of the resistance art would get credit and recognition for their work. Curators from places like the Smithsonian were already looking as early as August 2020 to find possible homes for these meaningful creations—"history is happening right before us" (Zara 2020). One artist, Michael Zelehoski, even took some plyboards with their messages and created a sculpture out of them, resembling obelisks—intending to bring to mind the monument-toppling component of the 2020 uprising (Vartanian 2021).

As Carly, a forty-nine-year-old white woman and longtime protester in Columbus, Ohio, also mentioned, some monuments that racial justice activists have been fighting for a long time finally came down during the uprising of 2020. At the university (Columbus State Community College) where she works, it was difficult to get upper administration to capitulate to ongoing concerns about the statue of Christopher Columbus for many years prior.

> I do think the protests forced people to make changes . . . like at the college, for example . . . even back in the '90s, we were doing protests about the Columbus statues in the '90s, and the Santa Maria there was in the river by downtown, but there was really no real "here, we'll get rid of them," the Columbus statues and stuff and then at Columbus State, we had been the last few years really kind of like pushing because we had a Columbus statue like was the focal point of our campus, it was right in the middle of the campus, it was gigantic, it was in all the marketing materials. And we had . . . community sessions, where we talk about it and it was always . . . "Well, yeah, it's problematic, but oh my goodness, to take it down, that would just be too much, we can't do that, maybe we could put a little plaque by acknowledging the racism and genocide, but we can't really get rid of it, it's so huge." And then just out of nowhere went in the midst of all the protests, the college was just like, yeah, let's get rid of it well . . . previously, that would always happen, like every year on Columbus Day around Thanksgiving someone would come in and spray paint it. . . . People kept spray painting, and I think it was just that momentum of we're really doing stuff, and then it was that easy, that statue is gone!

Carly raised a few important points: that resistance art is not necessarily a new tactic, but it gained "momentum" during the 2020 uprising. Instead of the "graffiti" being quickly covered up and the demands behind it squelched or silenced, 2020 was different because administration began not only listening but acting in many cases, especially in areas with long histories of ongoing struggle over these public symbols. The Southern Poverty Law Center found that over 230 monuments "have been dismantled, hauled away, vandalized or given new names" since the murder of George Floyd in 2020—as one *New York Times* writer put it, they have been "coming down like dominoes" (Burch 2022). This component of the uprising cannot be understood as simply defacing public property but rather as the reimagining of a new society where the dignity of every human being is valued.

As Perhamus and Joldersma (2020) note, these monuments—to figures whose claim to fame is stealing land and defending slavery—are often placed in public places like schools and courthouses, sending powerful and ominous messages about to whom these spaces belong. "More than resistive and destructive, the monument topplings are visionary and productive" (Perhamus and Joldersma 2020, 1322). What may be missed in public representations of resistance art is the productive component of the work. When I personally visited the Robert E. Lee statue in Richmond, Virginia, in August 2020, I witnessed a very different space than I was able to perceive from the publicized photographs of a statue with graffiti on it. This space had to be fully perceived with all five senses. There was a community garden, makeshift basketball hoops, music playing, and perhaps the most moving component was the carefully constructed, candlelit memorials to dozens of different victims of police brutality circling the entire perimeter of the statue's base. A laminated, weather-proofed photo of each person, along with their name and their story, was surrounded by flowers at each point on the circle. As Kelli, a forty-four-year-old Black woman in Richmond, Virginia, recalled, these kinds of public tributes were not uncommon during the uprisings, and she used her social media accounts to share these components of the uprising with those not physically present.

> I was thinking about keeping my business open, so therefore I was here to protect it. I knew people were at home that weren't going to come downtown at all, and the first night of protest, I went outside and I went on Facebook. And from the Maggie Walker statue I showed—because I also am very protective of the ancestors—and at that point, they were trying to take down the statues . . . and so I just wanted to make sure that Maggie statue was protected. And praise God, there was a ring around her, people had flowers around her, people were standing around her. So but I did stand there in one of the largest crowds and when the energy started to shift, I caught that on my Facebook live . . . and I will say this: I think that my non-Black friends were more scared for me than I was, but more so, they got to feel the energy of why people were angry. Although they were scared and they wanted me to get home, they wanted me to keep recording because they wanted to watch and they wanted to just maybe wrap their head around what

they were seeing. Why the younger generation was having that aggressive energy. ... They're angry because you lied to them, because you didn't explain slavery and the enslaved population, you didn't explain that the Confederates lost and they have been praised on Monument Avenue, you have a lie. And because we have kept this brutal part of four hundred years out of our history books and so now these kids want explanations. And they are out in the streets because they want explanations; they want justice.

An interesting dynamic occurred in Kelli's city of Richmond, the former capital of the Confederacy. There is a major thoroughfare called Monument Avenue, including statues of Jefferson Davis, Robert E. Lee, and other white male Confederate heroes, and then only much more recently added (after continuous advocacy of community citizens demanding change) statues of Arthur Ashe (African American tennis hero from Richmond) and Maggie Walker (African American business leader also from Richmond). Because so many young people were relatively new to the movement, Kelli feared that protesters wouldn't discern which statues were monuments to enslavers and which were descendants of the enslaved persons. Much to her relief, not only had the marchers spared the Maggie Walker statue from defacement, but they had placed flowers around her—much like the tributes placed around the base of the Robert E. Lee statue to those killed by police. A key aspect of Kelli's quote is just how central the monuments became to the uprising and how participants' actions were not simply destructive toward these artifacts. *Even though much of it appeared spontaneous, it was an outgrowth of years of work* community members had been doing to raise awareness about the racial bias in the selectivity of whom we memorialize versus whom we ignore. In attempting to correct the record from its white supremacist omissions and errors, there was not merely a tearing-down but also a building-up and creating at the same time and in the same spaces. This work can be considered an *antiracist racial project,* according to the parameters defined by Omi and Winant (1994) in their racial formation theory, as these material objects got reorganized and redefined by uprising participants.

Grief Support, Mental Health, Fighting Isolation

Artists contributed their poetry, music, and artwork to the movement, and some grief was expressed through this art. But those with different skill sets contributed other talents. There were clergy, there were yoga instructors, there were teachers, there were social workers, there were simply good listeners and huggers—all of them contributed in some way to this collective mental health support system.

Emerging from home during a deadly pandemic without a vaccine yet available did not just make a public statement; it also helped to be less alone with the heavy weight of the multiple tragedies happening in the world. Communities found strength within one another.

As multiple interviewees in Minneapolis recalled, when George Floyd was first murdered, the news was not immediately met with an organized protest march but rather with what could more aptly be described as a "vigil" or more of a somber gathering. Jim Bear, a forty-four-year-old Native American man there, explained,

> So I had gone to the site on Thirty-Eighth and Chicago there, which would become George Floyd Square, but it was a site where he was killed. I had gone there early afternoon on Tuesday and people were just starting to gather, and I don't even know that I would really call that a protest. But it was sort of the initial gathering that the protest then grew out of it. So I don't know the purpose of your research, if you want to call that, yeah. . . . I don't think I would necessarily call those protests; they were more just kind of community solidarity.

By the time of these interviews (2021), the killing of Daunte Wright by former officer Kimberly Potter had already happened, fueling a similar community mobilization for which Jim Bear explained clergy played a particular role.

> The day that [Daunte Wright] was killed . . . I was part of some clergy chaplains that sort of did an emergency response to the site where—so he actually died two blocks away from where he was shot, so he was shot at certain intersection, and so there's three sites happening in the city of Brooklyn Center. There was crowds forming at the police precinct there, and there is a crowd forming at where Kimberly Potter shot him, and then there was a crowd forming where he actually died, which is about two blocks away, and so I responded to where he died, along with a number of other clergy folks, and we just held a vigil there. And Daunte his mother and other family members of Daunte came and shared, and we just held a very impromptu vigil. A couple of speakers and some prayers being offered, but then we were up against timeline because there was a hard curfew of seven o'clock at that time and . . . it's still very much light out, you got another two hours of daylight here or so, but yeah, so we tried our best to finish up by seven o'clock by the curfew there.

Clergy are called for "emergency response" in these incidents, which allow grief to be shared and the grief-stricken to support one another.

Several participants shared it was important for them to feel the "unity"—as Charles, a thirty-six-year-old Black man in Columbus, described it (quoted in the previous chapter) when he went to support the family in the wake of Casey Goodson's murder by law enforcement there. Faith, an eighteen-year-old Black/white biracial woman in Williamsburg, Virginia, was also quoted in the previous chapter describing the uprising as "a healing and like grieving time where you could feel and touch one another." Nicole, a twenty-seven-year-old Black woman who participated in Washington, D.C., also featured in the prior chapter, recalled how comforted she felt by a "keynote speaker" there who focused on mental health, telling the crowd it was okay if it was too traumatizing for them to watch every shooting, keep up with every news story, because it can cause repeated trauma. Many interviewed honestly did not know what they would find. Charles was a new protester, but Faith and Nicole had both attended protests in years prior, noting that the 2020 uprising included more of these mental health and collective grief components. Certainly, the timing during a deadly pandemic and lockdown added to the imperative of this kind of "wraparound" care. Although she was a new protester, Janay, a twenty-eight-year-old Black woman in Atlanta, dived right in, attending fourteen different events in her city (one of only eight people in the sample to be in the double-digit participation level), and with all the marching, she eventually needed some balance. So she decided to lead a yoga class, which she included as part of her synopsis of her uprising participation.

> I also had a protest yoga event that I put on with a few people at a gym I used to work with, so kind of just getting together with people that have been protesting, and we did the social-distance yoga in Piedmont Park to . . . get people to know each other, but at the same time give people time to kind of reflect on how they were feeling but also have them realize that they are other people that are going through the same feelings that they are walking for. Anyone of any race, any profile, any sexual orientation, to kind of just release how they felt and just kind of relax from everything they're protesting usually lasted about two hours, according to my watch we walked about fifteen miles a day.

Janay called it "protest yoga," but she contrasted the yoga with the marching, which she characterized as more vigorous and intense. The yoga, unlike marching, was a space to "relax" and "release" but also connect with others experiencing similar emotions. This was another component of the uprising not necessarily in the protest/march category but a chance to support others going through similar emotions in a quieter setting.

On news reports, marching, chanting, and carrying signs are typical representations of protests. Yet conceptualizing this as an uprising is broader, more readily encompassing quieter spaces with supporting, grieving, caring for each other.

Sally, a thirty-six-year-old white woman in Louisville, Kentucky, emphasized how calm most of the community spaces were when the police were not there.

> And the way that they address protest, they address it in like protesters are rioters and we're problematic and we're the ones, causing the problems—which, in fact, I mean every time I was down there, it was so peaceful, I was offered hot dogs, pizza, water—times you were just sitting there just kind of talking with the community.

When tragedy affects a community, it is not just individual mental health care that is needed but collective care in community. A study by Bor et al. (2018) noted that police killings have a "spillover effect" on the mental health of African Americans, even those who do not directly live in the community or know the family of the victim. As Virginia Tech researchers found after the tragedy there, "tragedies not only produce grieving individuals, they also produce grieving communities" (Hawdon and Ryan 2011, 1377). Thus, this was an uprising of *collective grief, which called for collective healing*. Although certainly anger is one stage of grief and can aid in the healing process, many also need to process in other ways. These quieter spaces became an important and necessary component of the uprising.

Logistical Supports

Many logistical supports are needed for successful direct action demonstrations, including on-site as well as off-site roles and responsibilities. Everyone in this sample participated on-site in at least one gathering, but several held additional support roles aside from that, both on and off location. Jessica Williams (2017) of Direct Action Movement in Australia identifies several crucial supporter roles in demonstrations, including marshal, police liaison, legal observer, first aid (medic), community liaison, and media liaison. During the 2020 uprising, for those too concerned about their health during the pandemic to participate on location but still wanted to support, Chandra Steele (2020) of *PC Magazine* listed several suggestions, including supporting bail funds, donating to legal defense funds, providing mutual aid, and supporting medics. Some older (age thirty-eight to fifty-three) veteran protesters who had been participating in this kind of work for decades knew these various roles and understood them well. Whenever support roles were mentioned, it was almost always to note how much people do not realize how organized a "protest" is and all that goes into coordinating it.

Rev. TM, a fifty-three-year-old white man in Minneapolis, had decades of direct action experiences, including most recently working with Indigenous groups at the Standing Rock reservation to protest the Dakota Access Pipeline. From direct action trainings at the Highlander Center, King Center, and elsewhere, he learned that there is a high level of organization, including supporting roles of which some are unaware.

> In protests or in events like this—and like I said, I trained a lot in civil disobedience—they're organized and, well, there's a front line, and a second line, third line, and a fourth line and where you're most useful in the midst of that, and where you're willing to be arrested, or were willing to do this. And so, it's very clearly organized, and so I'm part of that organization and I know where my role is and I try to be on that role. And whether I'm on the side, or in the center, or in this row or that row—and so yeah, so it's pretty—I mean once melee happens and it's less scripted, there's a lot of spontaneity as well, but the training helps us kind of be present in the midst of the spontaneity.

A recurring theme especially among older, more experienced protesters was that some "events" they attended were not always in the protest category, but they were still part of the uprising. Moreover, as alluded in chapter 3, they often felt their level of organization was well above that of law enforcement—providing a calmer, more predictable structure as opposed to instability. Part of this structure, then, is not everyone is a front-line participant. Rev. TM saw his role as changing over time due to being white but especially due to his age: "This was a different feel; it was really a call to solidarity, I understand, in my own life I used to be a young energetic activist and now I'm really called to be in support and solidarity of young activists." So he felt not as much as a "protester" as he did a clergy support person at several uprising events.

Rev. Lane, a thirty-eight-year-old white woman in Rochester, New York, highlighted several of the supportive roles mentioned by the Direct Action Movement on their website (Williams 2017), including legal observer and medic. As leader of a congregation, she provided logistics (building space) as well.

> During that time, I attended myself probably about three of those protests; however, I serve a congregation that opened its doors up for three weeks, four weeks to house a group—the Rochester Street Medic Collective. We essentially opened our building to be a medic triage site and also to be a storage site for a bunch of their equipment. As well as a place where our medics could come back and have a meal at the end of the very long days that they were having, and also to be a place where folks could be medically treated. At that same time our congregation also made the decision to open up its restrooms to people who are attending the protests; the city of Rochester would not open any public restrooms for folks who

> are gathering and we had hundreds, if not up to over one thousand people down in Martin Luther King Jr. square park without a restroom. Our congregation is situated half a block up for Martin Luther King Jr. square; we're right at Clinton in Court Street, right across from what's over here Washington Square park. And so we made the decision to open up our restrooms and also to put out some supply tables so when some of the racial justice actions, following the death of George Floyd were happening pretty much every Saturday here in Rochester, we were out in front of our congregation with restrooms open and like tables with snacks, bottles of water, sunscreen, masks. Just supplies that would help folks as they were protesting.

Rev. Lane mentioned many material logistics needed—medics, supplies, restrooms, food and water, sunscreen, masks. But nonmaterially, being available and ready for bail is a crucial supporting role in the uprisings as well as the role of legal observer, which Rev. Lane also discussed.

> One of the issues there was that none of the cops wore masks during this pandemic—every, all the protesters were wearing masks and the cops were not, which was concerning. Also, just to have cops kind of surrounding an area like that created a really unwelcoming atmosphere; thankfully, they had folks there who were legal observers. And so, for me, as someone who has those cues from the past, I can see, Oh, thank goodness, you know these folks are being at least observed, they have these legal observers here, maybe that will help cops to stay a little bit more on point or whatever.

In the United States, the National Lawyers Guild patented the term "legal observer" (LO), and they have been a notably marked presence in their green hats at protests since the 1960s. Anyone can train to be an LO—they do not have to be lawyers—and they use photo, video, and handwritten notes that can come in handy for any court cases that may arise out of the event (McMahon 2020; Truong 2020). As noted in chapter 3, one of the things that upset several interviewees is that the clearly designated roles of both legal observer and medic are well known to law enforcement officers at these events, or at least they should be. So when this understood agreement, usually followed in most other such events, was violated, it added to the sense of outrage at injustice for participants.

Hood Scholar, a thirty-eight-year-old Black man and longtime community organizer who participated in Minneapolis, also addressed how some don't realize the level of organization at protests, as well as the breach of agreement when the medic was assailed by police. Additionally, he remarked on the power of community-based mutual aid, which emerged beautifully and spontaneously.

> It's actually more organized than what it seems—so we really have people who are like-minded people often support, and there are people who are like on the front lines like engage with the police, so there's literally like a medic pass you have to wear.... You can clearly identify them as medics, and a police officer would know if she [nurse who got shot by rubber bullet] was wearing this thing.... Like I don't know if you saw the picture of when I was handing out water [to] ... hundreds of people.... There were places I went to what I didn't see any cameras, but a whole lot of work was being done ... bread, eggs, toilet paper.... So what we were doing was organizing and collecting supplies.... So I took some pictures, but other than that, right, it was no cameras down there, was no news station there ... making sure that babies had diapers, older folks had their formulas, their prescriptions.

Although chapter 3 presented his story of the rubber bullet hitting the medic and chapter 4 presented the system of mutual aid in Minneapolis, I combine these stories together again here to emphasize that this is all part of the logistics coordinated behind the scenes. Again, we see the dissatisfaction with media not showing these most beautiful parts of the uprising—community members helping other community members, often in ways that did not involve chanting, marching, or holding signs. They provided material needs for one another in a way the authorities did not.

Likewise, Jordan, a twenty-six-year-old man who identified as Black/mixed, also passed out water in the Atlanta area. It was his first time participating in protest, but he realized right away there were many other supporting roles besides marching, so he shifted more into those roles after his initial protest attendance.

> My main goal, which is to say the same for my friends and family, anybody with social media, I'm starting to use my platform for change, also just supporting in general the cause. I brought waters, I passed out waters, I had a shirt on, people were staying hydrated and everything. Just helping and writing for the cause. ... I think everybody on the park out there definitely contributed in some way to helping with motivating change and at least starting the conversation towards change.

Jordan mentioned a supporting role, covered more in the next section as well, in terms of dialogue with family and friends, on social media. But the act of contributing and distributing water is a crucial logistical support, particularly in the summertime heat. It can quite literally be lifesaving.

RJ, also a first-time protester in his twenties and an African American man in

Washington, D.C., was moved to see other community members there besides protesters to support the needs of those marching.

> The best thing about being out there that day was that there were medics ... not official live hospital medics and whatnot but people that knew what they were doing as far as making sure people were able to stay hydrated or if somebody needed to know urgent care or whatnot they had equipment to provide that for them.

RJ literally described this as the "best thing" about his day of participation. As we have established, this is a time of a community deep in grief and isolation. To be able to witness the selflessness of people who simply showed up, not to take a selfie with a sign but to really serve others' needs, was incredibly moving and special to see.

Protesters on the ground need provisions of various sorts. Kelli, a forty-four-year-old Black woman who owns a coffee shop and community gathering space called the Urban Hang Suite in Richmond, Virginia, was not necessarily looking to be the one "marching with a sign," but with her business located so close to uprising events, she felt compelled to be there. At first, she stood in front of her business during protests to protect it from any potential vandalism, by letting them know it was a Black-owned business. But eventually, her business became a "hub" similar to Rev. Lane's congregation in Rochester, New York.

> I also was a hub for organization that was out protesting and doing things for citizens for eviction rights, and so they would come and put water and pamphlets and stuff under my desk in my coffee shop. I got these little tables up front, so they could come and get it anytime they needed it or refill it. I give them coffee and things of that nature. But I mean, just looking at them, from the night before, whether it be their eyes because of the tear gas, or the actual bruises from the rubber bullets, or just as great on their knees from whether they were running into kind of get out the way, I saw a lot of the physical damage to places but also saw a lot of the physical damage to people, those that were out there.

Storage, beverages, and restrooms were all logistical supports she provided to nearby activists. Eventually, they had "protest kits" available given all these injuries. During our interview, Kelli marveled at how far things have come since her earlier activist days, with technology, internet, and social media.

> I was very shocked to know that the kits—actually that you can purchase, to get ready for stuff like this. And how advanced ... it has become ... the fact that there was the full package. ... There's a theater lab basement downstairs and they would make the packages—it would have water and food and just the stuff for

your eyes, all the things—that you just came and picked up a package. I'm like, wow.

Although Kelli was not preparing these "protest kit" packages herself, the activists she provided storage space for were doing it at her location. These kits include food, water, and masks, along with solution (or sometimes milk) to soothe one's eyes from tear gas or pepper spray. Supports like this contributed to the uprising's ability to sustain as long as it did.

Jim Bear, a forty-four-year-old Native American man in Minneapolis, affirmed the importance of providing supplies, and it is all about figuring out what your own personal contribution will be.

> Just know your comfort level. And there's no shame in saying, I'm here for this, but if things start turning violent, then I don't want to be here for that. But then find those people that are willing to be present for that and see you know what kind of needs there. So maybe you're not one who's going to be there when the tear gas starts flowing and all that, but maybe you're one that's going to be dropping off gallons of milk and water and stuff in preparation for when all that happens.

An uprising only sustains over a long haul due to these kinds of supports, both on- and off-site. Jim Bear also stressed that people of color have higher risk of being injured and targeted at these events, so the ways in which participants are racialized also is a deciding factor in which support roles they undertake.

Logistical supports include both material and nonmaterial components. Another support role is lay security for protest marchers, a position more likely to be held by white participants. Although I observed this practice as a highly organized feature of my hometown's protest marches, including preparatory training for those interested in serving in this capacity, it was surprisingly difficult to find anything yet written on this component. In contrast to legal observers and medics, who are clearly marked and have been serving in these capacities for decades, information about lay security who protect protesters from attacks is sparser. Vehicle ramming (as terrorism) has gotten heightened attention in the United States in the years since the 2017 killing of Heather Heyer in Charlottesville, Virginia, but it is hardly a new tactic, and organizers are increasingly realizing that law enforcement is doing little to prevent it. If anything, there is a legal trend to protect those who harm and kill during this "unintentional" practice (Bidgood 2021; Bloom 2020). One report in the transportation industry even identifies vehicle ramming ("metal against marchers") as a troubling addition to the list of causes of pedestrian deaths, urging better attention to and protection from this practice, while also asserting that it has a low overall death toll, so is not as serious as some other problems (Jenkins and Butterworth 2020). Almost any news article I found on lay security during the 2020 protests was instead about white armed militias who claim to be protecting their community from "Black Lives Matter." There is plenty news about all the ways protesters are harmed, maimed, and even killed by both law enforcement and white supremacist militias but precious little on what is done to protect them from these harms. NPR did a piece on a Latinx lay security group called Security Latinos De La Lake in the Minneapolis–Saint Paul area, but they were not part of the actual protest marching and were organized more to protect the surrounding businesses from damage (Fadel 2020). The closest comparison seemed to be the "Wall of Moms"—a mostly white or light-skinned group of women in Portland, Oregon, who stood in front of other protesters, chanting things like, "Moms are here, feds stay clear" to protect the activists from police violence (Henderson 2020). This group's primary focus was protection from law enforcement attacks rather than the violence from civilian terrorists. However, there was eventually concern from activists of color that these white women were garnering far more media attention than those who had been doing the work for much longer in communities of color, so some group members ultimately withdrew to other less visible activities (Henderson 2020).

Blake, a twenty-one-year-old White man who participated in Williamsburg, Virginia, as part of the lay security team there, quoted in chapter 3 about his work, seemed mindful about the importance of whites not taking over while in this role. Blake sought to offer logistical support to activists on the ground once he saw that this was another option besides traditional marching.

> I attended almost every single one we had in Williamsburg, so I'd say that got to between ten and twenty. My involvement with them was I actually ran security for them, so I made sure that any disgruntled or outwardly displeased individuals couldn't do any harm to the groups. So I started out, I went to one of the first protests that we had in Williamsburg at the courthouse and I saw that they only had one or two people protecting the large group of people there. So at the end of it, I decided that I wanted to help in a way, more than just standing with the group, but making sure the group had the opportunity to give their voice, and putting myself on the wayside, to make sure that people could speak their point of view and all that. But at the end of my first protest, I went and spoke with the people who were running security there, and I was like, hey, sign me up!

While media may portray protesters as aggressors, in fact once anyone attends or witnesses protest as Blake did, it becomes evident they are in a vulnerable position, going through heavily trafficked areas on foot and unarmed. Also, as established in chapter 3, most law enforcement presence was often inconsistent and more focused on protecting property than the First Amendment rights of people assembled. Thus, Blake's security role was both intervening in contentious verbal exchanges (monitoring levels of interaction and potential for escalation to violence) as well as keeping an eye out for vehicles at risk of car ramming, by hovering around the protest site. At times, members of the security team noted license plate and vehicle description to share with law enforcement after each day's events, trusting they would investigate any ongoing threats.

Whether legal observer, medic, lay security, providing supplies, bail money and pickup, or providing mutual aid for community provisions, all supporting roles were crucial in sustaining the momentum of the uprisings. For every media sound bite showing a confrontation between protesters and law enforcement officers, or impassioned sign holders marching and chanting, there are various "quieter" supporting roles that don't make the news. Organizers collected funds to buy diapers and food and pick up prescriptions. Lay security kept their bodies between protesters and onlookers, some impatient with traffic being stopped. This "uprising" was not just an uprising of protesters; it was an uprising of mutual aid, of community members supporting one another and providing for each other, at a time of tremendous isolation and uncertainty—a beautiful uprising indeed.

Extension Efforts: Media, Video, Conversation

The final category of supporting roles for uprising participants includes all of the various extension efforts that carry the racial injustice conversations beyond protest sites and into the greater community. Several interviewees mentioned their commitment to spread information about racial injustice and why they were marching to those who were not there, especially those who did not get the magnitude of the problem. Some preliminary evidence suggests protest activities can swing the pendulum of public opinion toward greater concern about the grievances raised by the movement. For example, one study of over three thousand U.S. voters surveyed just before both the 2016 and 2020 elections revealed that more people perceived racial discrimination as a problem by the second wave of the survey, after the summer 2020 uprisings had taken place. This study also examined vote switching, finding that this increased support for government help for minorities drove a segment of the population to switch their allegiance from Republican to Democratic candidates in 2020 (Mutz 2022). The uprising not only potentially influenced how people voted in the subsequent election, but it had some cultural impact in terms of influencing public discourse about racism. For instance, a study of mentions and searches on online platforms like Google, Twitter,

Wikipedia, as well as the news demonstrated that usage of terms like "diversity," "systemic racism," "mass incarceration," and "white supremacy" spiked in usage after the 2020 uprising took place (Dunivin et al. 2022). While certainly neither cultural change in discourse nor support for any particular party or candidate directly translates into support for antiracist policies and practices, the sheer volume of people mobilizing in 2020 for racial justice likely had some indirect influence on eventual political processes, according to political scientist Maneesh Arora, who along with her colleagues studied the wax and wane of support for BLM in the months following the uprising (O'Brien 2021). Even though the rapid spike in public concern about racial discrimination in June 2020 was not sustained long at its initial higher levels, it did nevertheless have an impact in some ways, such as voting behavior, policy agendas like police reform, and building coalitions of activists, who may have further policy influence down the line.

Several interviewees understood this chain of influence at some level because they articulated the need for protest participants to be mindful about how they explain to others why they were out there. As Kelli, a forty-four-year-old Black woman in Richmond, Virginia, put it, when asked what advice she would give to others wanting to get involved, "If you're going to inform industries, make sure you're informing in your household to make sure that you're taking it a step further than 'I was in the streets last night protesting this,' so when you come home and you share that with your grandparents, your aunties, and your children, on your own—anybody in your family. Then whether that's the elders or the youth that you're explaining to them why, you have a clear reason to why you are out there and you're able to share that experience so that again that kind of trickles down through the generations of how important it is, or why it was important for you to be out."

Kelli framed this as part of people's responsibility, not even an option; if they are going to participate in active protests, they should have a clear rationale for explaining to others the importance of their actions. Earlier in the interview, Kelli recounted how she used her various social media feeds—part of her community-oriented business as an entrepreneur—to not only live stream from the protest sites but to have conversations with others who were questioning why the actions had to happen, educating them as to the ongoing history of racial inequality, particularly in this Richmond area. Moreover, Kelli specified this educational dialogue should ideally be multigenerational.

Janay, also an African American woman, only twenty-eight years old in Atlanta, and first-time protester, participated in many events in her area and recognized that whether people were participating or not, social media and internet was an important tool for educating on the issues central to the uprising.

> All throughout the country, everybody was speaking out in their way, shape, and form, whether it be through protesting or through just the internet or through social media, I think that's super awesome. I had a lot of friends that I told them if they didn't feel comfortable protesting, I get it, but to speak out in their own ways, and I think that that was accomplished through protesting that everyone now is starting to realize that as a country, we're willing to speak out and we are not afraid to speak out. And I think that is something that is a huge factor that is very important that was distributed through the protesting.

As established in earlier chapters, first-wave BLM organizing that primed the awareness level for the 2020 uprising's perfect storm to happen could not have happened to the level it did without social media and technology, especially people's phone/video recording and sharing capabilities. Janay explained how these media work hand in hand with protesting on the ground.

While headlines stated more Americans supported racial justice protests than ever before in June 2020, even with the highest polling estimates, that still left at least a quarter of Americans—often a vocal minority—who were skeptical, including then-U.S. president. Ever since 2013 ignited the "Black Lives Matter" versus "All Lives Matter" debate, social media was a hot spot for such public arguments. Yet often the modern context has been "homophilic clusters" of "echo chambers" for many, particularly on platforms like Facebook, and not just in the United States but globally (Cinelli et al. 2021). Some participants talked about expanding their reach beyond those who already agreed with them, beyond their immediate area and beyond their usual allies. This was relevant for Patrice, a twenty-two-year-old racially mixed woman in the Detroit area whose mother was white and father was African American, because her family networks were diverse in their views of the uprising, including those who were more "conservative."

> I've always tried to share—if there's ever racial equality or gender inequality or even immigration—anything like that, I always try to share any information that I see because . . . you can make an educated opinion and then things can get better. And so I feel like people, especially my high school and undergrad, kinda like trust me to be a source to put information out there. And so, there were several people messaged me and asked for more information on what the protests are or where they're happening or why people are so upset, or what I think the best way to change it. And so I just think it's important to spread information . . . because I feel like a lot of times—white people, especially—are kind of raised [to] view certain issues differently than minorities or people who are targeted by police. And so, I feel like as somebody who's very nice, I have a unique perspective, sometimes

> . . . that's where I'm like, wow, like I think white people might actually understand this. And so I try to share that and even with my family and stuff. My family knows I was going out and protesting and they're definitely more conservative than I am, and it opened the door to having a lot of conversations about race and policing, what I think about it. So if it's not with my peers and it could be with older people who are like, "Well, I saw your daughter was out" or they like bring it up to their friends, and then it kind of just changes the way people think about things.

Rather than just relying on news clips of strangers protesting, when participants shared accounts of themselves in the uprising, it put the human face of a loved one in place of a stranger and might have made them more open or receptive to new perspectives about racism and the need for racial justice. Patrice felt she could communicate with more conservative whites in her family in a way they might be more willing to understand since it came from her, a loved one. Patrice used social media as a way to start dialogue between those who are concerned about racial justice and those who are more unsure or have difficulty fully grasping why people participated in the uprising.

Social media thus expanded the uprising's reach beyond just preaching to the choir. Helen, a forty-four-year-old African American woman in Williamsburg, Virginia, felt that her social media posts about her family's participation in the uprising, as well as her other interactions on social media platforms, were an important component of the uprising in and of themselves. It rejuvenated relationships and connections across oceans and nations.

> It superseded my expectations but to also see how powerful social media is—which, social media, yes, we know it has that negative aspects, but how it brought communities together. . . . My department chair from Hawaiʻi who I love so much, we still stay in contact, we speak at least once a month—she called me from a protest, and she's a cancer survivor, and she's white and Hawaiʻi has its own racial strife. She was there, and she called me and she sent pictures, and said because I love you. And to see it happening in New Zealand, and all over the place—that it's more than a moment, like this is a reality that must change! So it's superseded anything that I thought would actually happen and to know that there are steps, there are things that have been done on the level of law. Now, is it going to take a while? Unfortunately, yes, but to see that the protests of 2020 were motivators for that, like that in itself . . . was all worth it, and even now it's still worth it.

Helen's mention of Hawai'i and New Zealand demonstrates how social media played the role of connecting people during the uprising. As previously discussed, protests against racist police brutality have been happening for decades but often stay local to areas where the latest event has taken place. One might have to travel to New York, or Baltimore, or Ferguson to join with others protesting injustice or simply watch from afar and express solidarity. The uprising events were so proliferated that people in seemingly every corner of the world stood up at the same time, and part of those extension efforts connected people through social media. It amplified what already felt big at one's local level to something even bigger shared with others across the miles.

Finally, Faith, an eighteen-year-old Black-white biracial participant, also in Williamsburg, Virginia, brought it full circle by combining the logistical supports discussed in the previous section with "emotional" and "verbal" support—other forms of extension efforts. Again, this was in response to the question prompt about dos and don'ts advice she would give to others who might want to get involved.

> Verbal support is key, too, or emotional support. Like if someone's going protesting and you can't come, send them with some waters or the protective gear, if it's a bigger event where they can get hurt. Pay some bail money, people who are arrested, get people out of jail, because most likely they didn't do anything wrong and they were just thrown in there. And if you feel up to protesting, then get out there and inside, as scary as they make it look in the one picture where someone's getting tear gas; not all have to get that, like smaller protests. They don't all have to get violent, but sometimes people feel the need to get violent, and if they do, then you can remove yourself from the situation without getting caught up in the middle.

The prior section of this chapter discussed bail money as a logistical support as well as water and protective gear, but the verbal and emotional support matters too. As Faith mentioned, people may be scared and need encouragement. Elsewhere in her interview, because she was quarantined from school, she spent more time than usual on social media and saw posts critical of her (and other people's) participation in the uprising. By not only offering encouraging words and solidarity (whether on social media or directly) but offering logistical support, these actions from people not attending can provide important support functions to those who are.

A Beautiful Uprising for All Five Senses

It was an uprising of artists and poets, of yoga teachers and shared grievers, of lay security and legal observers, of medics and mutual aid, and clergy providing sanctuary. It was an uprising of people too afraid to leave their homes but who sent bail money, water, protective gear, and encouraging words. It was an uprising of monument toppling and creating new spaces where community members expressed their fears and dreams—in graffiti, music, dancing, chanting, holding vigil, and shared silence. All this at a time of tremendous social isolation and uncertainty of a global pandemic. As an antiracist racial project, the uprising succeeded in building a community that would not be silent in the face of injustice, a community that felt less alone in its pain. This antiracist racial project may not have been united in its diagnoses for solving the problem, as we shall see in the next chapter, but it at least reframed the narrative that the *victims of racist violence are not to blame for their own victimization and that state-sanctioned justifications for racist violence must be questioned and challenged and authorities held accountable.*

This uprising used a mix of old and new social movement tactics, many of which weren't depicted in mass media coverage of the events. Visual and performing artists have historically been part of social movements (Everhart 2012), but the wooden plyboards and monument toppling were more uniquely characteristic of the 2020 uprising. Candlelight vigils and collective grieving are also certainly not new to 2020. Ratliff and Hall (2014) propose a typology of six different types of protest activities: (1) Literal, Symbolic, Aesthetic, and Sensory (includes art), (2) Movement in Space (i.e., marches), (3) Solemnity and the Sacred (includes vigils), (4) Civil Disobedience (tends to get the most media attention), (5) Institutional and Conventional (i.e., press conferences), and (6) Collective Violence and Threats. The 2020 uprising used some combination of all of these, and in fact, between 1960 and 1995, across over twenty-three thousand different protest events in the United States, Wang and Soule (2016) coded fifty-seven various tactics used, including fireworks, drumming, laying wreaths, singing, praying, bell ringing and meditation, as well as more violent and disruptive actions. What these studies fail to do is conceptualize a single "uprising" that was more than just a series of unrelated individual protest events but rather a collective harmony of various events that stretched over weeks, even months, and combined into one ultimate historical event—the racial justice uprising of 2020. Although this is a small set of participants so far, what these exploratory findings suggest is that *protest tactics from the past few decades came together into the 2020 uprising, yet with some unique new additions*—mainly filling the vacuum left by law enforcement in combating white supremacist vigilantes. Plyboards became an unplanned necessity due to those interruptions, and resistance art added to those barriers became a way to refuse to let the movement be silenced.

Likewise, mutual aid and other logistical supports are not new to social movement activity either. This chapter opened with the story of Georgia Gilmore in Alabama during the Montgomery bus boycott, selling baked goods to fund the movement, and the U.S. South during the civil rights movement of the mid-twentieth century is full of such stories. Isaac, Coley, and Cornfield (2020) identify three different pathways to participation in early years of Nashville civil rights movement in the 1960s—core cadre, soldiers, and supporters. Likewise, several participants in the current study moved through multiple roles during the course of the 2020 uprising—marching as a "soldier" at some point but then becoming a "core" by leading a host congregation, or a "supporter" by streaming a protest event or funding various activities. What is newer is how quickly with technology a supporter on the other side of the world can hop onto GoFundMe or Venmo and contribute to diapers and prescriptions in Minneapolis instantaneously. As Spade (2020) points out, mutual aid can be considered a radical method of social change because it bypasses the traditional bureaucracies of institutional aid, which often require meeting certain conditions and requirements, instead deeming all are worthy of support, no questions asked. In so doing, it makes a public statement that the traditional institutional arrangements have failed us—the Black Panthers' breakfast program and free clinics were one such notable example (Spade 2020). Whether the logistical support was material/financial or giving of one's time and services (e.g., medics and legal observers), uprising participants continued in a long social movement tradition with some of these activities. However, again due to the law enforcement vacuum left, a supporter role less studied yet is the lay security. In protecting protesters from counterdemonstrators, angry passers-by, and potential car ramming, lay security (often white men, allies) seem to play an interesting role worth more attention in future work. Especially since white ally roles have historically become problematic in antiracist movements, more understanding is needed about how this role developed and under what contexts has it potentially been effective.

Technology, internet, social media are all modern developments that catapulted racial justice 2020 into this beautiful uprising, and of course, these developments did not begin in 2020. Scholars by now have documented just how crucial these media were to the development of the Black Lives Matter social movement (e.g., Carney 2016; Edrington and Lee 2018; Mundt, Ross, and Burnett 2018), such that the infrastructure was well in place when 2020 happened. This meant that most of the "first-time protesters" in this sample were likely to have been following #BLM, perhaps even considering themselves allies or members well before this, but without an active protest in their area to attend until 2020. Regardless of whether they were first-time protesters or more seasoned veterans, most participants understood it as their responsibility to engage in extension efforts, using whatever social media they had at their disposal. As noted in chapter 3, this became imperative once it became evident that mainstream media narratives were not characterizing correctly what was transpiring on the ground at the protest sites. Whether it was critics or skeptics of the movement, persons who supported but did not feel safe enough to come out, or people participating at other locations besides their own, participants used social media to connect with others about what they were seeing and to advance dialogue about antiracist solutions. The work of this uprising was much more than just marching and holding up a sign.

Some traditional quantitative measures of "protest" do not get at the full range of components of this uprising. For my study, I have defined the stretch of time between March and December 2020 as the uprising period, but we do know that the apex of the activity was the month between late May and late June of that year. However, the more we expand the timeline, the more we can find a range of beauty as far as these different components. Galleries around the country are beginning to display some of the resistance art that is now a part of history, and public spaces that once held monuments to white Confederate figures or spots of racial tension are now under contentious renegotiation. Just what has become of these various spaces alone further emphasizes the discordant harmony of the anger, pain, and grief and how it is dispersed so unequally among society. For example, the intersection of Thirty-Eighth Avenue and Chicago Street in Minneapolis became a memorial space now known as George Floyd Square, even maintained by an officially recognized 501(c)(3) nonprofit organization, with visitors from around the globe coming to pay respects and tribute (J. Jones 2021). In Richmond, Virginia, the spot with the graffiti-adorned Robert E. Lee statue was unofficially renamed Marcus-David Peters Circle (after an African American teacher killed by police), the base of the statue will go to a museum, and a local sculptor will replace it with a new monument giving voice to various constituents of the community (Duster 2021). Yet in Louisville, Kentucky, most news stories still use the name "Jefferson Square Park" to refer to the spot that participants only named as "Injustice Square Park," and whatever art, flowers, and tributes that community members laid there in honor of Breonna Taylor and others have been cleaned and disposed of on more than one occasion, with city officials citing need for "sanitation" as justification (Barton 2021). It is no wonder that participants in this study hold so many different convictions on what needs to happen next because the problems have so many different manifestations depending on the location.

Art alone is symbolic and cannot solve the problems by itself. Yet it provides a medium through which people connect with one another, support one another, remind one another there is still some beauty left in the universe despite all the carnage racism causes. In filmmaker and writer Rachel Raimist's "My Beautiful, Broken Minnesota," she reminds the reader that racism and corruption in policing was hardly new to Minneapolis by the time the world was suddenly all watching in 2020. Although her multiracial family experienced myriad "microaggressions" while residing in Minneapolis—including a police raid to their home not unlike Breonna Taylor's—Raimist nevertheless highlights the beautiful solidarity she experienced there and celebrates the potential in human connection. As in many cities, "in Minneapolis the arts and creative expression outlets were an important part of building community, partnerships, and understanding" (Raimist 2021, 31).

Although as we shall see in the next chapter, much policy change is still waiting to happen, organizers emphasize that much of the impact of this global uprising was most felt on the micro and local levels. While mutual aid is hardly new, new organizations were created and more community members were connected to much needed services as a result of the uprising. This was particularly felt in Minneapolis, with people all over the nation and world transferring money and supplies electronically with a simple click (Marcus 2021; Woodward 2020), but in many other areas of the country too, racial justice organizations that received a sudden influx of funds had to make decisions about what to do with it. Quickly disillusioned by the ability of politics to make big changes in policing, the funds that were at first being used to meet legal and medical needs of those injured on the ground while protesting began to also go to the same needs in communities of color disproportionately impacted by the pandemic (Salinas 2021). The uprising not only led people to where they could both give and receive mutual aid but to where they could share their grief and mental health needs collectively. As Dani McClain (2021) wrote, the traditional psychological approaches to "post-traumatic" stress and grief are less helpful for African Americans (and some other people of color) in the constant cross fire of systemic racism for whom "the 'post' in 'post-traumatic' never seems to come" (McClain 2021). The first-wave BLM movement was cultivating a focus on Black joy and self-care before the 2020 uprising, such as Tricia Hersey's "nap ministry" founded in 2016, but again, 2020 drew way more attention. The ongoing stress and grief caused by systemic racism is a public health issue. Directing more community members to an awareness of this fact as well as to resources for addressing it was certainly an accomplishment of the 2020 uprising—as component of this antiracist racial project. However, this only puts band-aids on the impacts of racism rather than getting to its source and its root. Let us examine in the closing chapter how close to the root 2020 got us and how much work remains.

CHAPTER 6

After 2020

What's Next?

> As it stopped being mainstream and in their faces and the world open back up, it was easier for you to revert back to your comfort. Because you weren't forced to look at this anymore.
>
> —Kelli, Virginia

> But for a reckoning to occur, there has to be more than just an acknowledgement of injustice. There has to be action.... For those whose commitments to justice remain, there appears to be a long and cold winter ahead, because the racial reckoning of the current moment is moving full speed ahead, with no signs of quieting anytime soon.
>
> —Hakeem Jefferson and Victor Ray, 2022

By October 2020, when many Americans took their "black square" off their social media profiles, returning to business as usual, journalist Adam Serwer wrote an *Atlantic* piece titled "The Next Reconstruction?" where he questioned whether the 2020 uprisings would be able to secure any impactful antiracist change: "How far will the possibilities of this moment extend? We could consider two potential outcomes—one focused on police and prisons, and a broader one, aimed at eliminating the deeply entrenched systems that keep Black people from realizing full equality, a long-standing crisis Americans have tried to suppress with policing and prisons rather than attempting to resolve it" (Serwer 2020). Most study participants fell squarely along one of these two ways of thinking about the problem. Moreover, it was rare that they extended the conversation unprompted into the broader ways racism is structured into society. Whereas most went beyond the "bad apple" approach of individual officer accountability and restitution in cases of shooting unarmed civilians, to various questions of reframing public safety as an institution, a conspicuous few looked beyond policing and prisons to all other institutions where racism also runs rampant.

As early as June 2020, journalist Nikole Hannah-Jones wrote a *New York Times* magazine piece, "What Is Owed?" asserting this historic moment of racial uprising, where the world was watching, would be an opportune time to finally cash that forty-acres-and-a-mule check that came back marked "insufficient funds"—the check that Dr. King referred to in his oft-quoted speech (the part that does not get quoted quite as much). Hannah-Jones (2020) made the case for reparations, as many have before her, identifying it as a significant means of narrowing the persistent racial wealth gap, among other things. Examining patterns like residential segregation and its connection to the racial wealth gap, as well as educational, economic, and environmental injustices are all important components of antiracist justice. Both the Movement for Black Lives (M4BL) and Black Lives Matter (BLM) organization websites include the BREATHE Act as part of their demands, which "paints a vision of a world where Black lives matter through investments in housing, education, health, and environmental justice" (Black Lives Matter Global Network 2022). Yet divestment from police, rather than investment in reframing these other institutions, seems to be the part of the conversation often heard the loudest. Also, the George Floyd Justice in Policing Act gained more traction in Congress overall (bans chokeholds, limits qualified immunity, requires body cameras, requires reporting, makes lynching a federal hate crime) than the BREATHE Act which involves other entities besides police—yet even the tamer George Floyd Act failed to pass Congress in 2021 (Alcindor 2020; Inskeep and Johnson 2021; D. Jones 2021). One would hope that activists on the ground were "dreaming big" during 2020, but as available paths forward quickly began to narrow, it is not altogether surprising some of their visions for the future did the same.

This is not a survey research project. My hunch is that if I were to have given interviewees a list of antiracist policy changes needed in society, most if not all of them would check "all of the above!" I do not believe these racial justice advocates stand in opposition to broad, bold societal change. However, I kept the invitation to the topic wide open to see where they went with it because I believe the direction they chose tells us something about how they see the world. So one of my closing questions was, "Were your objectives achieved? If not, what needs to happen next?" Their answers to this "what's next?" question fell into one or more of three broad categories that I am calling individual, intermediate, and systemic. Unanimously, all thirty interviewees mentioned some type of *individual*-level changes needed, including themselves and others (e.g., educating themselves, dialogue with others), as well as changes within policing at the level of individual accountability within the existing system. Additionally, the vast majority (twenty-two out of thirty) advocated various institutional changes but all limited to institutions of policing, prison, and public safety. These included things like better training (i.e., implicit bias and deescalation), higher education-level requirements to join the force in the first place, and better mental health screening for police. I placed these suggestions into an "*intermediate*" category, along with any discussions of improvements of prison and parole systems, as well as decriminalization of marijuana, which several understood as a racial justice issue.

I reserved the final "*systemic*" category for those taking that additional step beyond the criminal justice system—which Serwer states above has essentially been used to "suppress" the nation's long-standing racism rather than solve it. Yet I would argue it has hardly suppressed but indeed exacerbated racial injustice. It was the rare interviewee who mentioned the school-to-prison pipeline, for example. The BREATHE Act does include a provision to get police out of schools (the Justice in Policing Act does not). But examining the education system as a whole and its many racial inequalities is a broader way of thinking about racial justice than just merely examining the ways in which the criminal justice system interacts with it. It was also the rare person who mentioned voting rights, residential segregation, or reparations for African Americans. Only ten of the thirty interviewees ventured unprompted beyond the criminal justice system to what could be changed at a systemic level. None of these "systemic" thinking participants were under the age of twenty-eight, and the vast majority were over thirty—all but three were over forty.

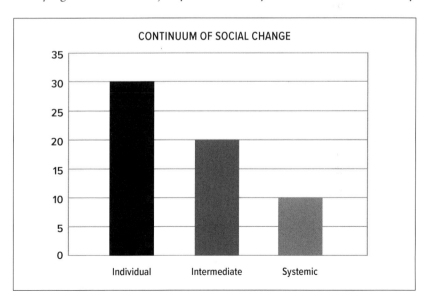

The majority were not first-time protesters either. This pattern suggests it might take a while in one's walk for racial justice to come to an awareness of the broader roots of racism, as opposed to just examining the crisis case we are marching about this time.

Once the guilty verdict in the Derek Chauvin case happened (the verdict for Kimberly Potter and the verdict for Travis and Gregory McMichael along with William Bryan—killers of Ahmaud Arbery—had yet to take place), I wanted to know whether participants viewed the verdict as the turning of tide toward greater accountability in cases of racist violence, or whether it was an exception or fluke. This was part of examining the research question of whether they felt the uprising made a substantial difference in any ways. This question was either treated with cautious optimism or downright skepticism among the participants. None felt that this single verdict could usher in a new pattern by itself. Many stressed the video evidence and other exceptional factors about Floyd's murder, along with the pandemic lockdown where more people were watching than ever, made the uprising something virtually impossible to see again. Not that unjustified violence is not happening every day to African Americans and other people of color, unfortunately, but rather that the circumstances of its exposure to the public are not often able to be replicated to the degree that Floyd's horrific death was. Moreover, daily mobilization of marching around the world for weeks on end is unsustainable and unrealistic just to obtain the basic justice legally entitled to all citizens. Also, this question felt particularly irrelevant to protesters in Louisville, Kentucky, for example, who took to the streets well before the summer and were still awaiting any sort of semblance of justice in Breonna Taylor's killing as well as other related local murders at the hands of the state. So picturing what future racial justice might look like post-2020 uprising is admittedly difficult, when immediate realities of getting just basic accountability in individual cases is elusive and ongoing.

Nevertheless, these interviewees took brave risks, visioning a more racially equitable society than currently exists. So let us explore their blueprints for next steps. Although some extend further beyond the criminal justice system than others, every suggestion is a contribution of some kind, and any would bring greater racial justice than we have had.

Level One: Individual-Level Change

When asked if their objectives had been accomplished, and if not, what needed to happen next, some echoed individual-level goals discussed in chapter 4—connecting with others, sharing grief within community, raising awareness (in themselves as well as others), making a public stand against injustice, and supporting each other, for example. These goals were more immediate and they felt they had achieved them. However, even with the vague "awareness" objective, several felt there was still much work left in educating others about the extent of racism. Plenty referred to racism deniers in their circles who they were committing themselves to educating or figuring out ways to "translate" policy solutions like "defund the police" into words their contacts might be more likely to understand and thus support.

Rabbi M, for example, who also discussed intermediate-level changes, described his commitment to having conversations with others, framing it as his responsibility as a white ally. His own spiritual tradition in Judaism provided a model for seeing this role as a translator of sorts. He said, "In Hebrew, we have a term; it's called the 'mature mind,' and it means 'translator.' And in the Talmudic times, the person would stand up for the community and read from the Torah scroll and the mature mind would stand right next to him or her and translate for them." So he felt BLM activists were already creating powerful ideas for solutions, and his goal was "not to change the work of these activists; I think they're doing amazing work—it's to add to it and amplify it." While supporting intermediate-level societal changes like reframing public safety and defunding the police, Rabbi M, a fifty-one-year-old white man, acknowledged that the combination of his race, class, and gender as well as his position in his community as a spiritual leader would allow him to "amplify" the voices of visionary Black activists by having conversations with other white, suburban people like himself who still needed convincing that "defund the police" was worthwhile.

> I think that the very question of 'What does public safety look like?' what does it mean? I think . . . 'defund the police' . . . immediately shuts down so many people, right? And I feel like I can be the person who can help support these activists of color and say, 'Great, Mr. [or] Ms. suburban fifty-year-old white person. You don't agree with that, so let's talk together. What does public safety look like? Do you agree that unarmed people shouldn't be shot and killed by the cops? Yes? All right, great, so we're in agreement! Now, what does that even look like? What policies have to be in place? Are you aware, right, that only 17 percent of crimes in Minneapolis have been violent crimes, have been solved by the police in the last decade? That's 83 percent that haven't. Most of the crimes, or most of the times the cops are called, it's because of truancy, or homelessness, or a mental illness issue, or an addiction issue. Shouldn't we have people who are trained to do that?' And oftentimes I'll have people say, "Oh that's an interesting point," right? Like, "You wouldn't go to your dentist to have an appendectomy, would you?" Well, "No, of course, not, Rabbi." Well, like, "Why would you call the po-

lice when somebody is having a mental health crisis?" Right, so part of what I view my role as is to help these really wise visionary prophetic activists.

As opposed to prophet, the rabbi sees himself as messenger and translator, communicating the importance of these changes to others who will hopefully become supporters, even if previously hesitant.

The individual-level contribution of conversation and "dialogue" was a popular go-to for many participants. Several talked about the need to educate others as well as themselves. Helen, a forty-four-year-old Black woman quoted in chapter 4 for seeing her role as a mother empowering her children as one important motivator for her participation, raises that objective again here in this quote, along with self-education, so she can more effectively dialogue with others.

> I think my initial goal was met like I said empowering my children. I also wanted to see some type of personal change in being able to engage in those conversations with people. Because before it was okay, [but now] it's too exhausting, I shouldn't have to keep having this conversation, but realizing it doesn't matter how exhausted I am, those conversations still need to occur. With me reading literature, me just basing my own internal biases that might be there as well, so just knowing that, although I am Black, there's still a whole lot I need to learn and so much I need to engage with.

Several African American participants defied the notion that they somehow just automatically understand the history of racism by being Black. Some, like Helen, discussed a commitment to redoubling their efforts at engaging in these difficult conversations by seeking out new information and resources. Helen refers to this as "personal change" at the individual level. Helen is also one of the rare ten individuals in the sample who spoke about changes beyond the criminal justice system, perhaps because she is a high school teacher and a parent; in a subsequent section, we will examine her discussions of the role of education, youth, and voting rights in more detail. However, I want to highlight that individual-level strategies were also advocated even among those who also saw the bigger picture.

Another respondent, Monica, a thirty-three-year-old white woman in Tampa, Florida, who was tear gassed at her very first and last protest she attended, focused a lot of self-education and unlearning prejudices as individual-level strategies. Ultimately, she also endorsed reimagining public safety and police reform (intermediate level), but much of how she answered the "what's next" question was at the individual level.

> In our society as a white woman, I have privilege. I did see myself as an ally before, but . . . I and other white people need to do more. . . . I'm looking for different

> ways that I can be more involved, but I've also been doing a lot of personal reflection and reading a lot of books on just what it means to be an ally and what it means to be antiracist and how to confront your own prejudices and actually help people.... How can I, in my everyday life, how can I help and dismantle the systems that are in place ... to listen and to learn and unlearn things that I've learned throughout my life.... I think that police institutions are a way to keep people of color down. And I know that people talk about reform of police departments a lot, but I don't if something is fundamentally racist I don't know how you change that. I think we need to work as a society to dismantle these institutions that do keep people down, and I think that starts with us doing the inner work with unlearning whatever prejudices we might hold.... I think it has to start there because if people believe keep believing that these institutions are fundamentally good or don't need to change them, we're not going to get anywhere. So I think that it does need to come with people again examining our own prejudices and standing up to things that keep people down and saying it's not okay. And I wish I had all the answers. I wish I knew that there was like a magic pill to fix everything, but I think it's very complicated and it permeates many different areas of our society, but I think we all need to start looking at ourselves first

Monica recently completed a social work degree, so elsewhere in the interview she asserted many police calls would be better handled by social work professionals, endorsing "defund the police" and explaining that most people don't understand what that means. However, in almost every sentence in the above quote, Monica comes back to "we need to start looking at ourselves first." This focus on "inner work" was an oft-mentioned component for individual-level solutions, especially among whites.

Yet African American protesters were also passionate about having conversations to advance people's understanding of the depth of the problem of racism in society. Kelli, a forty-four-year-old Black business owner and longtime activist in Richmond, Virginia, met the unique moment in history with cautious optimism, feeling vindicated that others seemed at least momentarily willing to have the conversations she wanted to have for a long time.

> I think my ways of protesting have been on different levels.... People know that I have a Black business that is about community and working with others, actually standing and listening to leaders and activists and politicians talk about how we can make change, to posting things on my platform. I have a large audience on my social media platform. And I was able to be very vocal just by just saying a lot and then having my non-Black friends send mediums or send me messages or come by the coffee shop, or just wanna get more knowledge, or understanding, or sym-

pathy, or help, or whatever they needed to do.... We have been fighting this fight for a long time, and especially in Richmond, and so selfishly I had some I-told-you-so moments.... I've been creating events, experiences and elevating people, places, and things within the Black culture of Richmond because you all have ignored it for years here. And y'all called us racist because we were doing these things. And now you watched a man be murdered in front of you, and then you seen your kids question whether or not you're a racist—for you to kind of have a eye-opening experience of "oh my gosh, they have been struggling" for a minute. So I think that that's what I've gotten a little bit of fulfillment out of. Being able to kind of let my shoulders down a little bit, knowing that the lens are different and my voice is being heard different. But I still got my guard up because, again, we still dying in the hands of police, we're still dealing with racism, disparities with racial injustice, so again, we're still not in the clear.

Although conversations may not seem like much in the grand scheme of all political demands for racial justice, Kelli felt some vindication for whites to appear (at least temporarily) more supportive than before. Notably, Kelli was called "racist" (by "non-Blacks") for emphasizing Black history, but yet in this moment, she felt "my voice is being heard different." Kelli is one of many interviewees who mentioned social media as a tool for advancing antiracism. Notably, Kelli is one of the few in the sample to discuss systemic change as well. But she frames these dialogues as a component of the work necessary to marshal broader support for systemic change.

Several participants referred to this work and its impact as "raising awareness." Faith, an eighteen-year-old who identifies as Black/white biracial, stated,

> My personal objective was to raise awareness and try to feel like I made some sort of an impact in talking to people. So one time, my hairdresser had asked me if I felt that I was really doing anything by doing the protests. I had to answer that with yes, because I brought awareness to a cause mainly is the main reason. ... Going out there ... they will ask questions, and then also when you destroy things and get a big media presence, people start paying attention and they want to stop and get whatever it is to go back to normal and not have something be in the news, so you're threatening to keep putting things in the news ... so people would feel less, I would say, daring and bold to complete these racist actions when they're going to be consequences, and they can see that people do actually care. ... So I think that my objective was to bring awareness to people who wouldn't typically participate and to feel like I made some sort of impact in just be there to support people. ... So it was nice to be able to talk to people and hear their stories, and it brought awareness to the cause. But I would say, like donate, become

> educated, and educate neighbors or friends, educate anyone, anyone who's acting ignorant and has a bumper sticker on their car that doesn't make any sense, just give him some choice words about how they can fix their actions and not offend people as much for their cars. But anyways, I would say, like make sure they especially like education, education is key. Get involved on social media, talk to people, donate to different causes.

Faith felt she gained, as well as spread, awareness—learning from other people's stories and then answering questions from passers-by and people who "typically wouldn't participate," or skeptics, about why she marched. This was not Faith's first protest; she had been doing them a few years, but she is still young and developing her consciousness. So while at different types of uprising events, she learned strategies for talking to people with "bumper stickers" (of the "All Lives Matter" type or "Blue Lives Matter") by listening to speakers and other participants. These conversations were both in person and on social media.

Media as a route to awareness also came up in the coverage of the protests—Faith emphasized that destruction of property plays a role. Elsewhere in her interview, she noted that property is covered by insurance, thus replaceable. Although she did not participate in property destruction, even the simple action of laying in the street for 8 minutes 46 seconds and briefly inconveniencing people whose traffic path for the evening was disrupted, was something she felt would raise awareness. In her view, these could be seen as a "consequence" for racism. In other words, even if some people don't care about an unarmed African American getting shot and killed unjustly, if they care about property being destroyed, traffic being disrupted, or even simply having to watch it on the news, then maybe they will perceive those as "consequences" enough that they don't want to have to see it happen again. In the absence of clear consequences for the offending officers, Faith framed the disruption caused by protests as a different type of public consequence. So awareness occurs at several levels, and many protesters felt like they were facilitating in that process by participating.

Sharon, a thirty-nine-year-old Black/Panamanian woman who, like Faith, participated in Williamsburg, Virginia, also invoked dialogue as a social change strategy. As one organizer of the local movement, she discussed changing the route of the marchers over time so that it would be more likely to confront tourists eating outdoors, as opposed to being by the courthouse, which was less proximate to bystanders.

> I desire to have that dialogue that does change minds because ... when you have a nice protest, there is hard noes and hard yeses on both sides. And you got one person standing on the side of the protest and they're just watching it. Next

thing you know and then you have someone that comes up to them and just start talking to them out of the protest . . . all the way down [the] street, we're back by the courthouse still talking. . . . Because you don't have to fully agree, but you have to at least acknowledge that there's a reason that we're out here that's where we need. That right there got me so excited, every time I saw somebody come from off the side and join the protest. Even if they just went from the end of [street name] listening, because I knew that you were going to go back to your hotel room, back to your resort, or wherever, and you were going to have a conversation about what you just did.

Sharon counted it as a small victory each time someone from the sidelines ended up joining in the marching as a result of chatting with her about why she was doing it. Again, she was one of few people who looked beyond the criminal justice system to more systemic changes, especially with respect to housing segregation, elsewhere in the interview. However, she also identified dialogue as a component of the process.

Making individual-level donations to "causes" related to racial justice is something that Faith above and also Beth, a thirty-four-year-old white woman in Louisville, discussed. Beth was a first-time protester in 2020, who also identified conversations with friends and family as an action strategy.

> I don't think I personally accomplished anything. I still feel like there's so much work to be done. I think what I realized after is yes, protesting is great. And it's important and I'm not saying that it's not, but after protesting, I sort of redirected my focus for me. Just to see where I could help out like financially, I think, because for me, I think, yes, you can protest, but there are so many other things structurally that are wrong. Just as a whole, so I donated to bail bond funds, things like that. I've tried to only eat at Black-owned businesses, things like that. I've tried to just restructure the way that I live basically instead of protesting. . . . And even not that it's necessarily my job, but I've tried to educate more my white friends and just pass on some more knowledge. . . . Sometimes it's not that people that don't want to learn; I think it's the way it's explained to them. I think I have a good way of explaining it to people that are close to me that they'll trust me and listen to me, so I've tried to be more vocal in that way.

Supporting Black-owned businesses is an individual-level strategy a few others mentioned as well as making donations to racial justice groups. Like the rabbi quoted at the beginning of this section, Beth is another white person who feels she can "translate" antiracist understandings to other whites in a way they might be more willing to listen. She does mention "there are so many things structurally that are wrong" without going into much detail. This lack of specificity in policy recommendations was not uncommon for new protesters.

A couple of times, interviewees were frank that they were not sure what to recommend. Again, this was on the part of first-time protesters, and there was a sense that the problem was almost too large or perhaps inevitable. This was mostly African American men participants. Charles, a thirty-six-year-old Columbus, Ohio, resident, became part of the uprising fairly late in the year by attending a protest about the killing of Casey Goodson, with the main objective of letting the family know they were not alone. In a prior chapter, he was quoted about how heartened he was to see people of many racial backgrounds there, not just African Americans. This was his very first time participating in anything like this. So when asked what he would recommend to stop the killings and injustice, he responded,

> Recommendations, wow, what could I recommend it to make a solid saying; that's a powerful question. I think people just need to live in unity, and I don't know how we can get there . . . because if it's a racial thing, you got some really hard work to do. I don't know what I could recommend. Can you recommend unity? [Interviewer: Of course.] Yeah, I mean everything is bad times. Just unity. And I don't know if these cops are just scared because of somebody, or if it's just, hey, I don't know.

Charles finds it incomprehensible why officers would act in such arbitrary manner. Suggesting eradicating racism would be "really hard work," he is not denying the magnitude of the problem. Indeed, it is a lofty wish to expect those caught in the cross fire of it all to also formulate elaborate solutions because just shouldering grief alone is enough to exhaust the creative mind.

Likewise, Tucker, a twenty-nine-year-old African American man in Columbia, Maryland, also new to protesting in 2020, could not fathom a certain answer on solutions, especially since the same things kept happening for so long without end. He hoped a future visionary would know the answer.

> I can't even wrap the honest answer. I don't know how to answer because I haven't seen a lot; I keep seeing the same things . . . my grandparents, my parents, all saying the same thing, and marching doing stuff like this, you haven't seen the videos Rodney King getting beat, Emmett Till getting killed, and it's still the same thing with Michael Brown and Trayvon Martin and then you got Philando Castile and you got a plethora of other names, so honestly I don't have to answer what we could do. You just gotta keep moving forward; that's how things got to keep on. Keep our heads high and just keep being resilient and knowing that these things don't come. We gotta stay together; that's the thing, we got to stay together and

> let a leader emerge. We got to stay together and let a leader emerge, and once that leader emerges, we just got to support them wholeheartedly. And then we can go from there.

Tucker's answer does not provide action steps in the traditional sense we might expect, but his response says so much. To keep moving forward in the context of these multigenerational assaults without justice is an act of collective resistance in itself. To not stop speaking out when the steady drumbeat is nearly incessant across these generations, to "stay together" and "keep being resilient," to not settle for defeat is a decision. Tucker sees an answer in the power of collective togetherness when a leader does emerge, to "support them wholeheartedly." In the meantime, he believes that speaking out, saying this is not right, is preferable to simply surrendering, even if he knows "these things don't come."

RJ, also a first-time protester and a twenty-nine-year-old African American man in the D.C. area, agreed that continuing to speak out and raise awareness could be a pathway to greater accountability for individual officers in these cases of wrongdoing.

> We need to say something about it, because if we just charge it to the game, but this is normal, this is not normal, this should not be normal.... I would say, moving forward, just to keep the awareness level as high as possible. Because stuff is going to keep happening, and it's a lot of different things in our communities that can be better as a whole, but when you're talking about a public service, accountability, or lack thereof, that affects us more so than our private community or private family lives or private friend lives. Like when this is happening in a public for people that should be working for the people, protecting the people, that makes your private setting harder. You have to worry about . . . if you have beef with someone around the corner and you guys are dealing with them with something, you call for public service that can help you with that.... So like now, you're dealing with two situations on top of the original so. Things like that, I just say moving forward, just keeping the awareness level high, still standing up, stepping out, speaking out about what you see, what you see going on, and hopefully there's some accountability come before moving forward.

RJ's ideal is that officers bring calm and resolve when intervening in a conflict, as opposed to adding more stress to it, but when officers fall short of the ideal, they should be held accountable—if not, the people must demand it by making the public aware.

In one way or another, the quotes above address protest as a means of bringing awareness to racial injustice. Individual-level efforts—whether it is discussions with friends, family, or community, or accountability of officers, or supporting Black-owned businesses, or using social media to raise awareness—are certainly a part of the process of rectifying racial injustice. However, to bring more systemic changes, other levels of action are also necessary.

Level Two: Intermediate-Level Change

A majority of the interview sample (twenty-two out of thirty) went beyond individual-level solutions to describing changes that should happen within the entire system of policing. The only participants (eight) who did not get around to discussing these criminal justice policy changes were mainly first-time marchers on the younger side of the sample (twenties and thirties except one), as noted above. Many who cited dialogue and social media posts as part of their social change strategies described conversations about police reform and even reorganizing public services altogether ("defunding" the police). Although reform (i.e., bias training, better screening/hiring practices) and complete reorganization of public services are two very different approaches, for the purposes of this analysis I place them all in this intermediate category mainly because they do not look beyond criminal justice to other institutions where racism is embedded. Within this intermediate category, a variety of possible social change strategies were discussed. There were also a mix of first-time as well as veteran protesters within this category.

Changing how police departments handle internal investigations of officer-involved shootings, as well as the way they seek to hire and train new recruits, were some policing-level changes suggested. Jordan, a twenty-six-year-old who participated for his first time in Atlanta and identified as Black/mixed, focused his suggestions on police departments and how they conduct their own investigations; he deemed this too much of a conflict of interest, ethically not sound, and an invitation to corruption, in need of change. After discussing how Derek Chauvin's murder (as opposed to manslaughter) charge was a welcome change toward justice, I asked if that was the main change he would like to see. He replied,

> Oh no, the larger objective is for change in the Justice Department in general, to see more openness with investigations. I think police should be subjected to a third-party investigation because it's kind of unfair that they're the only people allowed to investigate themselves. Like that'd be kind of weird like if I went out, broke the law, and said, Oh well, I'm gonna investigate myself and tell you if I broke the law or not. No, nobody's going to do that, I'm sorry. But you just had a president that literally just almost got impeached for that. . . . Now, fortunately, you're seeing police option of getting fired for making racial, making racist re-

> marks, for doing racial things to other officers, so you have to wonder how many of these individuals who possess the same powers of Chauvin are slowly slipping through the cracks. But I will tell a lot of people I have a lot of faith in the next generation of police officers; I think a lot of maybe the younger officers saw what they didn't want to see with Derek Chauvin and now understand like they see somebody that they know who they don't want to be, and now, maybe hopefully these police officers [will] . . . finally do something about these crooked officers that they just let go on and start holding police officers accountable for when you have a legal process. Because ultimately, that's where it's going to start to where now they have to change from their inside. Unfortunately, we can want all the change we want as civilians, but if the department itself doesn't want to change, unfortunately I don't really see it changing.

Jordan was a bit hard to categorize because at times he focused on "crooked officers" as if the problem is isolated "bad apples" (which would place him more in the individual category), but he also spoke about the organizational patterns of seeking manslaughter (or lesser) charges rather than murder for officer-involved shootings, and the pattern on internal investigations. Both require changes at the organizational level rather than simply purging individual officers. Jordan expressed a mix of hope and pessimism as to whether his suggestions would come to pass.

Likewise, Michelle, a twenty-four-year-old white woman protesting for her first time in Dallas, Texas, also was pessimistic about greater accountability for officers happening on its own.

> We don't know yet how these protests if they result in anything. We've seen convictions and stuff, but we don't know if anything is actually changing or if it's just for show—there's so many murders that go completely under the table, and no one takes a look at. And if it's not big on social media and no one hears about it, I'm sure the cop who did, that is on paid suspension and then a year later, when it dies down or however long later, he'll just come back to work or get a new job. So I don't know yet the results of any of these protests. I feel like it was a success, but at the same time, I feel like there just needs to be so much more to happen—legislation-wise and police-wise, there needs to be— I don't know how you can reform a system that is so deeply rooted in hate and racism and bigotry. I kind of feel like we need to abolish it and start from the ground up. . . . There's a lot that could be done for reform. I mentioned mental health checks, background checks . . . if they have any type of discrimination in their hearts toward a minority group that they should never be a police officer. And so there's a lot that could be done, but it's almost too big to reform, and it kind of needs to be French Revolution–style taken down.

Michelle raised the problem of offending officers being on paid leave or suspension and then either coming back or getting hired somewhere else. She also suggested that initial screening at the hiring point for police could be beneficial and perhaps preventative. At the same time, she also wondered whether the system was beyond reform. It was not uncommon for interviewees to show skepticism whether their own suggestions for reform would be enough to solve the problem.

Abby, an eighteen-year-old white woman who marched in Nashville, Tennessee, also discussed better training and hiring of police, even as she endorsed defunding the police. She offered other suggestions understanding that defunding the police may not be popular enough to happen.

> There's quite a few things—for one, I think police need more training. We always say, defund the police; I do highly agree with that. But if we're going to have them in place, because a lot of people don't want to defund the police . . . they need to take more training. Most states don't require police to take deescalation training, and I think they need that. They also need to have bias training to acknowledge and address implicit biases that they have. Like hairdressers and tattoo artists have more training and do more school than police officers, and they're not holding a gun or a weapon or a taser. So I think police officers need to have something that's comparable to a genuine undergraduate bachelor's or master's degree to be able to be a police officer.

Abby advocated more education and training for police—not just on operating weapons but rather on deescalating conflict and identifying bias. Although the amount of training and education required for officers does vary greatly by jurisdiction and amount of need (depth of hiring pool), and in some places there may indeed be more training for police than for hairdressers and tattoo artists, the fact that the amount of training does not inspire public confidence is disconcerting regardless.

Nicole, a twenty-seven-year-old African American woman protesting in Washington, D.C., had recently worked for her city's emergency dispatcher office, so she was well familiar with the testing used to screen for mental health and potential bias. Her perception was that anyone desiring a job could easily game the system and figure out how to pass through the screener whether or not the test was an accurate reflection.

> I know when I was at the police department, we had to take a bias training. But if you're racist, I just skip to that, click it, you just get the answers right, this is about money, so you're going to put down what they want to hear. So everybody's like, oh, we're doing bias training with the iPads on computer. So you don't have

> really a Black person coming in there talking to you or someone a minority coming into a big police academy meeting and saying, hey, you know these stops that you're doing when you see these kids with hoodies, that's a fashion statement for you. When you see it, it doesn't have to necessarily put fear into you to the point that you're going to stop no other reason they're not doing anything crazy. When you see a nice car with a Black person in it, they don't automatically have to be a drug dealer; they could be a lawyer, a doctor, a social media influencer because now they're getting paid big bucks. . . . So I think that the media depicts minorities as rough and lacking education and being disrespectful, and of course, if I was a white person and I was watching [the media] day in, day out, that when I did have an encounter with a live person, I myself would, you know, be extra.

Nicole's concern was that the bias training she witnessed firsthand was basically virtual education questions to click through, including no actual interaction with people of color. In her estimation, until white officers have actual meaningful interactions with "minorities" enough to supplant the infectious media images of "gang member" and "drug dealer," they are unlikely to be able to perform their jobs equitably without relying on racial profiles and stereotypes. Nicole was one of only ten interviewees who also suggested changes outside of the criminal justice system, examining racism more systemically. However, she identified changes needed within policing as well.

Others went past the initial screening of recruits to the way the police organize their work once hired. It is not altogether unsurprising, given the ballot initiative during the 2021 election, that most of the Minneapolis residents in the sample spoke of reorganizing public safety so that social workers and other related professionals respond to emergency calls rather than police. Although the measure did not pass, it was obviously hotly debated, and most acknowledged its merit for addressing some of the ongoing problems. Jim Bear, a forty-four-year-old Native American man in Minneapolis, explained,

> I would say at this point, what do we have to lose? It's certainly worth exploring what it would look like to do away with the Minneapolis Police Department and put in some kind of public safety system that will have something akin to police officers but will also have well-trained sort of emergency response. People so that when you have someone who is being accused of passing off a counterfeit $20 bill, you don't need four people with guns there for that. I mean, hell, a counterfeit twenty, I've unknowingly passed off counterfeit money, and I present it and the teller's like, oh man, this is counterfeit, and I look and I'm like, hey, you're right, and that was the end of that transaction, right? No police called, nothing like that. So we just have so many situations where people have guns—are not neces-

sary to that situation, don't need to be there, actually make it worse when they're there. So yeah, I don't know if I would put myself solidly in the camp of defund the police, but I'm strongly leaning that way. What we're doing now is not working, and doing it better or with more money is not going to work any better because we've thrown money, we've increased police budgets, we've thrown money at this problem, hired more officers, we've done all these things, and all it ends up doing is leading to more Black and brown people being arrested, put in jail, leading to a larger community rift, between the people who are overly policed and those who are doing the policing.

Using the $20 counterfeit bill example (the offense for which the police were called when they killed George Floyd in May 2020), Jim Bear maintained that a gun was not needed for that situation at all, nor for many other situations in which police are called. In fact, in many situations the presence of police just aggravates it. Although Jim Bear does not put himself "solidly in the camp of defund the police," he does agree with public service reorganization and is critical of overpolicing.

Justin, a fifty-year-old white man and Minneapolis resident, also felt emergency response should be supplemented more by social workers as opposed to just police.

> There needs to be a radical shift in how the public are treated by police officers, particularly people of color but people in general. Why should my tax dollars go to pay for someone to swear at, beat, kill other members of my community? So I do think there's something's terribly wrong with the police and that needs deep, deep reform to really get to a place of protect and serve, rather than increasing armed confrontations. And I do feel like this was a messaging lag—defund the police terrified enough people that made it more difficult to do that, but my own town, I live in Golden Valley. Now, they just announced that they're going to have a social worker embedded at the 911 call center to field calls instead. So to make some changes, and I think those are incremental steps, I think we need to go much, much further, but progress is progress.

In chapter 3, Justin compared the standard of professionalism he must follow with clients (not swearing or disrespecting people) to what he saw police officers do, so here again he stressed that tax dollars should not go toward supporting this behavior. Justin raised an important point that even if citywide ballot initiatives don't pass, they still bring the idea of incremental changes to the attention of citizens and policymakers, and portions of what is in the policing bill can find their way into smaller neighborhoods, towns, and other areas.

Although not in Minneapolis, Patrice, a twenty-two-year-old woman who participated in both Troy and Detroit, Michigan, and identified as Black-white biracial, also endorsed additional social workers as part of emergency response, among other changes.

> I definitely think the way that police are trained—so in undergrad, I minored in criminal justice and majored in political science, so I had a lot of knowledge about what was going on and the demographics of these crimes, how it happens, and the way that police are being trained was something that we were learning about at the time. And it definitely is primarily, they are taught self-defense and how to use guns versus like how to be respectful and how to interact with people. And so that would be the biggest thing I would say . . . is training, I definitely agree that social workers should be incorporated into especially nonviolent policing situations more because they have been taught and trained how to deescalate situations and . . . what the best way is to communicate with different people. I also think that people should make more of an effort to have police live in the neighborhoods that they police because a lot of times police will live in different neighborhoods [and work in] Detroit, and so they don't know what it's like . . . to live in Detroit and to have this fear of police and to be targeted and things like that. . . . Those are the three main ones I can think of right now.

Community policing and social workers as emergency responders were mentioned repeatedly. Patrice noted social workers are trained on how to communicate across differences and deescalate conflict, whereas police are not. As a criminal justice major in college, she understood that these crucial "nonviolent" skills were not nearly as much a key component of police training as they needed to be.

Yet policing is but one component of the criminal justice system. Others incorporated additional elements of the system in need of reform in their comments, such as legal changes and prisons. As Rev. TM, a fifty-three-year-old white man in Minneapolis, stated,

> But there's a lot of work left to do. I mean, obviously there's still prisons that are packed to the gills, we still criminalize Black and brown bodies more than white bodies and it's in the systems, in the inside, the correction facilities are inhuman. And in the fact that we don't restore rights of people who are out and if served their time is still a huge piece of injustice. So there's lots of issues that need to be tackled. The work is never done; it won't be done in my lifetime. But it doesn't mean I'm not going to keep doing it.

Prison reorganization as well as restoration of rights after time served are important changes needed in Rev. TM's view. Blake, a twenty-one-year-old white man in Williamsburg, Virginia, also focused on the overrepresentation of "Black and brown" people in the prisons, correctly identifying that drug laws are one of the main culprits of that discrepancy. Blake mentioned marijuana laws in particular.

> I feel a strong need for reform in the law enforcement system. We need to start hiring and putting social workers into police precincts because half the things that police officers are being called to go out to are things that they aren't trained to deal with, and we should be putting people who are trained to deal with these things on the front lines, I think. We already made a very big step in the decriminalization of cannabis in Virginia, at least, because I do not feel like Black individuals, or white individuals for that matter, should be getting locked up for years for having cannabis . . . just the skewed amount of Black individuals versus white individuals who are getting arrested and incarcerated for marijuana and all that. I believe, I think it's closer to like three to one or four to one as far as like if you get arrested for having a tiny bit of cannabis on their person versus white people. . . . So that's one step we have taken in the right direction, but I feel like what we need to do is make it so it's not a race-based system and . . . it's based on the law, not who the people are who are breaking the law if that makes sense.

While agreeing with others about adding social workers to emergency response teams, Blake also raised the importance of reevaluating drug laws, particularly when they have been known to be unequally enforced depending on race. Using the state-level law change as an example emphasizes pursuing institutional change at local and state levels rather than federal as a more expedient path to addressing entrenched racial inequalities.

Understandably, the one (retired) state senator in the sample (Bill) stressed the importance of local-level action as well. Bill noted California already implemented the changes included in the George Floyd Policing Act (proposed federal legislation that never passed) a long time ago, as well as some other changes he deemed more progressive than the federal suggestions.

> Certainly, we've seen initiatives in Sacramento in the legislature. There's been a lot, even before the uprising—in criminal justice reform, of sentencing reform—we've had progressive majorities in both houses in Sacramento and Governor Brown and Governor Newsom, we've tried to—if not eliminate the death penalty, increase sanctions for police who engaged in excessive use of force. Creating more open records on police brutality and use of force. On the sentencing, eliminating life without possibility of parole for youth offenders who engage in a felony that can historically could get them sentenced to life without possibility of parole, now we have a guaranteed review after twenty years, for fifteen-, sixteen-,

seventeen-year-olds who are sentenced to life in prison, it can no longer be without possibility of parole. So lots of criminal justice reform in the state. I guess one objective would be to see the federal government, Congress, move forward on some of the progressive legislation that was filed in the wake of the George Floyd murder. And yet everything seems to be getting stalled in the Senate, at the national level, whether its budget or voting rights or police reform.

Creating new sentencing terms and guidelines, particularly in the case of death/life sentences and youth offenders, have been some substantial changes applauded at the state level here by Bill, a seventy-year-old white man who attended protests in Monterey and Sacramento, California. Bill was one of the few who also made suggestions outside the criminal justice system, but he recognized the dire need within this system also. Despite progress at the state level in California, Bill was frustrated that these goals could not become a priority at the federal level.

Nate, a twenty-eight-year-old African American man also in California, is the only person in the sample with prior law enforcement background. As an undergraduate, he was poised to go into law enforcement but instead departed that path, served in the Peace Corps, now pursuing a doctorate in psychology, and was quite passionate about the underserved mental health needs of African Americans. Nate had many suggestions for changes at various levels of the criminal justice system, from police all the way to attorneys.

> If you're ever talking with people that are trying to change something in the system ... don't be military or paramilitary because they're not invading a country there, this is their community, wherever they're working is their community. And I personally don't believe that law enforcement officers should be focused on shooting individuals or detaining folks. We have National Guard for a reason, now these other trained military personnel in inner cities, waiting to be deployed are being trained and things like that—we don't need that! We need people that are trained in mental health. We need that; I truly believe that it starts from their training. If you're gonna have law enforcement trained, make sure they're educated in mental health. It sucks, but maybe they need a master's in something or in social work or something. Yes, it sucks, but they're already paying California six figures to be a cop, just with a high school diploma. So biggest thing to advocate—I'm not going to do the whole defund-the-police stance or anything, but I will say that if you're going to be a law enforcement officer, or if we're going to move toward the future, they need to start looking for more rehabilitative practices.... Putting people in cages changes their psyche.... I've seen people that literally just got a traffic ticket put [next to] people that are rapists and murderers because they don't separate folks ... and they learn how to become something

> they weren't.... I'm not talking about the folks that kill folks, murder, and breaking things; I'm talking about people that they get caught with marijuana, or they were tough, they were a little troubled.... So I'm saying like we need to change the criminal justice system.... The mental health field needs to take over the system.... Even lawyers need to have some sort of mental health classes, training. Just because you have a law degree when you're a judge or lawyer doesn't mean that you are acting in the best professional way behind the scene. Yes, it's a lot, there's a lot to that, and I just wanted to say it at the end because I've just seen so much trauma from all for some officers who—they literally don't know what to do with people who are different cultures, who speak differently than they do, look differently than they do, or who have trauma. They come from high school, just six months of training to shoot a gun.... That's it.

Nate covered a lot of ground throughout many aspects of the justice system—first, policing. He critiqued paramilitary garb for creating an ominous presence rather than building community relationships. With his Peace Corps background, elsewhere in the interview he also shared how when they go into a community, they learn it; they find out who is who in the community and build relationships, which Nate felt was a model that policing could do well to adopt. Nate also echoed others above that more education for police officers is needed as well as mental health training. Prison reform is a subject rarely touched on among the sample, but Nate's humble Alabama beginnings meant that he knew quite a few people for whom prison had made things worse, anything but rehabilitative. One of his biggest critiques was that prison is a "caged" experience, which it certainly does not have to be if one examines other societies, and that it also groups very different people together with different offenses and different needs. Finally, perhaps the most interesting and unique of his suggestions is that both police officers and lawyers/judges need not only mental health training but also better ability to communicate across cultural differences. While the training of police is becoming more and more scrutinized publicly, not much has been made of law school bias training, if any. However, police just select initial charges; they don't determine sentencing. The legal system is a crucial step in the pathway to the prison crisis to which Nate also referred. So his comprehensive examination of the system is instructive. Nate attended over forty different uprising events in multiple locations throughout the state of California in a variety of capacities. So even though he was a "first time" protester millennial, he clearly did a deep dive into the experience, following up with attending city council meetings and other action-focused steps other than just marches and vigils. He truly sought lasting changes, not just marching with a sign. However, even he did not make it to mentioning changes needed in other institutions besides the criminal justice system when I asked him what the next steps were.

Several participants, Nate included, did mention experiences with racism they and their families had, both with police and other institutions—particularly protesters of color. Mostly, these experiences were mentioned near the beginning of the interview when I asked them about the various factors that motivated them to participate in the uprising despite the pandemic quarantine. Several African Americans mentioned racism they had faced in schools and workplaces. So I doubt these participants, if asked differently, would agree the criminal justice system is the only institution in need of change. The catalyst for the uprising was primarily the crisis of the justice system and policing in particular. Thus, it is certainly not surprising that when asked what needs to change and what needs to happen next, this area is where most people focused. Yet ideally, changes in the criminal justice system would happen in conjunction with related changes in other social institutions, a topic to which we now turn.

Level Three: Systemic-Level Change

The rarest pattern in this sample (ten out of thirty) were those who looked beyond the criminal justice system to other institutional changes needed in society. The direction of these answers varied greatly but included voting and political changes, schools/education, jobs/housing, and a broader moral/economic look at apology and reparations for slavery and continued white supremacy. As Amy August (2021, 8) notes, "Police violence, while the source of many reprehensible social pathologies, is also the symptom of a much more insidious and pervasive disease." Understanding police violence as but one symptom of the much larger problem of systemic racism sharpens one's analysis.

When asked what advice would they give to others wanting to get involved, several protesters advised against just jumping into a protest without having a larger plan of what they hope to accomplish. At the most basic level, it was getting involved with voting and elections. As Kelli, a forty-four-year-old African American woman in Richmond, Virginia, stated,

> Because again, really have a clear position of why you're doing what you're doing. Are you really trying to make sure . . . larger voices are heard? So while you're out there, that there's an action plan, that there is a process that you have the direct attention of the elected officials that can actually make this change. Just do you have a clear plan of action?

As a student protester decades ago, Kelli recalled how multicultural students proffered more resources and representation through making demands to the administration. Today, there is not always a clearly delineated process for the pathway between marching, making demands, and making sure "you have the direct attention of elected officials" when social media channels have proliferated and no one is watching the same things. Kelli noted much changed since her earlier protesting days, including her fascination with how you can now order "protest kits" online. While certain key information and supplies are at people's fingertips in a way like never before, in other ways Kelli found the information flow challenging. She emphasized that protest should have a clear connection to action, including having the ears of elected officials.

Likewise, Jane, a thirty-one-year-old white woman protesting in Norfolk, Virginia, even though it was her first time participating in such an event, recognized the importance of making sure protest was not the last stand, staying directly connected to what happens in the ballot box. Jane was also self-critical that she believed she could do more.

> I guess I accomplished a goal in that I added to the numbers for the city of Norfolk for the demonstrations, if everybody had made the decision to stay home and we wouldn't have had a demonstration—like you said about voting, it takes everybody. And as far as after that, I probably could have attended more or looked into the reforms that my city and other cities had into place. . . . I guess I could have thought critically about specific changes to be made to ensure that this kind of thing doesn't happen as often or anymore. I didn't want to be just a bystander . . . protesting with them; that's not right. Maybe attend local meetings, I made it a point to participate in local elections. . . . I do admit that in the past, the presidential election is the only one, I think a lot of people think, but there's one coming up on November 2 through the gubernatorial election, absolutely the voting. And so even your small grassroots, all the way down to the grassroots, little, tiny organizations that you're allowed to have an opinion about, that's where it starts.

Elsewhere in the interview, Jane drew on her criminal justice background from college to explain how prosecutorial and judicial discretion is a huge problem, making decisions easily swayed by personal biases. She said "use of force" by police is typified by the same slippery standard of review. Jane echoed others that local-level government was the more successful place to start for making criminal justice reform at the ballot box.

Helen, a forty-four-year-old African American woman in Williamsburg, Virginia, got involved in voter registration drives as part of her uprising participation, so she was equally as passionate about the role of the electoral process in making change. As a schoolteacher and a mother, she also stressed youth involvement and addressing problems of racism in the schools.

> I know in this area, there were some WJCC [school district name] students that participated, but also took it a little bit further and try to engage with the school board to address the biases and the issues that they are seeing within education. . . . [Daughter name] did get together with a group of other students, I think there were maybe five of them, mostly minorities not think [daughter name] may have been the only Black student who started talking about things that they saw in their own school. And who met with the principals with administration and started having those ongoing conversations about microaggressions, things that I didn't even know happened, even though I'm there and it's there was a survey that was done students responded with their experiences, but to have that dialogue about what happens where African Americans and minorities are treated and things are done one way versus their counterparts, how the curriculum caters to only one aspect and even when you look at the advanced courses when you're looking at things such as [program within the high school]. You see certain things there and the way things are done that need to change, so they started those conversations. Are those conversations going to go anywhere? We don't know. But it does show that there is more work that needs to be done because we do know that that school-to-prison pipeline, it's a real thing. What the connection between the education and changing what's happening in America and changing policing, changing laws like that conversation I think was made more apparent and given life because of the demonstrations and the protests of 2020.

Helen's daughter faced microaggressions that she did not even know about as a teacher working in the same high school where her daughter was a student. In mentioning the curriculum, and the school-to-prison pipeline, Helen was one of the few to make the connection between the education system and the criminal justice system during her interview. Like many in the sample, Helen questioned whether any of this would actually happen. However, she credited the uprising with at least starting more movement on these problems than previously had taken place. She also felt hopeful about youth driving change. She said kids "should have the opportunity to talk to their school board leaders, the people in their districts that are supposed to represent them. They don't have that. . . . We need representation; they need voices." A repeated theme was that elected officials should be more responsive to the needs of the community they represent, just as citizens need to be more involved at the local level holding representatives accountable.

Janay, a twenty-eight-year-old African American woman in Atlanta, Georgia, was a first-time protester in 2020, but she jumped in with a fervor, attending fourteen different events, and her prognosis was that racial injustices are linked to a myriad of other social issues, traceable back to the political landscape writ large.

> I don't know where you start in fixing all the injustice. I think that a lot of people's eyes are open to what's injustice and . . . people are now willing to listen, but I think there needs to be changes, all the way from the top down. . . . We knew Trump was the worst choice for president, at least in my opinion, so I think, starting from the top down, we need to figure out when it comes with the House the Senate and things of that nature. I personally believe there's going to be a certain age cutoff like you can't be seventy, eighty almost another generation of our another century, and you're making laws for people that are twenty, thirty years old. . . . Now, do I think people who are twenty years old need to be in office? No, because I also feel like they're [inaudible] too. But I think there needs to be some balance that we need to find as a country. To get us all start to understand each other, and I think that we're making those steps, but I think that also, at the same time, we can't give up on making those steps. And how we go about making those steps? I'm personally not in government and not being a big government person, so I don't really know exactly how, but I think that there needs to be ways that we do bring in the demographic that is more of what is in right now. . . . The fact of like rumors were like we're going to lose gay marriage or women are going to be not able to have abortions in Texas like there's just such a wide spectrum of things, and I think that as a country, we got to figure out a way to get onto one page.

As with some other younger participants, sometimes they were not altogether sure on all the answers. However, Janay understood that the work of reform was beyond the justice system alone. Her concern extended to women's rights, gay rights, and especially the fact that many of the nation's leaders are a different generation altogether from a large segment of the population. As a young adult in her twenties, she is onto something here, that the politicians have not caught up with their generation's views on many of these social and political issues. For instance, a Guardian poll in 2020 revealed that a majority of Americans agreed "racism is a serious problem," but the proportion of those agreeing decreased with age—68 percent of thirty-five- to fifty-four-year-olds agree, 69 percent of adults over fifty-five agreed, but among younger adults, the agreement climbs to 80 percent of Americans recognizing racism as a serious problem (Smith 2020). Likewise, on the other issues Janay mentions—support for abortion climbs to 67 percent in the under-thirty age group, whereas it is only in the 53–55 percent range for the older age groups of Americans (Pew Research 2021). With gay marriage, similarly the support decreases with age—60 percent of older adults, 72 percent of middle-aged adults, but up to 84 percent of young adults support same-sex marriage rights (McCarthy 2021). It is easy to see, then, why Janay and other members of her generation who were leaders of the uprising would be impatient and frustrated with politicians still debating rights that from their perspective should not even be a matter of debate.

Nicole, another African American woman in her twenties who protested in Washington, D.C., but was also active in her local Virginia community at BLM protests of 2015, also painted with a broad brush all the various social and political issues that she felt went hand in hand.

> We're talking about protesting... but protesting has only gotten so far.... Okay, we're not, they weren't slaves. Okay, but then they weren't like sharecroppers—was even worse because now you're working for a fraction of the money that you deserve, but then you have to pay that money back to the owner of the farm, so it's like you're a slave, but they're made you think like [you're free, but] you're not honestly. Then after that, we have the Jim Crow South where it was supposed to be separate but equal, but it really wasn't. So we protest it all of this, and okay, now we're going to integrate, but then white people are moving out to the suburbs, so they're taking the stuff with them that make the area better. So, yes, you're integrating with somebody... [when] the great stuff is really out in the suburbs. ... Now you can get, we have affirmative action. Okay, but you're picking only a select few of Black people. It's just like over the years, yes, progress is made, but then, when you really look at it, it's like another form of discrimination that is blocking. Like we still have places that Blacks really aren't heavily populated in neighborhoods. You still have racism when it comes to trying to buy houses and get mortgages, APR loans or sometimes hire for Black people within their [network]... which doesn't help that people in the housing developments and you have a school system, if you really want to get the senior charter schools, it's like you mostly had to do private, and then when they get into private schools, they are not surrounded by people that look like them, which then in turn it hinders them because you have to fit in with the white society, but then, when you go home you feel ostracized.

Nicole here outlined the illusion of racial progress—political concessions that might have seemed like victories just had other problems of its own—"when you really look at it it's like another form of discrimination." Importantly, she goes well beyond the criminal justice system to examining the basis of economics, jobs, housing, and schools. (The discussion also goes on much longer than this excerpt provides.) Like many others, she feels protesting is only a small part of building the movement for justice and equality. Nicole is quoted in the previous section highlighting how computerized bias trainings for police do not get to the heart of the issues. In short, she has a lack of confidence in small policy changes that are billed as reform but end up just perpetuating the same inequalities in new ways. Taken together, Nicole's interview quotes illustrate that housing segregation, in particular, impedes progress and equality in both structural and interactional ways. The housing segregation is a resource issue due to lack of equal access to resources (jobs, schools, etc.), but then it is also a causal factor behind the lack of extensive cross-racial interactions that could reduce prejudices between groups. In other words, in the scenarios that Nicole described, whites are walking away with the greater resources, but they are also walking away with severe misperceptions about the groups outside of themselves, while they also have the power to act on those misperceptions in damaging and even deadly ways. Whites' unjust enrichment has dire consequences in the lives of people of color (Feagin 2020).

A mix of first-time and veteran protesters implicated residential segregation as part of the problem. Sharon, a thirty-nine-year-old Black/Panamanian woman in Williamsburg, Virginia, who was new to protesting but like Janay became very regularly involved in the summer, noted the segregation of her community.

> I feel like there's so much potential in Williamsburg, but Williamsburg is just so willingly segregated ... in terms of income and color. And willingly so this isn't like a unwilling segregation.... Like areas where I came from are rare because I'm friends with whites, Blacks, Mexicans like that you're friends with everybody, you have an understanding of different cultures, just because you grew up with those cultures.

Earlier in the interview, Sharon explained that her motivation for getting involved in the racial justice movement relatively late in life was that she lived in a racially integrated community in New Jersey where she did not perceive problems related to race at that time. So she was surprised to migrate to a new area of the country and find more segregation than she had experienced previously. Notice she described the segregation in several ways: segregation "of mind," which gets at the interactional part of the equation, as well as the fact that it is a "willing" segregation. Although she identified several areas of the criminal justice system that needed work, she also knew this was not the only institution to shoulder the burden of addressing racism in the community.

Likewise, Rev. Lane, a thirty-eight-year-old white woman in Rochester, New York, described many changes needed in criminal justice and law enforcement but also broadened the conversation to other components of society, particularly within her own community. None of the clergy I interviewed were new to protesting, and Lane was no exception. Lane credited earlier mobilizing in the years leading up to 2020 as making the uprising possible. While she was passionate about officer accountability and a civilian oversight board that would include subpoena power, she also was one of few to articulate how "defund the police" meant not only supplementing public safety calls with social workers but also investing the money from the public budget into other aspects of the community in meaningful ways.

> Abolition of the police, more jobs, more—certainly, more programs, more support for our community—those would be the things for me that would be the big-picture pieces. In Rochester especially, any sort of a plan to address childhood poverty would be amazing—we're in the top five in the country for childhood poverty. In the city, our school system is horrible—I'd like to see that addressed. These pieces, that if we were to not be funding this huge multibillion-dollar enterprise of the Rochester Police Department, it would just be amazing what we could try and put towards other things.

Like Helen and Nicole, Rev. Lane uplifted the importance of schools and the youth. She also emphasized there is a finite amount of resources, so the proportion of the city budget that is allocated to the police as opposed to other institutions speaks volumes about what is valued and prioritized.

My study suggests that more long-term involvement in protest increases the likelihood that participants see the bigger picture of social changes necessary to arrive at the movement's desired goals. Keep in mind, Rev. Lane quoted above was not as much a "marcher" in 2020 as she had been in prior years, but she was at the helm of a church that was providing sanctuary to marchers in various ways. This role kept her aware of a variety of occurrences that happened during the uprising: having to bail out the medic from a remote jurisdiction when the action was downtown, seeing white supremacists attack and vandalize church property, and hearing of journalists with press badges who were forced out of police union meetings. As a marcher in the middle of a crowd, one would presumably be less aware of these occurrences and therefore perhaps less privy to the conversations that occur beyond signs and slogans, to managing the logistics of dealing with the various institutions, when it comes to securing bail for congregants, filing police reports for damages, and monitoring ongoing negotiations between the police and the city that funds them.

It was indeed the slightly older protesters who had been around the proverbial block a few times who had the most vision connecting the bigger picture. Bill, a seventy-year-old white man and retired state senator in California, had been involved with racial justice since the 1960s when as a Berkeley law student he helped work on the case of the San Quentin Five. He was a white ally to the Black Panthers in the Bay Area from an early age. So he deeply understood that the problem was not to be simply solved by antibias training for police officers alone. In the previous section, he mentioned state-level reforms in California—ending the death penalty, increasing penalties for police use of force, and so on. Yet he ultimately framed this as much beyond the justice system.

> But you have to look in a broader historical perspective to the disenfranchisement of people of color in this country and globally. And the time of reckoning is way overdue, and I guess, I would just close with—I think it's been raised, but one of the most successful experiments in my lifetime, it was the end of the apartheid movement in South Africa and the use of Truth and Reconciliation Commissions to bring victims face-to-face with their oppressors. There's a woman professor at Sac[ramento] State who's on a board of an organization we serve together called Global Majority. Her husband and nine-year-old son were executed in front of her by South African police to terrorize her. She was the family member in the ANC [African National Congress], and through, she says, Nelson Mandela and Bishop [Desmond] Tutu, she participated in Truth and Reconciliation face the killers of her husband and her son and was able to share with them what they had taken from her and guarantee that they would shoulder a burden, as she would, for the rest of her life. And we've never had that in the United States since the legal abolition of slavery in the continued Jim Crow of our justice system and our economy. We need political leadership in Washington and in communities that will convene what may feel like uncomfortable opportunities for people to share their stories in their histories. It's long overdue, and I don't see the healing taking place until there's some conscious commitment to truth and reconciliation in the U.S.

Bill emphasized we may need to look globally, outside the United States, for alternative models of how to face a nation's history that has been built on racist exploitation since its founding.

Likewise, Hood Scholar, a thirty-eight-year-old African American man who participated in community organizing with his mother since his youth in Richmond, Virginia, and who traveled to both Ferguson, Missouri, in 2015 and Minneapolis in 2020 to offer his direct organizing skills to the movement, made the global connection. He holds a leadership role in an international Black freedom organization, and he asserted that "Black Lives Matter," which he had previously lent his support to, now seems too small of a slogan to contain all that needs to happen.

> The movement, the Black freedom movement which we are calling it teaching against the Black lives matter because isn't that we were out there in news call that's Black lives matter but we aren't Black lives matter . . . for the historic moment, are we are still working towards the Black freedom. Yes, let's learn things that we can use towards the movement. Yes, we learned a lot from that we learned some things, then it's time to do this, let's do that. Also, it gave us some things that we need because actually we planted some, like trainings and stuff and games from the things we need to train other members in our other chapters of the organization. So I guess, to answer your question, we didn't have any other immediate objectives . . . like we want to be able to meet this goal or anything like that, but it gave us the things we need for the movement, freedom movement for Black people to get free, which is connected to the larger movement way back with our ancestors.

Hood Scholar viewed the uprising as just a tiny moment in a much larger trajectory of growing, learning, and expanding the global Black freedom movement. Not unlike several of the broadest thinkers in this category, he has worn many hats in his lifelong journey in the movement—he is an ordained minister with a master's in divinity, a military veteran, and a PhD in American studies who wrote his dissertation on the dispossession of African Americans from their land. He even founded a Black Lives Matter chapter in the earlier days of the movement. Such experiences appear to allow marchers to see the bigger picture.

Rev. David, a white forty-eight-year-old man participating in Louisville, Kentucky, also was not new to racial justice demonstrations and similarly wore various hats over the years, occupying a variety of roles in the years of movement building. He did racial justice work in the past in Galveston, Texas, in Chicago, in Baltimore with the killing of Freddie Gray, and in New York with the killing of Eric Garner, among others. Also, in his role as a U.S. Army Reserve chaplain, he mentioned that being a federal officer was a helpful supportive role during protests to help bail out protesters when they get arrested. Yet in Louisville, his role was to support congregations who were attempting to provide sanctuary to protesters, but LMPD were violating their rights to do so. He arrived on-site to defend the congregations from these attacks (as described in more detail in chapter 3). Although his continued affiliation as a federal officer seemed to limit him somewhat in how radical of a position he could take with respect to the "defund the police" debate, he mentioned that even though he was "not solidly" all the way in the "abolition camp," he was "not far off." He saw it as far broader of a struggle than just criminal justice.

> This is not just about police accountability and it's not about police not doing things properly or following procedure; it's about systemic racism within the country, built in a country that was built on chattel slavery. And the biggest change we need is a national reckoning with the fact that we've never healed from being enslavers. And from our country's institutions being built by indenture—by chattel slavery. And until we find a way to heal around that, until we find a way to acknowledge it, and do reparations and heal around that, then we're still going to be in the position where people thinking they're doing the right thing, because it's what the culture has taught them—misuse the power and force they have that they have access to, to continue that white supremacy culture, to continue and defend that white supremacy culture. And that change, that's the deeper work; that's why I'm a minister, not a lawyer, because I think that change is religious in nature more than it is legal and policy in nature itself—our deepest values and beliefs and understanding of who we are.

Simple procedural changes within law enforcement cannot alone address a nation's systemic racism problem. Rev. David called for a "national reckoning" that is more of a moral imperative than a legal one. He and Bill were the only two in the entire sample to mention reparations at all—the policy solution suggested by Nikole Hannah-Jones at the opening of this chapter, a social change that encompasses both legal and moral aspects. Such refocus of the conversation on reparations emphasizes where the money is invested rather than from whom it is taken away (e.g., "defund the police"). Whereas "defund the police" is a new slogan, the reparations bill has been introduced every year but never passed since 1989, despite the only thing the bill does is establish a commission to examine the possibility of reparations (Freking 2021). Rev. David stressed that "white supremacy culture" has a long history, and the treatment that people were protesting, all over the globe, is much bigger than just what bias trainings or even sweeping criminal justice reform alone can undo. Seeing the bigger picture, while not as common among the interviews, broadens one's perspective—and not commonly expressed by one-time, first-time marchers. Nonetheless, the only way to begin is to start, and everyone must start somewhere. This uprising was most assuredly building the next generation of freedom fighters to take up this ongoing charge.

Moving Forward from Disparate Launch Points

Uprising participants held many goals, from micro to macro and beyond. They marched shoulder to shoulder all the while having divergent understandings of the problems as well as the root causes. They mobilized in many different cities, towns, and neighborhoods—not all of them even marched necessarily. They created art, they held each other as they grieved, they toppled monuments, and they dodged attacks from law enforcement officers as well as white supremacists and other militia. They live streamed video content for those who could not leave their homes during a global pandemic with no vaccine yet in sight. Their days, weeks, and even months of steadily showing up caused such a stir that the world could not help but begin to pay attention, even those who had never before acknowledged that racism was a serious problem. However, such a consistently disruptive effort is not ultimately sustainable for the long haul. Grassroots mobilization eventually transitions into policy change if it is to be successful. Interviewed about one year after their participation, most were either cautiously optimistic, neutral, or downright pessimistic about how much change had taken place due to their hard work.

Most participants evaluated their short-term micro goals as relatively more successful than their institutional visions for eradicating racism on a broader scale. For example, those who said they wanted to add to the crowd numbers, stand up and not be silent, show opposition to unjust police killings, support grieving families, raise awareness, and be together with others who felt the same as they did felt that they had accomplished what they set out to do. Parents who participated felt they created teachable and enriching moments for their children, instilling a sense of social justice and standing up for themselves and each other. Participants of color in particular felt they were able to stand in solidarity with each other, and they found such goals to be more realistic and achievable than the idea of completely ending racist police violence, which many felt had always been part of history and thus probably always would be. In other words, the younger generation just saw themselves as advancing the same struggle their parents, grandparents, and ancestors had fought. Basically, they perceived they were holding tight to not retreat from what little progress had been made as well as just fighting for survival. As mentioned in chapter 4, their positions often mirrored a critical race theory perspective, the permanence of racism (Bell 1993). White participants felt they were learning how to be better allies as well as modeling for other whites best practices (i.e., not taking over or trying to become leaders/voices of the movement). The white interviewees strove to differentiate themselves from other whites who may only have been there because so many other social gatherings were closed or canceled but were not seeking to make long-term commitments to antiracism ("performative allies"). In contrast to these "fair weather friends," those whites interviewed one year later were attempting to continue their work in various ways, some more small scale than others. Others were longer term activists for whom 2020 was just a continuation of what they had already been working on. The longer term racial justice warriors were more likely to advocate for social changes beyond the criminal justice system as well.

There is evidence well beyond this study that there were plenty of "fringe participants" in the 2020 uprisings—not doing racial justice work before the uprisings or continuing the work afterward. In their national survey study conducted in 2020, Gause and Arora (2021) estimated about 20 percent of the uprising participants attended for reasons not related to Black Lives Matter. When listing their grievances, they were more related to dissatisfaction with government's handling of the coronavirus pandemic or general human rights concerns such as labor and health care. Whites and Republicans were the two groups most likely to be there for non-BLM reasons. But "even among Black, Democratic and independent protesters, 15 to 17 percent say they attended for reasons not aligned with BLM goals" (Gause and Arora 2021). Yet, even if they were not all there for the same reasons, the fact that they at least showed up added to the totals, which likely influenced political outcomes such as the November 2020 presidential (and other) elections. In another article about this research, Arora states, "Even those who express support for the movement do not necessarily agree with the larger policy or structural goals of the movement" (O'Brien 2021). They may not have agreed with defunding the police or reparations, but their presence added to a public perception that this was a problem urgently in need of addressing right away. There was a temporary interest convergence that dissipated once a new U.S. president (Joe Biden), who at least appeared to care and empathize, arrived on the scene as the world was watching. Even as those not new to the movement understood, Biden attending the funeral of George Floyd was certainly more than Donald Trump would have done, but for changes beyond such "optics," neither leader would ultimately deliver.

In the uprising aftermath, many symbolic changes occurred. Notably, most of the successful social changes that could be chalked up to the 2020 uprisings were not mentioned by participants in this study when asked what needs to happen next. For example, no one in this study mentioned that Confederate monuments needed to come down, but many were toppled in 2020, more than ever before (Perhamus and Joldersma 2020). Likewise, no one mentioned they wanted to see more "diversity, equity, and inclusion" job positions expand fivefold in 2020, but that is exactly what happened (Goldberg 2022), likely in response to the uprising. No one mentioned getting rid of characters like Washington Redskin and Aunt Jemima, though certainly these were welcome antiracist changes and long overdue. Recall Native American respondent Jim Bear dates his very first protest activity back to a Super Bowl in 1992 in Minneapolis when the Washington team played there. It is not the case that these are undesirable changes, unwanted, or unwelcomed, but rather, they were not the central objective. Some cultural shifts began to occur, but legal and structural changes were slow in coming.

As Keeanga-Yamahtta Taylor (2021) noted in the New Yorker, "True to their sensibilities, elected officials quickly tugged the low-hanging fruit of symbolic transformation." One such example was the cultural symbol of making Juneteenth a federal holiday. It was a nod to the legacy of chattel slavery that shaped the enduring systemic racism experienced in the United States and beyond, as well as a tribute to the courage and sacrifices made by those who fought the long struggle to emancipation. But passing a bill for a holiday would be far easier to accomplish politically than legislation with palpable consequences for people's lives. Citing a barrage of public opinion statistics, though, Taylor makes the case for some indirect effects that could potentially influence public policy shifts—namely, changes in people's willingness to acknowledge systemic racism's lingering impact, and even some widespread agreement on the fact that some public safety calls are better handled by social workers than police. It was not even substantial legal/structural change yet, but the mere potential for such cross-racial solidarity in public opinion on these basic matters of human rights was already enough to prompt an ongoing backlash to what little progress there was.

What structural changes, if any, resulted from the 2020 uprisings? There was a guilty verdict for Derek Chauvin in the murder of George Floyd. After I completed the interviews for the present study, this Chauvin verdict was followed by not only a guilty verdict for Officer Kimberly Potter in the death of Daunte Wright (Bogel-Burroughs 2022) but also guilty verdicts for the three killers of Ahmaud Arbery, plus federal hate crime charges in which the three were also found guilty (McCausland 2022). As some noted, even getting charges, much less a trial, much less a guilty verdict, were all small victories that community organizers were not accustomed to seeing in most related cases before this point. The 2020 uprisings likely contributed to this changing pattern. Yet these are individual cases, and many more go unprosecuted. More to the point, none of these legal resolutions of cases eliminate the tragedy or bring the slain person back to life. These verdicts are but paltry consolations, and much more is required in pursuit of equality—namely, reorganization of structures, services, and resources, reprioritizing whose lives matter most. Not as much swift condemnation when things go wrong but proactive policies and procedures to ensure things go right. This requires broader, large-scale societal change than a single verdict here and there.

Why can ambitions for social justice sometimes shrink to not far beyond the landscape of what is offered or seems permissible? Accountability for bad apple officers does not seem like much if the cases keep happening much more than what even makes the news. Social behavioral exchange theorists like George Homans posit the satiation-deprivation principle, that a reward is no longer valuable to someone if they get it all the time (Appelrouth and Edles 2015). So the reverse should also be true—that if a basic reward hardly ever comes, then it may seem outsized in its importance when it finally is given. And simple justice after someone's death should be considered a given anyway, not a reward or even a concession. Oppressors can count on being able to control effectively a population if they so sparsely hand out what's justly due that when they finally do extend the basic human right, it seems like a victory. Activists become stuck fighting on the lower end of Maslow's hierarchy of needs (survival) instead of boldly visioning a society organized more equitably. This type of long-scope vision extends beyond the tiny "wins" but can be hard to hold on to when wallowing in the mire of the everyday grind of the movement work. Much like capitalists that depend on exploitation wearing down workers (whose labor is expended providing for basic needs) rendering them too burned out to organize for better pay and benefits, so too white supremacist structure of society has whittled down those fighting for justice and perhaps constricted some to a more myopic vision of the problems. There are even journalists writing about "activism fatigue" (Kramer 2017) and "social justice fatigue" (Arteaga 2020), comparing it to the literature on job or career burnout, offering tips for self-care and other ways to recharge. Of course, these pieces place the onus on the individual and not the system that created the necessity of having to fight for these basic rights.

Longtime advocate for abolition of prisons, scholar-activist Angela Davis reminded readers in 2020 that today's calls for more humane policing were not unlike earlier calls for a more humane slavery. Reform of an existing institution that basically retains the current institution with a few tweaks is likely not to eliminate the ongoing problems. A. Davis (2020) wrote, "Abolitionist approaches ask us to enlarge our field of vision so that rather than focusing myopically on the problematic institution and asking what needs to be changed about that institution, we raise radical questions about the organization of the larger society." In other words, "defund the police" is not about the police—it is about visioning new possibilities for all the other institutions of society. "Such new possibilities would include rewarding jobs, critical education, decent housing, accessible health care, recreation, and art for all" (A. Davis 2020). Recall that several participants, when asked what needed to happen next, included a caveat, something like, "I won't go as far as saying defund the police, but . . . " And then after their "but," they went on to articulate new visions for the organization of society that cared for mental health needs, that treated all humans with respect, that skillfully deescalated conflicts without use of violence. Activists have clearly been shamed as unpatriotic for boldly articulating new visions and thus have been conditioned to camouflage their ideas into what they perceive as more socially acceptable language and presentations. This ultimately cuts short the vision of what is possible.

But one cannot solely fault 2020 uprising participants for scaling back their ambitions, when such stringent and vocal backlashes to racial progress began with a vengeance the moment any concessions to racial justice began. From the January 6, 2021, white supremacists making an attack on the U.S. Capitol to the local and state laws banning any sort of teaching of race or African American history, to the U.S. Supreme Court cases in 2023 ending race-conscious admissions, the counterattack to the 2020 racial justice uprisings was swift and mighty. In the corporate world, citing the work of sociologist Adia Harvey Wingfield and others, analyst Kimberly Adams (2023) finds "companies these days are a lot quieter about social justice issues than they were in 2020, which is exactly what many expected: public support, then backlash, then retreat." Among nonprofits, the post-2020 outlook was equally dismal—as the Philanthropic Initiative for Racial Equity reported, far more grants were pledged than granted to racial justice efforts (Tomkin 2021). As interest convergence theory predicted, these pledges for racial justice were largely symbolic, often never materialized or else quickly retreated. Brennan Center for Justice's Theodore Johnson (2021) echoed this assessment when he stated in his book When the Stars Began to Fall that the backlash was highly predictable and that unless/until moral issues are attached to national interests, racial justice as a moral imperative will not gain traction for long.

Most of these uprising participants understood that 2020 was a unique moment in history, like none seen in their own lifetimes and thus probably not likely seen again in the near future. For these and other reasons, they wanted to make sure they were a part of this antiracist racial project. In his analysis of earlier periods of radical social transformation, both national and global, Gal Beckerman (2022) wrote that activists "need spaces to come together in the quiet when revolutions are only impassioned conversations among the aggrieved and dreaming. Because without those spaces, we risk a future in which the possibility of new realities will remain just beyond our grasp." It is true, as one respondent put it, that many of the foot soldiers in the 2020 uprising may have now "taken down their black squares," no longer quite as vocal as they once were about ending racism. There may not be the same level of marching in the streets, but this type of surge is ultimately unsustainable for the long haul, and other work is happening that may be quieter but could potentially be transformative, nonetheless. From their various vantage points, my hope is that they are pushing forward in new ways—ways that don't shrink from the thought of "what they will let us accomplish" and instead reflect what they dream of accomplishing. They made history, and now it is time to make sure their work was not in vain.

APPENDIX

Uprising Participants

	Pseudonym (* if real)	Location of Protest	Age	Gender Pronoun	Racial Identity	First Time Protest?	Interview Date	# **
1	Carly	Columbus, Ohio	49	She/her/F	White	No	5/21/21	3
2	Helen	Williamsburg, Va.	44	She/her/F	Black/African	No	5/27/21	7
3	Monica	Tampa, Fla.	33	She/her/F	White	Yes	6/4/21	1
4	Kelli*	Richmond, Va.	45	She/her/F	Black/African	No	7/8/21	3
5	Hood Scholar	Minneapolis, Minn.	38	He/him/M	Black/African	No	6/4/21	7+
6	Jordan	Atlanta, Ga.	26	He/him/M	Black/mixed	Yes	7/14/21	1
7	Faith	Williamsburg, Va.	18	She/her/F	Black/white	No	8/3/21	8
8	Blake	Williamsburg, Va.	21	He/him/M	White	Yes	8/4/21	15
9	Sharon	Williamsburg, Va.	39	She/her/F	Black/Panamanian	Yes	8/4/21	20+
10	William	Rutherford County, N.C.	53	He/him/M	White	No	9/3/21	2
11	Janay*	Atlanta, Ga.	28	She/her/F	Black/African	Yes	9/23/21	14
12	Michelle*	Dallas, Tex.	24	She/her/F	White	Yes	9/25/21	3
13	Sally	Louisville, Ky.	36	She/her/F	White	Yes	9/27/21	7
14	Beth	Louisville, Ky.	34	She/her/F	White	Yes	9/28/21	3
15	Nicole	Washington, D.C.	27	She/her/F	Black/African	No	9/30/21	1
16	Charles*	Columbus, Ohio	36	He/him/M	Black/African	Yes	10/2/21	1
17	RJ	Washington, D.C.	29	He/him/M	Black/African	Yes	10/8/21	1
18	Tucker	Columbia, Md.	29	He/him/M	Black/African	Yes	10/8/21	1

	Pseudonym (* if real)	Location of Protest	Age	Gender Pronoun	Racial Identity	First Time Protest?	Interview Date	# **
19	Patrice	Detroit & Troy, Mich.	22	She/her/F	Black/white	No	10/9/21	2
20	Isabel	Denver & Aurora, Col.	23	She/her/F	White	No	10/10/21	7
21	Jane	Norfolk, Va.	31	She/her/F	White	Yes	10/13/21	1
22	Abby	Nashville, Tenn.	18	She/her/F	White	No	10/15/21	2
23	Rabbi M*	Minneapolis, Minn.	51	He/him/M	White	No	12/7/21	20+
24	Rev. TM*	Minneapolis, Minn.	53	He/they/M	White	No	12/9/21	35+
25	Jim Bear*	Minneapolis, Minn.	44	He/him/M	Native American	No	12/10/21	30+
26	Justin*	Minneapolis, Minn.	56	He/him/M	White	No	12/15/21	15
27	Rev. David*	Louisville, Ky.	48	He/him/M	White	No	12/15/21	2
28	Nate*	Monterey, Ca.	28	He/him/M	Black/African	Yes	12/19/21	45
29	Bill*	Monterey & Sacramento, Ca.	70	He/him/M	White	No	12/20/21	3
30	Rev. Lane*	Rochester, N.Y.	38	She/her/F	White	No	12/21/21	3

*** *number of protests attended in 2020*

REFERENCES

Adams, Kimberly. 2023. "Businesses Are Quieter on Social Justice Issues as Support for Black Lives Matter Dips." Marketplace, June 20. Retrieved on December 29, 2023 at https://www.marketplace.org/2023/06/20/businesses-social-justice-black-lives-matter-support/.

Alcindor, Yamiche. 2020. "What's in the Justice in Policing Act?" *PBS News*, June 12. Retrieved on February 1, 2022 at https://www.pbs.org/newshour/politics/whats-in-the-justice-in-policing-act.

Ali, Kecia, Julia Watts Belser, Grace Y. Kao, and Shively T. J. Smith. 2020. "Living It Out: Feminism during COVID-19: Full Catastrophe Mentoring: A Conversation." *Journal of Feminist Studies in Religion* 36:107–116.

Andone, Dakin, and Chuck Johnston. 2017. "Report on Charlottesville Rally Faults Police over Planning, Failure to Protect Public." *CNN News*, December 2. Retrieved on December 1, 2021 at https://www.cnn.com/2017/12/01/us/charlottesville-riots-failures-review/index.html.

Appelrouth, Scott, and Laura D. Edles. 2015. *Classical and Contemporary Sociological Theory: Text and Readings*. 3rd ed. Thousand Oaks, Ca.: Sage.

Arteaga, Noelia. 2020. "Overcoming Activism Fatigue." *Stanford Daily*, July 23. Retrieved on March 2, 2022 at https://stanforddaily.com/2020/07/23/overcoming-activism-fatigue/.

Associated Press. 2021. "Key Events since George Floyd's Arrest and Death." *Associated Press*, June 25. Retrieved on May 18, 2022 at https://apnews.com/article/derek-chauvin-trial-timeline-ad67932d2bf727dd4c23e17e63a97224.

August, Amy. 2021. "Coloring in the Progressive Illusion: An Introduction to Racial Dynamics in Minnesota." In *Sparked: George Floyd, Racism, and the Progressive Illusion*, edited by Walter R. Jacobs, Wendy Thompson Talwo, and Amy August, 1–14. Saint Paul: Minnesota Historical Society Press.

Barton, Ryland. 2021. "Louisville Cleans Out 'Breonna's Square' Again." *89.3 WFPL News*, February 8. Retrieved on March 23, 2022 at https://wfpl.org/louisville-cleans-out-breonnas-square-again/.

BBC. 2016. "Philando Castile and Alton Sterling—Latest U.S. Police Shooting Black Victims." BBC, July 7. Retrieved on May 21, 2022 at https://www.bbc.com/news/world-us-canada-36733673.

BBC. 2021. "George Floyd: Timeline of Black Deaths and Protests." *BBC*, April 22, 2021. Retrieved on May 21, 2022 at https://www.bbc.com/news/world-us-canada-52905408.

Bebernes, Mike. 2020. "Why Was George Floyd's Death the Breaking Point?" *Yahoo News*, June 7. Retrieved on April 26, 2022 at https://news.yahoo.com/why-was-george-floyds-death-the-breaking-point-143440621.html.

Beckerman, Gal. 2022. "Radical Ideas Need Quiet Spaces." *New York Times*, February 10. Retrieved on March 2, 2022 at https://www.nytimes.com/2022/02/10/opinion/radical-ideas-need-quiet-spaces.html.

Beer, Tommy. 2021. "Trump Called BLM Protesters 'Thugs' but Capitol-Storming Supporters 'Very Special.'" *Forbes*, January 6. Retrieved on December 1, 2021 at https://www.forbes.com/sites/tommybeer/2021/01/06/trump-called-blm-protesters-thugs-but-capitol-storming-supporters-very-special/?sh=7f4adc163465.

Bell, Derrick. 1980. "*Brown v. Board of Education* and the Interest-Convergence Dilemma." *Harvard Law Review* 93:518–583.

———. 1993. *Faces at the Bottom of the Well: The Permanence of Racism*. New York: Basic Books.

Berg, Bruce L., and Howard Lune. 2012. *Qualitative Research Methods for the Social Sciences*. Upper Saddle River, N.J.: Pearson.

Bidgood, Jess. 2021. "In Harm's Way: The Car Becomes the Weapon." *Boston Globe*, October 21. Retrieved on March 16, 2022 at https://apps.bostonglobe.com/news/nation/2021/10/vehicle-rammings-against-protesters/tulsa/.

Black Lives Matter Global Network. 2022. "BLM Demands." Retrieved on February 2, 2022 at https://blacklivesmatter.com/blm-demands/.

Blades, Lincoln Anthony. 2016. "Philando Castile Killed by Police while Girlfriend Records on Facebook Live." *Teen Vogue*, July 7. Retrieved on May 21, 2022 at https://www.teenvogue.com/story/philando-castile-shooting-death-police-facebook-live-lavish-reynolds-falcon-heights.

Bloom, Mia. 2020. "Vehicle Ramming: The Evolution of a Terrorist Tactic inside the US." *Just Security*, July 16. Retrieved on August 24, 2024 at https://www.justsecurity.org/71431/vehicle-ramming-the-evolution-of-a-terrorist-tactic-inside-the-us/.

Bogel-Burroughs, Nicholas. 2022. "Kim Potter Sentenced to 2 Years in Prison for Killing Daunte Wright." *New York Times*, February 18. Retrieved on March 1, 2022 at https://www.nytimes.com/2022/02/18/us/kim-potter-sentence-manslaughter.html.

Bonilla-Silva, Eduardo. 2017. *Racism without Racists: Color-Blind Racism and the Persistence of Racial Inequality in America*. Lanham, Md.: Rowman & Littlefield.

———. 2020. "Color-Blind Racism in Pandemic Times." *Sociology of Race and Ethnicity* 8(3): 1–12.

Bor, Jacob, Atheendar S. Venkataramani, David R. Williams, and Alexander C. Tsai. 2018. "Police Killings and Their Spillover Effects on the Mental Health of Black Americans: A Population-Based, Quasi-Experimental Study." *Lancet* 392:302–310.

Bouchard, Kelley. 2016. "African-American Parents Say 'The Talk' Is a Life-and-Death Matter." *Portland Press Herald*, July 17. Retrieved on November 11, 2021 at https://www.pressherald.com/2016/07/17/african-american-parents-say-the-talk-is-a-life-and-death-matter/.

Buchanan, Larry, Quoctrung Bui, and Jugal K. Patel. 2020. "Black Lives Matter May Be the Largest Movement in U.S. History." *New York Times*, July 3. Retrieved on May 13, 2022 at https://www.nytimes.com/interactive/2020/07/03/us/george-floyd-protests-crowd-size.html.

Burch, Audra D. S. 2022. "How a National Movement Toppled Hundreds of Confederate Symbols." *New York Times*, February 28. Retrieved on March 9, 2022 at https://www.nytimes.com/interactive/2022/02/28/us/confederate-statue-removal.html.

Byrne, Matthew. 2020. "Police Departments Attempt a Charm Offensive amid Uprisings." *Truthout*, June 16. Retrieved on December 2, 2021 at https://truthout.org/articles/police-departments-attempt-a-charm-offensive-amid-uprisings/.

Callanan, Valerie J., and Jared S. Rosenberger. 2011. "Media and Public Perceptions of the Police: Examining the Impact of Race and Personal Experience." *Policing and Society* 21(2): 167–189.

Candclario, Chelsea. 2021. "What Is Performative Activism (and Why Does It Do More Harm than Good)?" *MSN News*, September 28. Retrieved on November 13, 2021 at https://www.msn.com/en-us/lifestyle/relationships/what-is-performative-activism-and-why-does-it-do-more-harm-than-good/ar-AAOUqxZ.

Cappelli, Mary Louisa. 2020. "Black Lives Matter: The Emotional and Racial Dynamics of the George Floyd Protest Graffiti." *Advances in Applied Sociology* 10:323–347.

Carnell, Susan. 2012. "Bad Boys, Bad Brains." *Psychology Today*, May 14. Retrieved on December 3, 2021 at https://www.psychologytoday.com/us/blog/bad-appetite/201205/bad-boys-bad-brains.

Carney, Nikita. 2016. "All Lives Matter, but So Does Race: Black Lives Matter and the Evolving Role of Social Media." *Humanity & Society* 40(2): 180–199.

Chavez, Nicole. 2020. "2020: The Year America Confronted Racism." *CNN*, December. Retrieved on May 16, 2022 at https://www.cnn.com/interactive/2020/12/us/america-racism-2020/.

Chevolleau, Sarah L. 2020. "Stay in Your Place!" *Journal of Global Faultlines* 8(1): 142–143.

Cinellia, Matteo, Gianmarco De Francisci Morales, Alessandro Galeazzi, Walter Quattrociocchi, and Michele Starnini. 2021. "The Echo Chamber Effect on Social Media." *Proceedings of the National Academy of Sciences* 118(9): 1–8.

Cinone, Danielle. 2020. "Bittersweet Symphony: Moving Elijah McClain Violin Vigil Is Stormed by Riot Police Who Pepper Spray Protesters in Jarring Footage." *The Sun*, June 28. Retrieved on December 3, 2021 at https://www.the-sun.com/news/1052735/elijah-mcclain-violin-vigil-riot-police-pepper-spray/.

Cobbina, Jennifer. 2019. *Hands Up, Don't Shoot: Why the Protests in Ferguson and Baltimore Matter, and How They Changed America*. New York: New York University Press.

Collins, Randall. 2020. "Social Distancing as a Critical Test of the Micro-Sociology of Solidarity." American Journal of Cultural Sociology 8 (October): 477–497.

Conlon, Kevin. 2022. "Ahmaud Arbery's Killers Found Guilty on All Counts in Federal Hate Crime Trial." *CNN*, February 22. Retrieved on May 16, 2022 at https://www.cnn.com/us/live-news/ahmaud-arbery-killing-hate-crimes-verdict/index.html.

Cowan, Jill. 2022. "Political Test for Gavin Newsom: Whether to Sign Injection-Site Bill." *New York Times* (August 19). Retrieved on August 22, 2022 at https://www.nytimes.com/2022/08/19/us/gavin-newsom-injection-site-bill.html.

Daniels, Jessie. 2021. *Nice White Ladies: The Truth about White Supremacy, Our Role in It, and How We Can Help Dismantle It*. New York: Seal Press.

Davis, Angela. 2020. "Why Arguments against Abolition Inevitably Fail." *Medium*, October 6. Retrieved on March 2, 2022 at https://level.medium.com/why-arguments-against-abolition-inevitably-fail-991342b8d042.

Davis, Dominic-Madori. 2020. "The Action Generation: How Gen Z Really Feels about Race, Equality, and Its Role in the Historic George Floyd Protests, Based on a Survey of 39,000 Young Americans." *Business Insider,* June 10. Retrieved on November 11, 2021 at https://www.businessinsider.com/how-gen-z-feels-about-george-floyd-protests-2020-6.

Deliso, Meredith. 2021. "Timeline: The Impact Of George Floyd's Death in Minneapolis and Beyond." *NBC News*, April 21. Retrieved on May 18, 2022 at https://abcnews.go.com/U.S./timeline-impact-george-floyds-death-minneapolis/story.

Disparte, Dante, and Tomicah Tilleman. 2020. "A Pandemic of Racism." *New America*, September 3. Retrieved on October 4, 2021 at https://www.newamerica.org/digital-impact-governance-initiative/reports/great-correction/.

Doane, Ashley "Woody." 2020. "Post-colorblindness? Trump and the Rise of the New White Nationalism." In *Protecting Whiteness: Whitelash and the Rejection of Racial Equality,* edited by Cameron D. Lippard, J. Scott Carter, and David G. Embrick, 27–42. Seattle: University of Washington Press.

Dreier, Peter. 2014. "Ella Baker, Ferguson, and 'Black Mothers' Sons.'" *Huffington Post,* December 22. Retrieved on October 7, 2021 at https://www.huffpost.com/entry/ella-baker-ferguson-and-b_b_6368394.

Dumas, Karen. 2020. "Opinion: What Role Should Whites Play in Black Lives Matter?" *Detroit News*, June 1. Retrieved on October 7, 2021 at https://www.detroitnews.com/story/opinion/2020/06/02/opinion-what-role-should-whites-play-black-lives-matter/5306655002/.

Dunivin, Zackary Okun, Harry Yaojun Yan, Jelani Ince, and Fabio Rojasa. 2022. "Black Lives Matter Protests Shift Public Discourse." *Proceedings of the National Academy of Sciences* 119(10): 1–11.

Durham, Simone N. 2022. "#BlackLivesMatter News Coverage: Examining Racial Projects and Hegemonic Imagery." *Understanding and Dismantling Privilege* 12(Special Issue 1): 6–27.

Duster, Chandelis. 2021. "Robert E. Lee Statue on Historic Virginia Street Removed." *CNN*, September 8. Retrieved on March 23, 2022 at https://www.cnn.com/2021/09/08/politics/robert-e-lee-statue-richmond-virginia-removal/index.html.

Ebrahimji, Alisha. 2021. "Runners around the World Dedicated 2.23 Miles to Shooting Victim Ahmaud Arbery." *CNN*, May 8. Retrieved on May 16, 2022 at https://www.cnn.com/2020/05/08/world/ahmaud-arbery-support-run-trnd/index.html.

Editorial Board. 2016. "The Moral Test of Government." *Chicago Tribune*, November 25. Retrieved on November 11, 2021 at https://www.chicagotribune.com/opinion/editorials/ct-disabled-illinois-care-rauner-edit-1127-jm-20161125-story.html.

Edrington, Candice L., and Nicole M. Lee. 2018. "Tweeting a Social Movement: Black Lives Matter and Its Use of Twitter to Share Information, Build Community, and Promote Action." *Journal of Public Interest Communications* 2:289–306.

Education Week. 2020. "Map: Coronavirus and School Closures in 2019-2020." *Education*

Week, March 6. Retrieved on May 16, 2022 at https://www.edweek.org/leadership/map-coronavirus-and-school-closures-in-2019-2020/2020/03.

Eichstaedt, Johannes C, Garrick T. Sherman, Salvatore Giorgi, Steven O. Roberts, Reynolds Megan E., Lyle H. Ungar, and Sharath Chandra Guntuku. 2021. "The Emotional and Mental Health Impact of the Murder of George Floyd on the U.S. Population." *Proceedings of the National Academy of Sciences of the United States of America* 118(39): e2109139118.

Everhart, Katherine. 2012. "Cultura-Identidad: The Use of Art in the University of Puerto Rico Student Movement, 2010." *Humanity & Society* 36(3): 198–219.

Fadel, Leila. 2020. "Armed Neighborhood Groups Form in the Absence of Police Protection." *NPR*, June 3. Retrieved on March 16, 2022 at https://www.npr.org/2020/06/03/868464167/armed-neighborhood-groups-form-in-the-absence-of-police-protection.

———. 2021. "Plywood Boards Bearing Art from Last Summer's Protests Represent Trauma and Strength." *NPR*, March 16. Retrieved on January 13, 2022 at https://www.npr.org/2021/03/16/977928940/plywood-boards-bearing-art-from-last-summers-protests-represent-trauma-and-stren.

Feagin, Joe R. 2020. *The White Racial Frame: Centuries of Framing and Counter-framing*. New York: Routledge.

Fernandez-Kelly, Patricia. 2020. "A Sociological Note on George Floyd's Death and the Pandemic." *Items* (Social Science Research Council), June 18. Retrieved on April 28, 2022 at https://items.ssrc.org/covid-19-and-the-social-sciences/society-after-pandemic/a-sociological-note-on-george-floyds-death-and-the-pandemic/.

Fine, Adam D., Zachary Rowan, and Cortney Simmons. 2019. "Do Politics Trump Race in Determining America's Youths' Perceptions of Law Enforcement?" *Journal of Criminal Justice* 61:58–67.

Fisher, Dana R. 2020. "The Diversity of the Recent Black Lives Matter Protests Is a Good Sign for Racial Equity." *Brookings*, July 8. Retrieved on March 27, 2022 at https://www.brookings.edu/blog/how-we-rise/2020/07/08/the-diversity-of-the-recent-black-lives-matter-protests-is-a-good-sign-for-racial-equity.

Fitzgerald, Toni. 2020. "What Are People Watching during Pandemic? News And Movies." *Forbes*, August 13. Retrieved on April 17, 2022 at https://www.forbes.com/sites/tonifitzgerald/2020/08/13/what-are-people-watching-during-pandemic-news-and-movies/.

Florido, Adrian, and Marisa Penaloza. 2020. "As Nation Reckons with Race, Poll Finds White Americans Least Engaged." *NPR*, August 17. Retrieved on April 28, 2022 at https://www.npr.org/2020/08/27/906329303/as-nation-reckons-with-race-poll-finds-white-americans-least-engaged.

Fondren, Precious. 2020. "The 'Say Her Name' Movement Started for a Reason: We Forget Black Women Killed by Police." *Teen Vogue*, June 11. Retrieved on March 27, 2022 at https://www.teenvogue.com/story/say-her-name-origin.

Franklin, Jonathan. 2021. "Aurora, Colo., Will Pay a $15 Million Settlement over the Death of Elijah McClain." *NPR*, November 18. Retrieved on December 3, 2021 at https://www.npr.org/2021/11/18/1056974723/city-of-aurora-pays-15-million-settlement-elijah-mcclain-death.

Freking, Kevin. 2021. "House Panel Votes to Advance Bill on Slavery Reparations." *AP News*, April 14. Retrieved on February 28, 2022 at https://apnews.com/article/race-and-ethnicity-discrimination-legislation-slavery-john-conyers-4929d09132b8a72e655d8a42c-c068a9d.

Garth, Hanna. 2021. "The 2020 Los Angeles Uprisings: Fighting for Black Lives in the Midst of COVID-19." In Viral Loads: Anthropologies of Urgency in the Time of COVID-19, edited by Lenore Manderson, Nancy J. Burke, and Ayo Wahlberg, 91–107. Chicago: UCL Press.

Gause, LaGina, and Maneesh Arora. 2021. "Not All of Last Year's Black Lives Matter Protesters Supported Black Lives Matter." *Washington Post*, July 2. Retrieved on March 27, 2022 at https://www.washingtonpost.com/politics/2021/07/01/not-all-last-years-black-lives-matter-protesters-supported-black-lives-matter/.

Gershon, Livia. 2020. "A Century of Black Youth Activism." JSTOR Daily, September 12. Retrieved on November 10, 2021 at https://daily.jstor.org/a-century-of-black-youth-activism/.

Gingrich, Jessica. 2018. "The Underground Kitchen that Funded the Civil Rights Movement." *Atlas Obscura*, December 31. Retrieved on March 9, 2022 at https://www.atlasobscura.com/articles/who-funded-civil-rights-movement.

Goldberg, Emma. 2022. "When Working for Racial Justice Means Taking Black History Month Off." *New York Times*, February 12. Retrieved on March 1, 2022 at https://www.nytimes.com/2022/02/12/business/black-history-month-diversity-inclusion.html.

Gould, Elise, and Melat Kassa. 2020. "Young Workers Hit Hard by the COVID-19 Economy." *Economic Policy Institute*, October 14. Retrieved on November 11, 2021 at https://www.epi.org/publication/young-workers-covid-recession/.

Green, Marcus Harrison. 2017. "What White Marchers Mean for Black Lives Matter." *Seattle Weekly*, December 27. Retrieved on August 25, 2024 at https://www.seattleweekly.com/opinion/what-white-marchers-mean-for-black-lives-matter/.

Griffith, Janelle. 2022. "Three Men Convicted Of Murdering Ahmaud Arbery Sentenced to Life in Prison." *NBC News*, January 7. Retrieved on May 16, 2022 at https://www.nbcnews.com/news/us-news/three-men-convicted-murdering-ahmaud-arbery-sentenced-life-prison-rcna10901.

Hagerman, Margaret Ann. 2013. "White Families and Race: Colour-Blind and Colour-Conscious Approaches to White Racial Socialization." *Ethnic and Racial Studies* 37(14): 2598–2614.

Hannah-Jones, Nikole. 2020. "What Is Owed?" *New York Times Magazine*, June 24. Retrieved on February 1, 2022 at https://www.nytimes.com/interactive/2020/06/24/magazine/reparations-slavery.html.

Harmon, Amy, and Audra D. S. Burch. 2020. "White Americans Say They Are Waking Up to Racism. What Will It Add Up To?" *New York Times*, June 22. Retrieved on May 16, 2022 at https://www.nytimes.com/2020/06/22/us/racism-white-americans.html.

Hawdon, James, and John Ryan. 2011. "Social Relations that Generate and Sustain Solidarity after a Mass Tragedy." *Social Forces* 89(4): 1363–1384.

Henderson, Brooke. 2020. "Early Members of 'Wall of Moms' Reflect on Where They Went Wrong as Protests in Portland Continue." *Fortune*, October 6. Retrieved on March 16, 2022 at https://fortune.com/2020/10/06/wall-of-moms-portland-protests/.

Hernandez, Joe. 2021. "Darnella Frazier, Who Filmed George Floyd's Murder, Wins an Honorary Pulitzer." *NPR*, June 11. Retrieved on April 26, 2022 at https://www.npr.org/2021/06/11/1005601724/darnella-frazier-teen-who-filmed-george-floyds-murder-wins-pulitzer-prize-citati.

Hoag, Alexis. 2020. "Derrick Bell's Interest Convergence and the Permanence of Racism: A Reflection on Resistance." *Harvard Law Review Blog*, August 24. Retrieved on May 16, 2022 at https://blog.harvardlawreview.org/derrick-bells-interest-convergence-and-the-permanence-of-racism-a-reflection-on-resistance/.

Holstein, James A., and Jaber F. Gubrium. 1995. *The Active Interview*. Thousand Oaks, Ca.: Sage.

Howard, Adam. 2016. "Racial Divide over O.J. Has Relaxed, but the Conversation Continues." *MSNBC,* February 1. Retrieved on December 1, 2021 at https://www.msnbc.com/msnbc/racial-divide-over-oj-has-relaxed-the-conversation-continues-msna786226.

Hurwitz, Jon, and Mark Peffley. 2005. "Explaining the Great Racial Divide: Perceptions of Fairness in the U.S. Criminal Justice System." *Journal of Politics* 67:762–783.

Inskeep, Steve, and Gina Clayton-Johnson. 2021. "The BREATHE Act Is a Counterproposal to Justice in Policing Act." NPR, March 23. Retrieved on February 1, 2022 at https://www.npr.org/2021/03/23/980234498/the-breathe-act-is-a-counterproposal-to-justice-in-policing-act.

Isaac, Larry W., Jonathan S. Coley, and Daniel B. Cornfield, 2020. "Pathways to Modes of Movement Participation: Micromobilization in the Nashville Civil Rights Movement." *Social Forces* 99(1): 255–280.

Jasper, James M. 2018. *The Emotions of Protest*. Chicago: University of Chicago Press.

Jenkins, Brian Michael, and Bruce R. Butterworth. 2020. "Metal against Marchers: An Analysis of Recent Incidents Involving Vehicle Assaults at U.S. Political Protests and Rallies." *Mineta Transportation Institute, San Jose State University,* October. Retrieved on March 16, 2022 at https://transweb.sjsu.edu/sites/default/files/SP1020-Metal-Against-Marchers.pdf.

Johnson, Odis, Jr., Keon Gilbert, and Habiba Ibrahim. 2018. "Race, Gender, and the Contexts of Unarmed Fatal Interactions with Police." *Fatal Interactions with Police Study*. Retrieved on January 31, 2019 at https://cpb-us-w2.wpmucdn.com/sites.wustl.edu/dist/b/1205/files/2018/02/Race-Gender-and-Unarmed-1y9md6e.pdf.

Johnson, Theodore R. 2021. *When the Stars Begin to Fall: Overcoming Racism and Renewing the Promise of America*. New York: Atlantic Monthly Press.

Jones, Dawn. 2021. "Black Lives Matter Flint and Law Enforcement Still Working for Change, but No Longer in Lockstep." ABC *12 News*, June 3. Retrieved on February 1, 2022 at https://www.abc12.com/news/black-lives-matter-flint-and-law-enforcement-still-working-for-change-but-no-longer-in/article_861a0d63-dc86-5ef6-a3d0-eee2a41d674c.html.

Jones, Justine. 2021. "A Celebration of Life at George Floyd Square." *Minneapolis Saint Paul Magazine*, October 13. Retrieved on March 23, 2022 at https://mspmag.com/arts-and-culture/a-celebration-of-life-at-george-floyd-square/.

Jones, Kay, Carma Hassan, and Leah Asmelash. 2020. "A Kentucky EMT Was Shot and Killed during a Police Raid of Her Home. The Family Is Suing for Wrongful Death." CNN, May 13. Retrieved on May 16, 2022 at https://www.cnn.com/2020/05/13/us/louisville-police-emt-killed-trnd/index.html.

Kaur, Harmeet. 2020. "The Coronavirus Pandemic Is Hitting Black and Brown Americans Especially Hard on All Fronts." CNN, May 8. Retrieved on May 16, 2022 at https://www.cnn.com/2020/05/08/us/coronavirus-pandemic-race-impact-trnd/index.html.

Kishi, Roudabeh. 2020. "Demonstration Trends in the U.S." *Armed Conflict Location and Data Event Project.* Retrieved on December 3, 2021 at https://acleddata.com/2020/09/23/demonstration-trends-in-the-united-states/.

Kishi, Roudabeh, and Sam Jones. 2020. "Demonstrations & Political Violence in America: New Data for Summer 2020." *Armed Conflict Location and Data Event Project.* Retrieved on December 3, 2021 at https://acleddata.com/2020/09/03/demonstrations-political-violence-in-america-new-data-for-summer-2020/.

Kishi, Roudabeh, Hampton Stall, and Sam Jones. 2020. "The Future of 'Stop the Steal': Post-election Trajectories for Right-Wing Conflict in the U.S." *Armed Conflict Location and Data Event Project.* Retrieved on December 1, 2021 at https://acleddata.com/2020/12/10/the-future-of-stop-the-steal-post-election-trajectories-for-right-wing-mobilization-in-the-us/.

Kishi, Roudabeh, Hampton Stall, Aaron Wilson, and Sam Jones. 2021. "A Year of Racial Justice Protests: Key Trends in Demonstrations Supporting the BLM Movement." *Armed Conflict Location and Data Event Project.* Retrieved on May 18, 2022 at https://acleddata.com/2021/05/25/a-year-of-racial-justice-protests-key-trends-in-demonstrations-supporting-the-blm-movement/.

Kramer, Jillian. 2017. "11 Change-Makers Share How They Deal with Activism Fatigue." *Self,* August 28. Retrieved on March 2, 2022 at https://www.self.com/story/activism-fatigue.

Lee, Trymaine. 2020. "Transcript: Into the Movement for Ahmaud Arbery." MSNBC May 12. Retrieved on May 16, 2022 at https://www.msnbc.com/podcast/transcript-movement-ahmaud-arbery-n1205406.

Lee, Trymaine, Jon Schuppe, and Sam Petulla. 2017. "25 Years since Rodney King Riots: Race, Rebellion and Rebirth in South L.A." *NBC News,* April 29. Retrieved on December 1, 2021 at https://www.nbcnews.com/news/us-news/ballad-south-l-race-rebellion-rebirth-n751471.

Levenson, Eric. 2020. "A Timeline of Breonna Taylor's Case since Police Broke Down Her Door and Shot Her." *CNN,* September 24. Retrieved on May 16, 2022 at https://www.cnn.com/2020/09/23/us/breonna-taylor-timeline/index.html.

Levenson, Eric, and Kristina Sgueglia. 2020. "There Were Two Calls between Amy Cooper and 911 about a Black Birdwatcher in Central Park, Prosecutors Say." *CNN,* November 17. Retrieved on May 16, 2022 at https://www.cnn.com/2020/10/14/us/amy-cooper-central-park-racism/index.html.

Li, Yao, and Harvey L. Nicholson Jr. 2021. "When 'Model Minorities' Become 'Yellow Peril'—Othering and the Racialization of Asian Americans in the COVID-19 Pandemic." *Sociology Compass* 15:e12849.

Lindeen, Ellen Birkett. 2020. "The Great White Awakening." *LA Progressive,* June 17. Retrieved on March 27, 2022 at https://www.laprogressive.com/racism/great-white-awakening.

Lisenby, Ashley. 2018. "Unarmed Black Women Are at Highest Risk When Interacting with Police, Study Finds." *Saint Louis Public Radio,* February 12. Retrieved on January 31, 2019 at http://news.stlpublicradio.org/post/unarmed-black-women-are-highest-risk-when-interacting-police-study-finds#stream/0.

Marcus, Josh. 2021. "'All We Have Is Each Other': The George Floyd Uprising and the Rise of 'Mutual Aid' Organizing." *Yahoo News*, April 30. Retrieved on March 23, 2022 at https://news.yahoo.com/other-george-floyd-uprising-rise-155205908.html.

Maxouris, Christina. 2020. "Here's What We Know about the Casey Goodson Jr. Fatal Police Shooting." *CNN*, December 12. Retrieved on May 18, 2022 at https://www.cnn.com/2020/12/12/us/casey-goodson-jr-what-we-know/index.html.

McAdam, Doug. 1986. "Recruitment to High-Risk Activism: The Case of Freedom Summer." *American Journal of Sociology* 92(1): 64–90.

———. 1990. *Freedom Summer*. Oxford: Oxford University Press.

McCammon, Sarah. 2020. "D.C. Police Officer on Why He Took a Knee with Protesters." *NPR*, June 7. Retrieved on December 2, 2021 at https://www.npr.org/2020/06/07/871751049/d-c-police-officer-on-why-he-took-a-knee-with-protesters.

McCarthy, Justin. 2021. "Record-High 70% in U.S. Support Same-Sex Marriage." *Gallup*, June 8. Retrieved on February 23, 2022 at https://news.gallup.com/poll/350486/recordhigh-support-same-sex-marriage.aspx.

McCausland, Phil. 2022. "3 White Men Who Murdered Ahmaud Arbery Found Guilty of Hate Crimes." *NBC News*, February 22. Retrieved on March 1, 2022 at https://www.nbcnews.com/news/us-news/ahmaud-arbery-trial-verdict-3-men-federal-hate-crime-trial-rcna17171.

McClain, Dani. 2021. "How We Survived a Year of Grief." *The Crisis*, January 1. Retrieved on March 23, 2022 at https://naacp.org/articles/how-we-survived-year-grief.

McDonald, Jermaine M. 2016. "Ferguson and Baltimore according to Dr. King: How Competing Interpretations of King's Legacy Frame the Public Discourse on Black Lives Matter." *Journal of the Society of Christian Ethics* 36(2): 141–158.

McMahon, Abbey. 2020. "The Green Hats at the Protests: National Lawyers Guild Legal Observers." *NW Sidebar*, August 20. Retrieved on August 24, 2024 at https://nwsidebar.wsba.org/2020/08/20/the-green-hats-at-the-protests-national-lawyers-guild-legal-observers/.

McTaggart, Ninochka, and Eileen O'Brien. 2021. *White Privilege: The Persistence of Racial Hierarchy in a Culture of Denial*. San Diego: Cognella.

Morales, Christina. 2021. "What We Know about the Shooting of Jacob Blake." *New York Times*, November 16. Retrieved on May 18, 2022 at https://www.nytimes.com/article/jacob-blake-shooting-kenosha.html.

Mueller, Amber L., Maeve S. McNamara, and David A. Sinclair. 2020. "Why Does COVID-19 Disproportionately Affect Older People?" *Aging* 12(10): 9959–9981.

Mundt, Marcia, Karen Ross, and Charla M. Burnett. 2018. "Scaling Social Movements through Social Media: The Case of Black Lives Matter." *Social Media and Society* 4:1–14.

Murphy, Heather. 2021. "Federal Judge Bans Tear Gas on Nonviolent Protesters in Columbus." *New York Times*, May 3. Retrieved on December 3, 2021 at https://www.nytimes.com/2021/05/03/us/columbus-police-tear-gas-ban.html.

Mutz, Diana C. 2022. "Effects of Changes in Perceived Discrimination during BLM on the 2020 Presidential Election." *Science Advances* 8(9): 1–9.

Myers, Justin Sean, and Joshua Sbicca. 2016. "Food Justice Racial Projects: Fighting Racial Neoliberalism from the Bay to the Big Apple." *Environmental Sociology* 3(1): 30–41.

Nawaz, Amna. 2020. "How This Year's Antiracism Protests Differ from Past Social Justice

Movements." *PBS News Hour*, October 28. Retrieved on March 24, 2022 at https://www.pbs.org/newshour/show/what-is-unprecedented-about-this-years-racial-justice-protests.

Nguyen, Thu T., Shaniece Criss, Eli K. Michaels, Rebekah I. Cross, Jackson S. Michaels, Pallavi Dwivedi, Dina Huang, et al. 2021. "Progress and Push-Back: How the Killings of Ahmaud Arbery, Breonna Taylor, and George Floyd Impacted Public Discourse on Race and Racism on Twitter." *SSM—Population Health* 15:100922.

O'Brien, Eileen. 2001. *Whites Confront Racism: Antiracists and Their Paths to Action.* Lanham, Md.: Rowman & Littlefield.

O'Brien, Shannon. 2021. "BLM One Year Later: What Shifts in Support Mean for the Movement and Race Relations in 2021." *Wellesley News*, August 4. Retrieved on March 27, 2022 at https://www.wellesley.edu/news/2021/stories/node/190341.

Offenharz, Jake. 2020. "'Round Up the Green Hats': NYPD Accused of Deliberately Targeting Legal Observers in Brutal Bronx Mass Arrest." *Gothamist,* June 8. Retrieved on March 15, 2022 at https://gothamist.com/news/round-green-hats-nypd-accused-deliberately-targeting-legal-observers-brutal-bronx-mass-arrest.

Omi, Michael, and Howard Winant. 1994. *Racial Formation in the United States: From the 1960s to the 1980s.* 2nd ed. New York: Routledge.

Pahwa, Nitish. 2020. "Why So Many Drivers Are Ramming into Protesters." *Slate,* June 12. Retrieved on March 16, 2022 at https://slate.com/business/2020/06/george-floyd-protests-cars-ramming-racism.html.

Patton, Stacey. 2020. "White People Are Speaking Up at Protests. How Do We Know They Mean What They Say?" *Washington Post,* June 2. Retrieved on October 7, 2021 at https://www.washingtonpost.com/outlook/2020/06/02/white-people-black-protests/.

Peoples-Wagner, Lindsay, and Morgan Jerkins. 2022. "10 Years since Trayvon: The Story of the First Decade of Black Lives Matter." *New York Magazine*, January 31. Retrieved on May 21, 2022 at https://nymag.com/article/black-lives-matter-2022.html.

Perhamus, Lisa M., and Clarence W. Joldersma. 2020. "What Might Sustain the Activism of This Moment? Dismantling White Supremacy, One Monument at a Time." *Journal of Philosophy and Education* 54(5): 1314–1332.

Pew Research. 2021. "Public Opinion on Abortion 1995–2021." *Pew Research Center*, May 6. Retrieved on February 23, 2022 at https://www.pewforum.org/fact-sheet/public-opinion-on-abortion/.

Pirtle, Whitney N. Laster. 2020. "Racial Capitalism: A Fundamental Cause of Novel Coronavirus (COVID-19) Pandemic Inequities in the United States." *Health Education & Behavior* 47(4): 504–508.

Putnam, Lara, Erica Chenoweth, and Jeremy Pressman. 2020. "The Floyd Protests Are the Broadest in U.S. History—And Are Spreading to White, Small-Town America." *Washington Post,* June 6. Retrieved on May 13, 2022 at https://www.washingtonpost.com/politics/2020/06/06/floyd-protests-are-broadest-us-history-are-spreading-white-small-town-america/.

Raimist, Rachel. 2021. "My Beautiful, Broken Minnesota." In *Sparked: George Floyd, Racism, and the Progressive Illusion,* edited by Walter R. Jacobs, Wendy Thompson Talwo, and Amy August, 29–32. Saint Paul: Minnesota Historical Society Press.

Ratliff, Thomas N., and Lori L. Hall. 2014. "Practicing the Art of Dissent: Toward a Typology of Protest Activity in the United States." *Humanity & Society* 38(3): 268–294.

Ray, Rashawn. 2020. "Bad Apples Come from Rotten Trees in Policing: The Pursuit of Racial Equity." *Race, Ethnicity and Immigration Colloquium*. Public lecture delivered via Zoom, September 8. Berkeley: Institute of Governmental Studies.

Ray, Victor. 2022. *On Critical Race Theory: Why It Matters & Why You Should Care*. New York: Random House.

Ray, Victor Erik, Antonia Randolph, Megan Underhill, and David Luke. 2017. "Critical Race Theory, Afro-pessimism, and Racial Progress Narratives." *Sociology of Race and Ethnicity* 3(2): 147–158.

Reynolds, Rema, and Darquillius Mayweather. 2017. "Recounting Racism, Resistance, and Repression: Examining the Experiences and #Hashtag Activism of College Students with Critical Race Theory and Counternarratives." *Journal of Negro Education* 86(3): 283–304.

Rivas-Drake, Deborah, Diane Hughes, and Niobe Way. 2009. "A Preliminary Analysis of Associations among Ethnic–Racial Socialization, Ethnic Discrimination, and Ethnic Identity among Urban Sixth Graders." *Journal of Research on Adolescence* 19(3): 558–584.

Romo, Vanessa, and Sharon Pruitt-Young. 2021. "What We Know about the 3 Men Who Were Shot by Kyle Rittenhouse." NPR, November 20. Retrieved on May 18, 2022 at https://www.npr.org/2021/11/20/1057571558/what-we-know-3-men-kyle-rittenhouse-victims-rosenbaum-huber-grosskreutz.

Russell-Brown, Katheryn. 2008. *The Color of Crime: Racial Hoaxes, White Fear, Black Protectionism, Police Harassment, and Other Macroaggressions*. 2nd ed. New York: New York University Press.

Russonello, Giovanni. 2020. "Why Most Americans Support the Protests." *New York Times*, June 5. Retrieved on April 27, 2022 at https://www.nytimes.com/2020/06/05/us/politics/polling-george-floyd-protests-racism.html.

Salinas, Marco. 2021. "With Efforts to Defund Police Backsliding, the BLM Movement Is Focusing on Mutual Aid." *The Progressive*, October 14. Retrieved on March 23, 2022 at https://progressive.org/defund-police-backsliding-salinas-211014/.

Sanchez, Ray, and Ashley Killough. 2021. "Former Dallas Police Officer Amber Guyger Asks Appeals Court to Throw Out Murder Conviction for Killing Botham Jean." *CNN*, April 27. Retrieved on May 21, 2022 at https://www.cnn.com/2021/04/27/us/amber-guyger-appeal-botham-jean-murder/index.html.

Sanchez, Ray, Melanie Schuman, and Anna Sturla. 2020. "Video Appears to Show Louisville BBQ Man Fired Gun before He Was Fatally Shot, Police Say." *CNN*, June 3. Retrieved on May 18, 2022 at https://www.cnn.com/2020/06/03/us/kentucky-david-mcatee-shooting/index.html.

Schmelzer, Elise. 2020. "When Does a Black Face Get the Same Equality? Aurora, Denver Police Use Force against Black People at Higher Rates than Other Races." *Denver Post*, August 9. Retrieved on December 3, 2021 at https://www.denverpost.com/2020/08/09/denver-aurora-police-use-of-force-race/.

Schrader, Stuart. 2020. "More than Cosmetic Changes: The Challenges of Experiments with Police Demilitarization in the 1960s and 1970s." *Journal of Urban History* 46(5): 1002–1025.

Serwer, Adam. 2020. "The Next Reconstruction." *The Atlantic*, October. Retrieved on January 31, 2022 at https://www.theatlantic.com/magazine/archive/2020/10/the-next-reconstruction/615475/.

Sherman, Lawrence W. 1990. "Police Crackdowns: Initial and Residual Deterrence." *Crime and Justice* 12:1–48.

Simon, Darran, and Ashley Killough. 2019. "Video of Botham Jean's Last Moments Played in Court. His Parents Weren't Ready." *CNN*, September 25. Retrieved on May 21, 2022 at https://www.cnn.com/2019/09/25/us/botham-jean-family-police-body-camera/index.html.

Smith, David. 2020. "Nine Out of 10 Americans Say Racism and Police Brutality Are Problems, Poll Finds." *The Guardian,* July 8. Retrieved on February 23, 2022 at https://www.theguardian.com/us-news/2020/jul/08/americans-racism-police-brutality-problems-poll.

Smith, Savannah, Jiachuan Wu, and Joe Murphy. 2020. "Map: George Floyd Protests around the World." *NBC News*, June 9. Retrieved on April 20, 2022 at https://www.nbcnews.com/news/world/map-george-floyd-protests-countries-worldwide-n1228391.

Spade, Dean. 2020. "Solidarity Not Charity: Mutual Aid for Mobilization and Survival." *Social Text* 38(1): 131–151.

Spalding, Diana. 2020. "When George Floyd Called Out for His Mama, Mothers Everywhere Answered." *Motherly,* June 4. Retrieved on October 7, 2021 at https://www.mother.ly/black-lives-matter/blm-moms-speak/george-floyd-called-for-mothers-everywhere.

Steele, Chandra. 2020. "How to Support Protesters from Home." *PC Magazine,* June 3. Retrieved on March 15, 2022 at https://www.pcmag.com/news/how-to-support-protesters-from-home.

Stott, Clifford, Otto Adang, Andrew Livingstone, and Martina Schreiber. 2008. "Tackling Football Hooliganism: A Quantitative Study of Public Order, Policing and Crowd Psychology." *Psychology, Public Policy, and Law* 14(2): 115–141.

Strong, Myron. 2020. "Collective Effervescence and the Election." *Norton Everyday Sociology Blog*, November 30. Retrieved on November 16, 2021 at https://www.everydaysociologyblog.com/2020/11/collective-effervescence-and-the-election.html.

Summers, Brandi T. 2020. "What Black America Knows about Quarantine." *New York Times*, May 15. Retrieved on April 28, 2022 at https://www.nytimes.com/2020/05/15/opinion/sunday/coronavirus-ahmaud-arbery-race.html.

Sweeney, Annie. 2021. "Punished by FOP for Kneeling in Protest, Chicago Police Officer Fights to Have Suspension Reversed on Principle." *Chicago Tribune*, October 6. Retrieved on December 2, 2021 at https://www.chicagotribune.com/news/criminal-justice/ct-met-fop-suspension-officer-protest-20211006-clzni3yucvgl5jjsicqyk3dpcq-story.html.

Tate, Julie, Jennifer Jenkins, and Steven Rich. 2022. "Fatal Force Database." *Washington Post*, March 25. Retrieved on March 27, 2022 at https://www.washingtonpost.com/graphics/investigations/police-shootings-database/.

Taylor, Keeanga-Yamahtta. 2021. "Did Last Summer's Black Lives Matter Protests Change Anything?" *New Yorker*, August 6. Retrieved on May 19, 2023 at https://www.newyorker.com/news/our-columnists/did-last-summers-protests-change-anything.

Thomas, Deja, and Juliana Menasce Horowitz. 2020. "Support for Black Lives Matter Has Decreased since June but Remains Strong among Black Americans." *Pew Research*, September 16. Retrieved on April 28, 2022 at https://www.pewresearch.org/short-reads/2020/09/16/support-for-black-lives-matter-has-decreased-since-june-but-remains-strong-among-black-americans.

Thompson, A. C., and Ford Fischer. 2021. "Members of Several Well-Known Hate Groups Identified at Capitol Riot." *Frontline*, January 9. Retrieved on January 14, 2022 at https://www.pbs.org/wgbh/frontline/article/several-well-known-hate-groups-identified-at-capitol-riot/.

Thompson, A. C., Pro Publica, Lila Hassan, and Karim Hajj. 2021. "The Boogaloo Bois Have Guns, Criminal Records and Military Training. Now They Want to Overthrow the Government." *ProPublica*, February 1. Retrieved on December 3, 2021 at https://www.propublica.org/article/boogaloo-bois-military-training.

Tillery, Alvin B., Jr. 2021. "From Civil Rights to Racial Justice: Understanding African-American Social Justice Movements." Department of State Briefing, Foreign Press Center, Washington, D.C., April 23. Retrieved on March 24, 2022 at https://www.state.gov/briefings-foreign-press-centers/from-civil-rights-to-racial-justice-understanding-african-american-social-justice-movements/.

Tomkin, Anastasia Reesa. 2021. "Philanthropic Pledges for Racial Justice Found to Be Superficial." *Nonprofit Quarterly,* October 7. Retrieved on December 29, 2023 at https://nonprofitquarterly.org/philanthropic-pledges-for-racial-justice-found-to-be-superficial/.

Tompkins, Lucy. 2022. "Here's What You Need to Know about Elijah McClain's Death." *New York Times*, January 18. Retrieved on May 21, 2022 at https://www.nytimes.com/article/who-was-elijah-mcclain.html.

Truong, Emily. 2020. "Professor Anne Berg Protects Your Right to Protest." *34th Street,* November 24. Retrieved on March 15, 2022 at https://www.34st.com/article/2020/11/professor-anne-berg-national-lawyers-guild-legal-observer.

U.S. Department of Justice. 2023. "Former Louisville Metro Police Department Officer Pleads Guilty to Using Excessive Force during 2020 Protest." Press Release, 23–536. Retrieved on May 19, 2023 at https://www.justice.gov/opa/pr/former-louisville-metro-police-department-officer-pleads-guilty-using-excessive-force-during.

USA Today. 2022. "COVID-19 Restrictions." USA Today, March 18. Retrieved on May 16, 2022 at https://www.usatoday.com/storytelling/coronavirus-reopening-america-map/.

Vartanian, Hrag. 2021. "Plywood Obelisks Reflect on a Year of Racial Justice Protests." *Hyperallergic*, May 24. Retrieved on March 9, 2022 at https://hyperallergic.com/648007/plywood-obelisks-reflect-on-a-year-of-racial-justice-protests/.

Vera, Amir, and Priya Krishnakumar. 2022. "From Trayvon Martin to Ahmaud Arbery: How Images Have Changed a Movement." CNN, February 26. Retrieved on May 21, 2022 at https://www.cnn.com/interactive/2022/02/us/travyon-martin-10-year-death-anniversary/.

Vinas-Nelson, Jessica. 2017. "Interracial Marriage in 'Post-racial' America." *Origins: Current Events in Historical Perspective* 10(12). Retrieved on November 11, 2021 at https://origins.osu.edu/article/interracial-marriage-post-racial-america/page/0/1.

Waldman, Katy. 2015. "Is Baltimore Beset by Protests, Riots, or an Uprising?" *Slate,* April 29. Retrieved on March 9, 2022 at https://slate.com/human-interest/2015/04/protest-versus-riot-versus-uprising-the-language-of-the-baltimore-freddie-gray-unrest.html.

Wamsley, Laurel. 2021. "March 11, 2020: The Day Everything Changed." NPR, March 11. Retrieved on May 16, 2022 at https://www.npr.org/2021/03/11/975663437/march-11-2020-the-day-everything-changed.

Wang, Dan J., and Sarah A. Soule. 2016. "Tactical Innovation in Social Movements: The Effects of Peripheral and Multi-issue Protest." *American Sociological Review* 81(3): 517–548.

Weitzer, Ronald, and Steven A. Tuch. 2002. "Perceptions of Racial Profiling: Race, Class and Personal Experience." *Criminology* 40:435–456.

Welsh-Huggins, Andrew. 2021. "Murder Charge for Ohio Deputy in Casey Goodson Jr. Shooting." *CNN*, December 2. Retrieved on May 18, 2022 at https://abcnews.go.com/U.S./wireStory/murder-charge-ohio-deputy-casey-goodson-jr-shooting-8151575.

Westerman, Ashley, Ryan Benk, and David Greene. 2020. "In 2020, Protests Spread across the Globe with a Similar Message: Black Lives Matter." *NPR*, December 30. Retrieved on April 28, 2022 at https://www.npr.org/2020/12/30/950053607/in-2020-protests-spread-across-the-globe-with-a-similar-message-black-lives-matt.

Williams, Jessica. 2017. "Supportive Roles." *Direct Action Movement*. Retrieved on March 15, 2022 at https://www.thedirectactionmovement.com/supportiveroles.

Wolfe, Jan. 2021. "U.S. Probes Phoenix Police Use of Force, Treatment of Protesters." *Reuters*, August 5. Retrieved on May 19, 2023 at https://www.reuters.com/legal/government/us-justice-department-launches-probe-into-policing-practices-arizona-2021-08-05/.

Woodward, Kerry. 2016. "Marketing Black Babies versus Recruiting Black Families: The Racialized Strategies Private Adoption Agencies Use to Find Homes for Black Babies." *Sociology of Race and Ethnicity* 2(4): 482–497.

Woodward, Samantha. 2020. "'A Culture of Care': University Students Engage in Citywide Mutual Aid." *Minnesota Daily,* October 12. Retrieved on March 23, 2022 at https://mndaily.com/262905 /news/a-culture-of-care-university-students-engage-in-citywide-mutual-aid/.

Yang, Maya, and Joanna Walters. 2021. "Kyle Rittenhouse Found Not Guilty after Fatally Shooting Two in Kenosha Unrest." *The Guardian*, November 19. Retrieved on December 3, 2021 at https://www.theguardian.com/us-news/2021/nov/19/kyle-rittenhouse-verdict-kenosha-shooting.

Zara, Janelle. 2020. "How Artists Are Using Plywood as a Canvas for Protest." *Architecture Digest*, August 18. Retrieved on March 9, 2022 at https://www.architecturaldigest.com/story/plywood-project-art.

INDEX

Abby, 59–60, 110–111, 165
Affirmative Action, U.S. Supreme Court ending, 186
African American history, bans on teaching, 186
Afropessimism, 118
Agents provocateurs, 79, 83, 88
Anti-Racist Action, 31
Antiracist racial project, 3–6, 26, 49, 127, 132, 147, 150, 186
Arbery, Ahmaud: conviction for killers of, 154, 184; killing of, 1, 8, 10, 38, 46, 54, 118
Armed Conflict Location and Event Data (ACLED) Project, 11, 56, 59, 128

Baker, Ella, 92, 101, 125
Beth, 160
Biden, Joe: administration of, investigated police department corruption, 90; attending George Floyd funeral, 19, 183; as creating improvements, in political office picks, 14; election of, as decreasing racial justice movement sustenance, 183
Bill, 34–35, 57, 87–88, 97, 124–125, 178–179
Black Lives Matter (BLM): as Black led, 23, 155; as catalyst for more Democrat Party support, 55; as catalyst for "say their names," 29; expanded gendered portrayals of police brutality, 105; focus on Black joy and self-care, 150; founding of, 15–19, 93; growth from 2015 to early 2020, 16–18; not all 2020 protests affiliated with, 79; outside agitators blaming for own damage, 86; as part of larger Black freedom struggle, 45; prior involvement as catalyst for 2020 involvement, 29, 33–34, 48, 51, 53, 118, 122, 148–149, 176; public support for, 143, 144, 183; support of BREATHE Act, 152; surge of "BLM protests" in 2020, 2, 11; as technology based, 50, 148–149; as youth led, 50
Black Panther Party, 34–35, 97, 179; free breakfast programs, 148
Blake, 39–40, 66, 84–85, 109, 114, 141–142, 169
Bland, Sandra, police killing of, 17, 29, 38, 53
BLM. *See* Black Lives Matter
Boogaloo Bois, 83, 87
BREATHE Act, 149, 153
Brooks, Rayshard, police killing of, 12, 38
Brown, Michael, police killing of, 29, 34–35, 38–39, 47, 51–53, 61, 102, 161
Bryant, Carolyn, 101

Carly, 30–31, 85, 94–95, 103–104, 130
Car ramming, 84, 90, 108, 140, 142, 148
Castille, Philando, police killing of, 33–34, 38, 53, 106, 161
Charles, 121, 133–134, 161
Charlottesville white supremacist violence of 2017. *See* Heyer, Heather
Chauvin, Derek: kneeling on George Floyd's neck, 48–52, 67; possible catalyst for culture change in policing, 164; trial and conviction of, 11, 75, 122, 125, 162; verdict as victory, 184; viewed as "bad apple," 58

Clark, Jamar, police killing of, 33–34, 38, 114
Coronavirus. *See* COVID-19
COVID-19, 2, 9–10, 27, 28, 41–47, 52, 54–55, 59, 86, 94, 96–97, 102, 103–105, 183
Critical race theory (CRT), 3, 118, 182; interest convergence, 3–6, 49, 55, 182–183, 186
Curfews, 79–88, 96

Diallo, Amadou, police killing of, 5, 29, 34

Facebook: as "echo chamber" for like-minded, 144; as movement mobilizer, 17, 36, 37–38, 76, 131; as place for law enforcement official statements, 8; as place where protesters were threatened, 105
Faith, 66–67, 112, 120–121, 134, 146, 158–159
Floyd, George: as catalyst for reform, 170; cried for mother before dying, 92; funeral, 113–114; George Floyd Justice in Policing Act, 149, 169; "George Floyd protests" misnomer, 2, 7, 20, 47, 121; George Floyd Square location, 123, 134, 149; passing counterfeit bill as only offense, 167; police killing of, 77, 89, 121, 125, 133, 137; protests anticipating trial verdict, 75. *See also* Chauvin, Derek; Frazier, Darnella
Frazier, Darnella: Pulitzer Prize honor, 47; video footage of George Floyd murder, 29, 47, 54–55

Garner, Eric, police killing of, 12, 16, 29, 39, 53, 89, 102, 180
Gilmore, Georgia, 127, 148
Goodson, Casey, police killing of, 13, 121, 134, 161
Guyger, Amber (Botham Jean), 20

Helen, 38, 95–96, 100, 104, 106, 109, 117, 145–149, 156, 173–174
Heyer, Heather, white supremacist killing of, 18, 20, 58–59, 108
Hood Scholar, 37–38, 41–42, 61–62, 123–124, 137–138, 179–180

Injustice Square Park, 80–81; officially named Jefferson Square Park, 149
Instagram, as movement mobilizer, 76
Isabel, 44–45, 76–77, 96, 111–112

Janay, 71–73, 80, 99, 119–120, 134, 143–144, 174–175
Jane, 173

January 6 attack on U.S. Capitol, 83, 186
Jean, Botham, killing of, 20
Jim Bear, 38, 48–49, 74–75, 86–87, 107, 113–114, 123, 133, 140, 166–167, 188
Jordan, 38, 41, 81–82, 97–98, 138, 163–164
Juneteenth, 113, 184
Justin, 64, 116, 124, 127, 167

Kelli, 31–32, 82–83, 112–113, 139–140, 143, 151, 157–158, 172–173
Kettling, as police intimidation technique, 69
King, Martin Luther, Jr., 89, 92, 127, 137, 152
King, Rodney, police beating of, 29, 57, 161
Ku Klux Klan, 30–31

Lay security, 140–142, 148
Lee, Robert E., monument, 131–132; renamed Marcus-David Peters Square, 149
Legal observers (LO), 137

Martin, Trayvon, killing of, 12, 15, 27, 32, 36–37, 38, 51–52
McClain, Elijah, police killing of, 20, 76–77
Michelle, 44, 110, 164–165
Monica, 70–71, 110, 156–157
Monument toppling, 12–14, 18, 25–26, 128, 130–132, 147, 149, 182–183

Nate, 51–52, 56, 78–79, 115–116, 170–171
Nicole, 36–37, 117, 122, 134, 165–166, 176–177
Noise Not Nazis, 31

Obama, Barack, statement about Trayvon Martin, 16

Parks, Rosa, 127
Patrice, 45–46, 62, 144–145, 168
Plywood board art, 25, 26, 103, 123–124, 129, 148
Potter, Kimberly, trial and conviction of, 133, 154, 184

Rabbi M, 33–34, 63–64, 82, 123, 155–156
Resistance art, 103, 129–130. *See also* Plywood board art
Rev. David, 69, 88, 180–181
Rev. Lane, 60–61, 75–76, 81, 98, 136–137, 177–178
Rev. TM, 32–33, 56, 73–74, 86, 98–99, 135–136, 168
Rice, Tamir, police killing of, 17, 29, 38, 52–53, 102, 161
Rittenhouse, Kyle, attack on protesters, 13, 84

Index

RJ, 40, 43–44, 63, 84, 118–119, 138–139, 162
Roof, Dylan, white supremacist shooting, 18

Sally, 73, 80–81, 135
"Say their names," 29
Scott, Walter, police killing of, 18, 89
Sharon, 42, 64–66, 104–106, 159–160, 177
Simpson, O. J., acquittal of, 57
South Africa, Truth and Reconciliation Commission, 179
Standing Rock, Dakota Access Pipeline, protests, 33, 99, 136
Sterling, Alton, police killing of, 38

Taylor, Breonna: awaiting justice, 154; memorial to, 149; police killing of, 1, 8–9, 10, 13, 29, 38, 46, 69, 77, 106, 118; police raid similar to, 150
Tiananmen Square, 74
Till, Emmett, killing of, 47, 61, 101, 161
Trump, Donald: discouraged masks as weakness, 45; election as catalyst for protest involvement, 33, 55, 59, 97–98; poor-choice president for racial justice, 175; statements on white supremacists and BLM protesters, 59; thinks rules do not apply to him, 80; as unlikely to attend George Floyd funeral, 191
Truth, Sojourner, 101
Tucker, 40, 43, 57, 161–162
Tumblr, as movement mobilizer, 37–38
Twitter: as movement mobilizer, 35, 37–38; as place to measure public concern about racism, 55

Wall of Moms, 141
Washington sports mascot: changing racist Redskins logo, 12, 183–184; protest in 1990s, 38, 183–184
Wells-Barnett, Ida, 92
William, 68, 102–103
Wilson, Darren, acquittal of, 37–38
Wright, Daunte: police killing of, 74, 133; verdict protests, 75; vigil for, 107, 133. *See also* Potter, Kimberly

Printed in the United States
by Baker & Taylor Publisher Services